SECOND EDITION

Basics
of
Biblical
Greek

WORKBOOK

Also by William D. Mounce

Analytical Lexicon to the Greek New Testament
A Graded Reader of Biblical Greek
Greek for the Rest of Us
Morphology of Biblical Greek
The NIV English-Greek New Testament
Pastoral Letters (Word Biblical Commentary)

SECOND EDITION

Basics
of
Biblical
Greek

WORKBOOK

William D.
MOUNCE

ZONDERVAN®

GRAND RAPIDS, MICHIGAN 49530 USA

ZONDERVAN.COM/
AUTHOR**TRACKER**

ZONDERVAN®

Basics of Biblical Greek Workbook: Second Edition
Copyright © 1993, 2003 by William D. Mounce

Requests for information should be addressed to:

Zondervan, *Grand Rapids, Michigan 49530*

ISBN-10: 0-310-25086-2
ISBN-13: 978-0-310-25086-9

Edited by Verlyn D. Verbrugge
Typeset by Teknia Software, Inc.

Printed in the United States of America

07 08 09 10 11 12 • 20 19 18 17 16 15 14 13 12 11

Table of Contents

Participles

Nonindicative Moods and μι Verbs

Track 2

Preface

This text is the companion volume to *The Basics of Biblical Greek*. Except for the first two chapters, each chapter is broken into six sections.

. "Parsing" contains ten individual words to parse.

. "Warm-up" are short phrases that center on the grammar learned in the current chapter.

. "Translation" gives you ten verses, usually from the New Testament (rarely from the LXX or Apostolic Fathers). I trust that by translating the Bible from the first day, you will be encouraged. Any word you don't know is given in the text in parentheses.

. "Additional" gives you another ten sentences to translate. The first five are either made up or are from the Septuagint or Apostolic Fathers. As a general rule, if you can translate these you are doing really well. The last five sentences are from a variety of sources, including my imagination. I single-spaced these exercises to save paper and so lower the price of the book, and because many teachers do not require students to do all the exercises.

In sentences 11-15, if you don't know the word but could figure it out from its lexical form, its lexical form is given in the footnotes. If you can't figure out the word, its meaning is given in the text in parentheses. In sentences 16-20 you are expected to use the lexicon. If the form is too difficult, or if the word is not in the lexicon, then I either give the lexical form in footnotes (if you can figure it out from the lexical form) or the meaning in the text in parentheses.

. "Summary" covers any new grammar learned inductively in the exercises.

. The verse references to the biblical examples are listed in "References." This is to help you not think subconsciously about the verse in English, which might happen if I list the reference with the verse. If the verse reference has a parenthesis around it, this means I altered the biblical passage a little. If there is a dash, one of my friends or I made it up.

In the Appendix you will find "Track Two." There are two different ways to work through the textbook. Track One follows the normal order of the textbook by covering all the noun system and then moving on to verbs. Track Two allows you to cover some of the verbal system earlier. The chapters in the textbook are the same. A fuller discussion is in the textbook, pages 71-72. When you are done with one of the tracks, you can use the other track for review.

I would like to review a few suggestions I made in chapter 2 of the textbook, since they are so important.

. Treat these exercises as if they were a test. Learn the chapter, and do the exercises without looking back. If you are stuck on a parsing or a verse, then move on. When you are done with the exercises, go back and review the textbook, and then come back and try to finish the exercises. If you do the exercises with the textbook open, flipping back and forth, you will not get a clear picture of what you know, or don't know.

. Remind yourself constantly why you are learning Greek. If you forget that you are trying to gain a facility in learning God's Word, you will most likely become discouraged.

. Be consistent in your studying. You cannot learn Greek by cramming, unless you are an exceptional learner.

. Work with someone. It is difficult to learn Greek on your own.

. Pay close attention to the footnotes in the exercises. They will give you hints, fine-tune your grammar, and point out theologically interesting facts.

. Have fun! Greek is a great language. Remember that. Don't lose sight of your goal. Laugh a lot. My second year Greek class was nicknamed "The Zoo," taught by Dr. Walter W. Wessel at Bethel College. It was a great class, and I have always tried to maintain that same combination of levity and seriousness in my own classes; it works.

A special thanks to Verlyn Verbrugge, Matthew Smith, Juan Hernández Jr., Glen Riddle, and Jonathan Pennington for their help.

William D. Mounce

Abbreviations

The Greek Old Testament

Gen	Genesis
Ex	Exodus
Lev	Leviticus
Num	Numbers
Deut	Deuteronomy
Josh	Joshua
Judg	Judges
Ruth	Ruth
1 Sam	1 Samuel
1 Kgs	1 Kings
2 Kgs	2 Kings
1 Chr	1 Chronicles

1 Esdr	1 Esdr
Tob	Tob
1 Mac	1 Maccabe
2 Mac	2 Maccabe
Ps	Psaln
Ode	Odes of Solomo
Eccl	Ecclesiast
Wsd	Wisdom of Solomo
PsSol	Psalms of Solomo
Is	Isaia
Jer	Jeremia
Dan	Dani

The New Testament

Mt	Matthew
Mk	Mark
Lk	Luke
Jn	John
Ac	Acts
Rom	Romans
1 Cor	1 Corinthians
2 Cor	2 Corinthians
Gal	Galatians
Eph	Ephesians
Phil	Philippians
Col	Colossians
1 Th	1 Thessalonians
2 Th	2 Thessalonians

1 Tim	1 Timoth
2 Tim	2 Timoth
Ti	Titu
Phlm	Philemo
Heb	Hebrew
Jas	Jame
1 Pt	1 Pete
2 Pt	2 Pete
1 Jn	1 Joh
2 Jn	2 Joh
3 Jn	3 Joh
Jude	Jud
Rev	Revelatio

Early Christian Literature

1 Clem	1 Clement
2 Clem	2 Clement
IMag	Ignatius to the Magnesians
IPhil	Ignatius to the Philadelphians

IRom	Ignatius to the Romar
Barn	Barnaba
Shep	Shepherd of Herma

General

NIV	New International Version
LXX	Septuagint (The Greek Old Testament)
A	Codex Alexandrinus
𝔐	Majority Text

p.	pag
pp.	page
f.	one following vers
ff.	more than one following vers

The Alphabet and Pronunciation

Write out and pronounce the Greek letters of the alphabet several times. It is essential to learn how to recognize, write, and pronounce each letter. You cannot continue until you have done so.

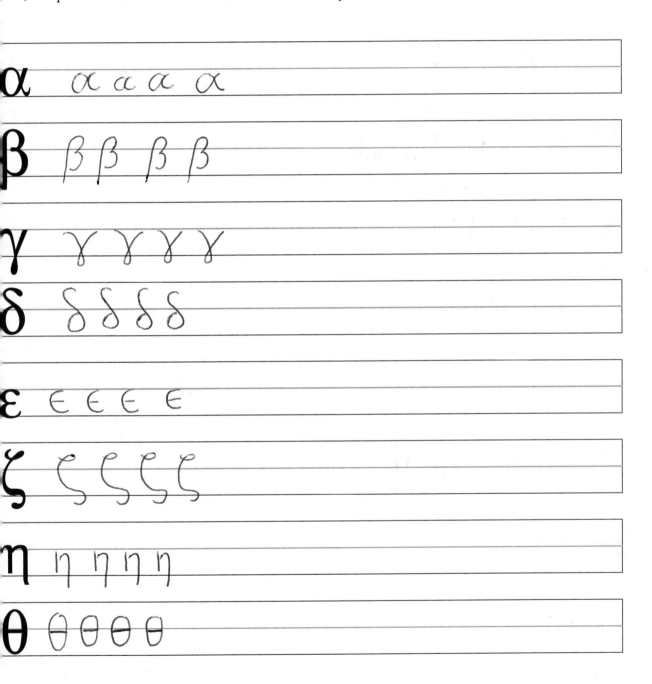

ι ι ι ι ι

κ κ κ κ κ

λ λ λ λ λ

μ μ μ μ μ μ

ν ν ν ν ν

ξ ξ ξ ξ ξ

ο ο ο ο ο

π π π π π

ρ ρ ρ ρ ρ

σ σ σ σ σ

ς ς ς ς ς

Grammar

1. What are the seven vowels?

    a. α

    b. ε

    c. η

    d. ι

    e. ο

    f. υ

    g. ω

2. When do you find the two different forms of sigma?

   a. At the beginning or middle of a word. σ

   b. At the end of a word. ς

3. What are the two breathing marks, and when do you find them?

   a. ᾿ Smooth breathing

   b. ῾ rough breathing

   Both are placed over the first vowel in words be with a vowel. They may be placed over a rho b a word.

4. How does the iota subscript affect pronunciation? It does not.

5. When is the diaeresis used? To indicate that two vowels are to be pronounced separately, not as a diphthong.

Punctuation and Syllabification

Syllabification

Divide the following words into syllables. If you are learning the rules, indicate which ones apply.

1. ἀμήν   ἀ μήν

2. γραφή   γρα φή

3. ἔσχατος   ἔσ χα τος

4. καρδία   καρ δί α

5. πνεῦμα   πνεῦ μα

6. προφήτης   προ φή της

7. σάββατον   σάβ βα τον

8. ἄγγελος   ἄγ γε λος

9. ἄνθρωπος   ἄν θρω πος

10. περιπατέω   πε ρι πα τέ ω

Reading

I cannot stress enough how important it is to learn to pronounce the language. After years of teaching Greek I assure you that if you do not learn to pronounce it, you will never master the language. As you are reading, do not worry about the meaning of the words.

Practice reading this selection over and over and over. Read it out loud until you can read it correctly in under 15 minutes. You can hear me read the passage on the CD-ROM included with the textbook.

ΙΩΑΝΝΟΥ Α 1:5–2:5

1:5 Καὶ ἔστιν αὕτη ἡ ἀγγελία ἣν ἀκηκόαμεν ἀπ' αὐτοῦ καὶ ἀναγγέλλομεν ὑμῖν, ὅτι ὁ θεὸς φῶς ἐστιν καὶ σκοτία ἐν αὐτῷ οὐκ ἔστιν οὐδεμία. 1:6 Ἐὰν εἴπωμεν ὅτι κοινωνίαν ἔχομεν μετ' αὐτοῦ καὶ ἐν τῷ σκότει περιπατῶμεν, ψευδόμεθα καὶ οὐ ποιοῦμεν τὴν ἀλήθειαν· 1:7 ἐὰν δὲ ἐν τῷ φωτὶ περιπατῶμεν ὡς αὐτός ἐστιν ἐν τῷ φωτί, κοινωνίαν ἔχομεν μετ' ἀλλήλων καὶ τὸ αἷμα Ἰησοῦ τοῦ υἱοῦ αὐτοῦ καθαρίζει ἡμᾶς ἀπὸ πάσης ἁμαρτίας. 1:8 ἐὰν εἴπωμεν ὅτι ἁμαρτίαν οὐκ ἔχομεν, ἑαυτοὺς πλανῶμεν καὶ ἡ ἀλήθεια οὐκ ἔστιν ἐν ἡμῖν. 1:9 ἐὰν ὁμολογῶμεν τὰς ἁμαρτίας ἡμῶν, πιστός ἐστιν καὶ δίκαιος, ἵνα ἀφῇ ἡμῖν τὰς ἁμαρτίας καὶ καθαρίσῃ ἡμᾶς ἀπὸ πάσης ἀδικίας. 1:10 ἐὰν εἴπωμεν ὅτι οὐχ ἡμαρτήκαμεν, ψεύστην ποιοῦμεν αὐτὸν καὶ ὁ λόγος αὐτοῦ οὐκ ἔστιν ἐν ἡμῖν.

2:1 Τεκνία μου, ταῦτα γράφω ὑμῖν ἵνα μὴ ἁμάρτητε. καὶ ἐάν τις ἁμάρτῃ, παράκλητον ἔχομεν πρὸς τὸν πατέρα Ἰησοῦν Χριστὸν δίκαιον· 2:2 καὶ αὐτὸς ἱλασμός ἐστιν περὶ τῶν ἁμαρτιῶν ἡμῶν, οὐ περὶ τῶν ἡμετέρων δὲ μόνον ἀλλὰ καὶ περὶ ὅλου τοῦ κόσμου.

2:3 Καὶ ἐν τούτῳ γινώσκομεν ὅτι ἐγνώκαμεν αὐτόν, ἐὰν τὰς ἐντολὰς αὐτοῦ τηρῶμεν.

2:4 ὁ λέγων ὅτι ἔγνωκα αὐτὸν καὶ τὰς ἐντολὰς αὐτοῦ μὴ τηρῶν, ψεύστης ἐστὶν καὶ ἐν τούτῳ ἡ ἀλήθεια οὐκ ἔστιν· 2:5 ὃς δ᾽ ἂν τηρῇ αὐτοῦ τὸν λόγον, ἀληθῶς ἐν τούτῳ ἡ ἀγάπη τοῦ θεοῦ τετελείωται, ἐν τούτῳ γινώσκομεν ὅτι ἐν αὐτῷ ἐσμεν. 2:6 ὁ λέγων ἐν αὐτῷ μένειν ὀφείλει καθὼς ἐκεῖνος περιεπάτησεν καὶ αὐτὸς [οὕτως] περιπατεῖν.

ΗΡΩΔΗΣ ΜΟΝΙ-

ΜΟΥ ΚΑΙ ΙΟΥΣΤΟΣ

ΥΙΟΣ ΑΜΑ ΤΟΙΣ

ΤΕΚΝΟΙΣ ΕΚΤΙ-

ΣΑΝ

ΤΟΝ ΚΙΟΝΑ

This inscription is on a column in the synagogue in Capernaum. The synagogue was built on top of a first century synagogue. The inscription reads, Ἡρώδης Μονιμοῦ καὶ Ἰοῦστος υἱὸς ἅμα τοῖς τέκνοις ἔκτισαν τὸν κίονα, of course without the accents. It means, "Herod (the son) of Monimos and Justos (his) son together with their children erected this column."

Review #1

Introduction

The review gives you the opportunity to evaluate your performance to this point. Treat it like a test.

Definitions

. What is a gamma nasal, and how is it pronounced?

Gamma becomes nasal before γ κ Χ or ξ
↳ pronounced like an "n"

. What is a diphthong?

Two vowels that produce one sound when pronounced.

. What is an improper diphthong?

A diphthong formed by a vowel and an iota subscript.

. Describe when an apostrophe is used.

An apostrophe fills in for the missing vowel which drops out when a preposition or conjunction ends in a vowel and the following word begins with a vowel.

Exercises

. Write out the alphabet.

αβγδεζηθικλμνξοπρστυφχψω

. How are the two sigmas used in one word?

σ to begin a word or in the middle of a word
ς at the end of a word

3. Give an example of a smooth breathing mark and a rough breathing mark.

    ἄνθρωπον
    ὑπέρ

4. Punctuation Marks. Match the Greek punctuation mark with its function.

    a. ,   semi-colon

    b. .   question mark

    c. ˙ (above line)   comma

    d. ;   period

5. Accents. Match the appropriate accent marks with their proper name.

    a. ´   circumflex

    b. `   acute

    c. ^   grave

6. How does an accent affect a translation?

    "Some words are identical except for their accents."

7. Syllabification. Divide the following words into syllables.

    a. διδάσκων   δι δά σκων

    b. διαμαρτυρόμενος   δι α μαρ τυ ρό με νος

    c. ἄνθρωπος   ἄν θρω πος

    d. λέγοντες   λέγ γον τες

    e. βάλλω   βάλ λω

Exercise 6

Nominative and Accusative; Definite Article

Introduction

Because this is your first full lesson with parsing and translating, I would like to offer some helpful suggestions. Your teacher may want to add a few more.

- Treat these exercises as though they were a test. In other words, do not keep looking back for the answers in the textbook. Learn the chapter and do the exercises. If you are not able to do all the exercises, go back, review the chapter, and redo the exercises.

- Write your vocabulary words on flash cards and go through them a couple of times before doing the exercises.

- Do not get frustrated because you do not know all the words in the exercises. One of the problems in introducing you to the New Testament this early is that there are things you just do not know. Because I want to give you the satisfaction of actually applying what you are learning by translating from the New Testament, I have given you the helps needed to translate each verse. So enjoy the fact that you are actually translating from Scripture, and remember that as time goes on you will need less help.

Inductive Methodology and the Footnotes

There are two different ways to learn a language, the "deductive" and the "inductive." The deductive emphasizes charts and a structure often foreign to the language. The inductive attempts to teach a language as it is naturally learned, learning grammar as you encounter it. However, if you are not immersed in the language and its culture, this method is difficult. I have tried to blend the two. One of the ways I do this is to teach the basic grammar in the chapter, and then as we meet some of the more unusual aspects of Greek grammar in the exercises, to discuss that grammar there. So please pay close attention to the footnotes in the workbook.

Parsing

Be sure to identify the word's stem and the case ending of each word.

	Inflected	Case	Number	Gender	Lexical form	Inflected meaning
1.	ἄνθρωπον	A	S	M	ἄνθρωπος	human being, man
2.	ὧραι	N	P	F	ὥρα ὥρα	times hours
3.	τήν	A	P	F	ἡ	the [definite article]
4.	βασιλείας	A	P	F	βασιλεία	kingdoms
5.	θεοί	N	P	M	θεός	gods
6.	τό	N/A	S	N	τό	the [definite article]
7.	λόγους	A	P	M	λόγος	words

Inflected	Case	Number	Gender	Lexical form	Inflected meaning
8. καιροί	N	P	M	καιρός	(appointed) times
9. τάς	A	P	F	ἡ	the
10. Χριστόν	A	S	M	Χριστός	Christ

Warm-up

The exercises in this section are short phrases that center in on the grammar you learned in the current chapter. They will not necessarily make a great deal of sense, and they are not always from the Bible.

As we have learned, the verb contains its own subject. λέγει means "he says," "she says," or "it says," depending on the gender required by the context. In our exercises, if a verb is third person singular, its definition is listed like this: ἐδίδασκεν (he/she/it was teaching). It is up to your understanding of the context to decide on the correct gender. This is true whether the subject is expressed or implied in the verb.

α. ἡ ὥρα ἔρχεται (he/she/it comes). The ~~time~~ hour comes

β. ἀγαπῶσι (they love) δὲ τὸν[1] θεόν. And they love God.

γ. ἔσωσεν (he/she/it saved) αὐτὸς ἄλλους. He saved others.

δ. βλέπω (I see)[2] νῦν τὸν Ἰησοῦν καὶ τοὺς ἀποστόλους. Now I see Jesus and the apostle

ε. ἡ ἀγαπὴ μακροθυμεῖ (he/she/it is patient). Love is patient

ζ. ἐγὼ γινώσκω (I know) ὅτι τὸ ἔργον τετέλεσται (he/she/it is finished). I know that the work is finished.

η. ἐποίησε (he/she/it made) ὁ λόγος τὸν κόσμον. The Word made the world.

Translation

The definition of any word that you do not know (except proper names and places) is listed after the Greek word in parentheses. I don't define the same word twice in the same verse. If you do not understand the form of the Greek word I have defined, and many times you will not, do not worry about it. The day's own trouble is sufficient. If two or more words that you do not know occur together, their meaning is given in the footnotes.

Remember to divide the sentence into its parts and to identify the subject, verb, and direct object (if any). Because you are just starting to read biblical Greek, we can only show you bits and pieces of verses. In a few chapters the sentences will be fuller and make better sense.

1. ἀποστέλλω (I send) τὸν ἄγγελον.
    I send the messenger.

---

[1] Notice how Greek uses the article in places where we normally would not. Greek often uses the article with proper nouns. In this situation you can drop the article in your translation if you think the context requires it.

[2] Hint: There is no expressed subject; it must be supplied from the verb.

αὐτοὶ τὸν θεὸν ὄψονται (they will see).

They will see God

ἐδίδασκεν (he/she/it was teaching) αὐτούς.

He/she was teaching them.

Διώκετε (Pursue!) τὴν ἀγάπην.

Pursue love.

ἐραυνᾶτε (You search)[3] τὰς γραφάς.

You search the writings.

πεπλήρωται (he/she/it has come) ὁ καιρὸς καὶ ἤγγικεν (he/she/it has drawn near) ἡ βασιλεία τοῦ θεοῦ.[4] *The time has come and the kingdom of God has drawn near.*

ἐτέλεσεν (he/she/it finished) ὁ Χριστός τοὺς λόγους.

Christ ~~has~~ finished the words.

τὸ σάββατον διὰ (for) τὸν ἄνθρωπον ἐγένετο (he/she/it was made) καὶ οὐχ ὁ ἄνθρωπος[5] διὰ τὸ σάββατον. *For the Sabbath was made for man and not man for the Sabbath.*

καὶ ἀπέστειλεν (he/she/it sent) αὐτοὺς κηρύσσειν (to preach) τὴν βασιλείαν τοῦ θεοῦ.[6]

And he/she sent them to preach the kingdom of God.

ἐραυνᾶτε could either be in the indicative mood stating a fact, or in the imperative mood stating a command, "Search!"

τοῦ θεοῦ means "of God."

Notice that there is no verb in the second half of this verse. When a Greek sentence is composed of two parallel ideas, verb(s) from the first half are often unexpressed but assumed in the second half.

τοῦ θεοῦ means "of God."

10. καὶ νῦν ἡ βασιλεία σου (your) οὐ στήσεται (he/she/it will continue).

And now your kingdom does not continue

Additional

The first five exercises in this section are either made up or are from another source such as the Septuagint or Didache. I want you to work with some verses whose English translation you probably don't know. The last five exercises are usually biblical verses, but the difference is that the helps I normally provide are absent. There will also be words you do not know; I want you to learn how to use the lexicon in the textbook. If the Greek word is too difficult to figure out, I will provide the necessary hints.

11. ὁ δὲ Παῦλος ἔφη (he/she/it said)· ἔπεμψα (I sent) ἄλλους ἀποστόλους.

But Paul said, "I sent other apostles.

12. τὸν Χριστὸν πιστεύουσιν (they believe) οἱ ἄνθρωποι ὅτι γινώσκουσι (they know) τὴν ἀγάπην αὐτοῦ (his).

The people believe Christ because they know his love.

13. Λαμὲχ δέ εἶπεν τοὺς λόγους.

And Lamech said the words

14. καὶ ἤρεσαν (they pleased) οἱ λόγοι τὸν Πιλᾶτον.

And the words pleased Pilate.

15. τὰ σάββατα φυλάξεσθε (you will keep).

You will keep the Sabbaths

16. τὰ ἔργα τοῦ θεοῦ αὐτοὶ πιστεύουσι (they believe).

They believe the works of God.

17. κύριον καὶ χριστὸν ἐποίησεν (he/she/it made) ὁ θεός αὐτόν.

And God made Christ Lord. And God made him Christ and Lord.

18. τὸ φῶς ἐλήλυθεν (he/she/it came) εἰς τὸν κόσμον καὶ ἠγάπησαν (they loved) οἱ ἄνθρωποι μᾶλλον τὸ σκότος ἢ τὸ φῶς.

Light came into the world and the people loved the dark be/more than the light.

19. καὶ ἐκρίνοσαν (they judged) τὸν λαὸν πᾶσαν (every) ὥραν.

And they judged the people every hour

20. καὶ αὐτοὶ ἦραν (they lifted up) τὰς φωνάς αὐτῶν (their).

And they lifted up their voices

Summary

The summaries at the end of the chapter cover what you learned inductively in the exercises and the footnotes. The summaries are limited to the first fifteen exercises; not everyone will do the final five exercises.

1. Sometimes the article can be dropped in your translation, while other times it is important. The grammar pertaining to the article can become quite complex, and I will point out different aspects of the article as we come across them. In this chapter we saw that Greek tends to use the article with proper nouns.

2. When a Greek sentence is composed of two parallel ideas, verb(s) from the first half are often unexpressed but assumed in the second half.

References

A "—" means the exercise is made up. If I altered an actual verse, its reference is enclosed in parentheses.

α. —; β. —; γ. —; δ. —; ε. —; ζ. —; η. —; **1.** Mk 1:2; **2.** Mt 5:8; **3.** Mk 2:13; **4.** 1 Cor 14:1; **5.** Jn 5:39; **6.** Mk 1:15; **7.** (Mt 7:28); **8.** Mk 2:27; **9.** Lk 9:2; **10.** 1 Sam 13:14; **11.** —; **12.** —; **13.** (Gen 4:23); **14.** —; **15.** (Ex 31:13); **16.** —; **17.** (Ac 2:36); **18.** Jn 3:19; **19.** Ex 18:26; **20.** (Lk 17:13).

Exercise 7

Genitive and Dative

Parsing

"(2x)" means the form has two possibilities.

Inflected	Case	Number	Gender	Lexical form	Inflected meaning
1. ἀγάπη	D	S	F	ἀγάπη	to love
2. κυρίοις	D	P	M	κύριος	to the lords
3. ἁμαρτιῶν	G	P	F	ἁμαρτία	of sins
4. τούς	G	P	M N	ὁ τό	the
5. ἀνθρώπῳ	D	S	M	ἄνθρωπος	to the human being/ to man
6. υἱούς	A	P	M	υἱός	sons
7. λόγου	G	S	M	λόγος	of the word
8. τά (2x)	N A	P	N	τό	the
9. αὐτοῖς (2x)	D	P	M N	αὐτό	to them
10. βασιλείας (2x)	G A	S P	F	βασιλεία	of the kingdoms / the kingdoms

Write Out the Forms of the Article

	masc	fem	neut
nom sg	ὁ	ἡ	τό
gen sg	τοῦ	τῆς	τοῦ
dat sg	τῷ	τῇ	τῷ
acc sg	τόν	τήν	τό

	masc	fem	neut
nom pl	οἱ	αἱ	τά
gen pl	τῶν	τῶν ~~τόν~~	τῶν
dat pl	τοῖς	ταῖς	τοῖς
acc pl	τούς	τάς	τά

Warm-up

1. ἄγγελος κυρίου   angel / messenger of the Lord

2. φωνὴν ἀγγέλων   voice of angels

15

707 330 8511 c

866   899   6440

707 469 0759 h

γ. ἡ ἀγάπη τοῦ Χριστοῦ
The love of Christ

δ. ταῖς ἁμαρτίαις τοῦ καιροῦ
The sins of the time/age

ε. φωνὴ θεοῦ καὶ οὐκ ἀνθρώπου
voice of God and not of man

ζ. ὁ κύριος τοῦ οὐρανοῦ
The Lord of Heaven

η. ὄψεσθε (you will see) τὴν δόξαν κυρίου.
You will see the glory of the Lord.

Translation

1. εἶπεν αὐτοῖς ὁ Ἰησοῦς.

Jesus spoke to them.

2. ἐλάλει (he/she/it was speaking) αὐτοῖς τὸν λόγον.

He was speaking the word to them.

3. τὴν ἀγάπην τοῦ θεοῦ οὐκ[1] ἔχετε (you have).

You do not have the love of God.

4. ἐπιμένωμεν (we should continue) τῇ ἁμαρτίᾳ;

Should we continue in sin?

5. ἀποστελεῖ (he/she/it will send) ὁ υἱὸς τοῦ ἀνθρώπου τοὺς ἀγγέλους αὐτοῦ.

The Son will send His messengers to the man.

---

[1] When the Greek sentence has a negation, you normally will have to add "do" or "did" to make your translation proper English. "Do" is present tense, "did" is past. Let context determine which is appropriate.

6. ἤγγικεν (he/she/it has drawn near) γὰρ ἡ βασιλεία τῶν οὐρανῶν.[2]

   For the kingdom of heaven has drawn near.

7. ἐπίστευσεν[3] ὁ ἄνθρωπος τῷ λόγῳ.

   The man believed the word.

8. γνωρισθῇ (he/she/it might be made known) νῦν ταῖς ἀρχαῖς καὶ ταῖς ἐξουσίαις.

   Now it might be made known to the rulers and to the powers (authorities).

9. ἡ ἀγάπη τοῦ θεοῦ ἐκκέχυται (he/she/it has been poured) ἐν ταῖς καρδίαις ἡμῶν (our).

   The love of God has been poured into our hearts.

10. [4] Ἀρχὴ τοῦ εὐαγγελίου Ἰησοῦ Χριστοῦ [[5] υἱοῦ[6] θεοῦ].

    The beginning of the gospel of Jesus Christ, Son of God.

Additional

1. ἐξουσίαν ἔχει (he/she/it has) ὁ υἱὸς τοῦ ἀνθρώπου ἀφιέναι (to forgive) ἁμαρτίας.

   The Son of man has power to forgive sins.

2. ἡ ἀγάπη γὰρ τοῦ θεοῦ διδάσκει (he/she/it teaches) τὴν ἐξουσίαν τοῦ κυρίου.

   For the love of God teaches the power of the Lord.

This word sometimes occurs in the plural, but it is preferable to translate it as a singular in English.

"He/she/it believed." This particular verb often takes its direct object in the dative and therefore you would not use the key word, in this case, with τῷ λόγῳ.

It is typical for the article to be dropped from titles, salutations, well-known phrases, etc. This first verse functions as the title to the gospel, and is not a complete sentence.

Square brackets are the editors' way of telling us that there is some uncertainty as to whether the enclosed words are authentic, i.e., original. This should raise the issue of "textual criticism" and your teacher will, sometime, tell you about it.

υἱοῦ is said to be in *apposition* to Ἰησοῦ Χριστοῦ. This is a common construction in Greek and should be learned well.

When a noun (or phrase) is used to further clarify the meaning of a previous word, that noun can be put in the same number and case as the word it is describing. Alternatively, it can be placed in the genitive case (which is called a *genitive of apposition*).

An easy way to translate an appositional phrase is to put commas before it, or a comma and "namely."

13. αἱ ἀρχαὶ τοῦ Ἰσραὴλ οὐκ ἐπίστευσαν (they believed) ὅτι ὁ Ἰησοῦς μισεῖ (he/she/it hates) τὰς ἁμαρτίας. *The rulers of Israel did not believe that Jesus hates sins.*

14. ὁ δὲ λόγος τοῦ Ἰησοῦ ἔχει (he/she/it has) ἐξουσίαν ὅτι ὁ θεὸς ἦν (he/she/it was) ἐν τῇ ἀρχῇ τοῦ κόσμου. *And the word of Jesus has power since God was in the beginning of the world.*

15. ἐγὼ ποιῶ (I do) τὸ ἔργον τοῦ ἀγγέλου αὐτὸς δὲ ἔχει (he/she/it has) τὴν δόξαν τοῦ θεοῦ. *I do the work of the messenger but he has the glory of God.*

16. οἱ δὲ υἱοὶ τῆς βασιλείας ἐκβληθήσονται (they will be thrown) εἰς τὸ σκότος. *But the sons of the kingdom will be thrown into the dark.*

17. εἶπεν αὐτῷ· ἐν ἁμαρτίαις σὺ ἐγεννήθης (you were born). *He said to him, "You were born in sins."*

18. λατρεύω (I serve) τὸν θεὸν ὅτι ἐγὼ πιστεύω τῷ εὐαγγελίῳ τοῦ υἱοῦ αὐτοῦ. *I serve God because I believe the gospel of His Son.*

19. καὶ σὺ εἰσακούσῃ (you will hear) καὶ ἵλεως (merciful) ἔσῃ (you will be) ταῖς ἁμαρτίαις τοῦ λαοῦ τοῦ Ἰσραὴλ καὶ οἴσετε (you will bring) αὐτοὺς εἰς τὴν γῆν. *And you will hear and be merciful the sins of the people of Israel and you will bring them into the*

20. αὐτή εἶπεν τῷ Ἰησοῦ ὅτι οὗτοι ὀργίζουσι (they are angry) τῇ βασιλείᾳ τῶν ἀνθρώπων. *She said to Jesus that they are angry at the kingdom of men.*

Summary

1. You can add "do" or "did" to your translation if necessary, such as when you are translating a negation.

2. Some verbs take their direct object in the dative, and a few even in the genitive.

3. Articles can be dropped in the Greek of titles, salutations, and well-known phrases.

4. Square brackets mark text whose authenticity is questioned.

5. *Apposition* is a construction that allows the author to use one noun to define another. The noun that is in apposition will either be in the same case and number as the word to which it is in apposition, or it will be in the genitive regardless of the case of the other noun. You can translate the noun by preceding it with a comma, or with "namely."

References

α. Mt 1:20; β. Rev 5:11; γ. (2 Cor 5:14); δ. —; ε. Ac 12:22; ζ. —; η. Ex 16:7; 1. Mk 1:17; 2. Mk 2:2; 3. Jn 5:42; 4. Rom 6:1; 5. Mt 13:41; 6. Mt 3:2; 7. Jn 4:50; 8. Eph 3:10; 9. Rom 5:5; 10. Mk 1:1; 11. Mk 2:10; 12. —; 13. —; 14. —; 15. —; 16. Mt 8:12; 17. (Jn 9:34); 18. —; 19. (1 Kgs 8:34); 20. —.

Exercise 8

Prepositions and εἰμί

ἐν τῷ εὐαγγελίῳ *in the Gospel*

εἰς τὴν οἰκίαν *into the house*

μετὰ τοῦ Ἰωάννου *according to John*

καὶ ἦν κύριος μετὰ Ἰωσήφ. *And the Lord was with Joseph*

οὗτός ἐστιν ὁ υἱὸς τοῦ θεοῦ. *This is the Son of God.*

θεοί ἐστε. *Ye are gods.*

ὁ θεὸς ἀγάπη ἐστίν. *God is love.*

Translation

Identify each preposition, the object of each preposition, and what word the prepositional phrase modifies.

ἔρχεται (he/she/it comes) εἰς οἶκον.

S/he comes into the house.

ἐξῆλθεν (he/she/it came out) ἐξ[1] αὐτοῦ.

It came out of him.

Δόξαν παρὰ ἀνθρώπων οὐ λαμβάνω (I receive).

I do not receive glory from men.

Notice the repetition of the preposition following the compound verb. This is considered good Greek, but in your translation you would not repeat the preposition.

19

4. ἐλάλησεν (he/she/it spoke) ὁ Ἰησοῦς ἐν παραβολαῖς τοῖς ὄχλοις.

   Jesus spoke in parables to the

5. καὶ ἐβαπτίζοντο (they were being baptized) ὑπ᾽ αὐτοῦ[2] ἐν τῷ Ἰορδάνῃ.

   And they were being baptized by him in the Jordan.

6. [3] κύριός ἐστιν ὁ υἱὸς τοῦ ἀνθρώπου καὶ τοῦ σαββάτου.

7. Καὶ ἐγένετο (he/she/it came to pass that) ἐν ἐκείναις[4] ταῖς ἡμέραις ἦλθεν (he/she/it went) Ἰησοῦ

   ἀπὸ Ναζαρὲτ τῆς Γαλιλαίας καὶ ἐβαπτίσθη (he/she/it was baptized) εἰς τὸν Ἰορδάνην ὑπὸ

   Ἰωάννου.

   And it came to pass in those days that Jesus went to Nazareth
   of Galilee and was baptized in the Jordan by John.

8. [5] Ὁ θεός ἀγάπη ἐστίν, καί ὁ μένων (one remaining) ἐν τῇ ἀγάπῃ ἐν τῷ θεῷ μένει (he/she/it

   remains) καί ὁ θεός ἐν αὐτῷ μένει.

   God is love, and one remaining in love remains in God
   and God remains in him.

---

[2]   αὐτοῦ means "his" when it is showing possession. When it is the object of a preposition it means "him."

[3]   Hint: What is the subject and what is the predicate in this verse?

      Hint: καί has more than one meaning. Do not assume it must mean "and" here.

[4]   "Those," modifying ἡμέραις.

[5]   Hint: How many complete thoughts are there in this verse? Divide it into its parts.

. καὶ ἔλεγεν (he/she/it was saying) αὐτοῖς· τὸ σάββατον (διὰ) τὸν ἄνθρωπον ἐγένετο (he/she/it was

made) καὶ οὐχ ὁ ἄνθρωπος (διὰ) τὸ σάββατον.

And s/he was saying to them: the Sabbath was made for man and not man for the Sabbath.

0. Καὶ ὁ Ἰησοῦς (μετὰ) τῶν μαθητῶν (disciples) αὐτοῦ ἀνεχώρησεν (he/she/it withdrew) (πρὸς) τὴν

θάλασσαν.

And Jesus withdrew with his disciples to the sea.

Additional

1. ὁ Ἰωάννης καὶ ὁ Πέτρος εἰσὶν μετὰ τοῦ Ἰησοῦ ἐν τῷ οἴκῳ τοῦ κυρίου.
John and Peter are with Jesus in the house of the Lord.

2. ἀλλ᾽ οἱ ὄχλοι ἐπορεύθησαν (they traveled) πρὸς τὸν Ἰησοῦν ἀπὸ τῆς θαλάσσης τῆς Γαλιλαίας.
*But the **crowd** traveled Jesus Sea of Galilee.*

3. καὶ εἶπεν ὁ θεὸς τῷ Νῶε καὶ τοῖς υἱοῖς αὐτοῦ μετ᾽ αὐτοῦ ...
And God said to Noah and to his sons with him...

4. μετὰ δὲ τὰς ἡμέρας τὰς πολλὰς[7] ... ἐτελεύτησεν (he/she/it died) ὁ βασιλεὺς (king) Αἰγύπτου καὶ κατεστέναξαν (they groaned) οἱ υἱοὶ Ἰσραὴλ ἀπὸ τῶν ἔργων καὶ ἀνεβόησαν (they cried out) ... πρὸς τὸν θεὸν ἀπὸ[8] τῶν ἔργων. *After many days the king of Egypt died and the sons of Israel groaned because of the work and they cried out to God because of the work.*

5. καὶ ἐκάλεσεν (he/she/it called out to) αὐτὸν ἄγγελος κυρίου ἐκ τοῦ οὐρανοῦ καὶ εἶπεν αὐτῷ· Ἀβραάμ, Ἀβραάμ, ὁ δὲ εἶπεν· ἰδοὺ (behold) ἐγώ. *And an angel of the Lord called out to him out of Heaven and said to him, "Abraham, Abraham," he said, "Behold me."*

6. οὐ γὰρ ἀπέστειλεν (he/she/it sent) ὁ θεὸς τὸν[9] υἱὸν εἰς τὸν κόσμον ἵνα κρίνῃ (he/she/it might condemn) τὸν κόσμον, ἀλλ᾽ ἵνα σωθῇ (he/she/it might be saved) ὁ κόσμος δι᾽ αὐτοῦ.

7. μεταβέβηκεν (he/she/it has been transformed) ἐκ τοῦ θανάτου εἰς τὴν ζωήν.
S/he has been transformed out of death into life.

The definition of διά with the accusative is "on account of." As is true of all the prepositions, this is only a basic definition, one that can be colored by the needs of the context. What is another English preposition that means the same thing as "on account of," and yet makes a better translation? As you become more comfortable with translating Greek, you will enjoy this kind of flexibility in your translating.

τὰς πολλὰς modifies ἡμέρας and means "many."

You can translate this ἀπό as "because of."

While we have said that this word is the "definite article" and is translated as "the," you are starting to see that it has a much wider range of meaning. Among other meanings, the word can be translated as a personal pronoun, in this case "his."

18. πιστεύετε (Believe[10]) εἰς τὸν θεὸν καὶ εἰς ἐμὲ (me) πιστεύετε.

    Believe in God and believe in me.

19. σὺ εἶ ὁ Χριστὸς ὁ υἱὸς[11] τοῦ εὐλογητοῦ (Blessed);

    Are you Christ, the son of the Blessed?

20. ἐξῆρεν (he/she/it took) δὲ Μωϋσῆς τοὺς υἱοὺς Ἰσραὴλ ἀπὸ θαλάσσης ἐρυθρᾶς (of red) καὶ ἤγαγεν (he/she/it led) αὐτοὺς εἰς τὴν ἔρημον Σούρ.[12]

    And Moses took the sons of Israel   Red Sea and led them into

Summary

1. Greek and English are not codes; there is not an exact one-for-one equivalence. This is especially true in vocabulary, and especially with prepositions. As you get to know the range of meanings a word can have, you will be more comfortable allowing the context to mold your choice of words. But remember, avoid allowing your knowledge of the English Bible to affect your word choice. Look at the context provided by the Greek verse.

References

α. Mk 1:15; β. Mt 2:11; γ. —; δ. Gen 39:2; ε. Jn 1:34; ζ. Jn 10:34; η. 1 Jn 4:8; **1**. Mk 3:20; **2**. Mk 1:26; **3**. Jn 5:41; **4**. M 13:34; **5**. Mk 1:5; **6**. Mk 2:28; **7**. Mk 1:9; **8**. 1 Jn 4:16; **9**. Mk 2:27; **10**. Mk 3:7; **11**. —; **12**. —; **13**. Gen 9:8; **14**. Ex 2:23 **15**. Gen 22:11; **16**. Jn 3:17; **17**. Jn 5:24; **18**. Jn 14:1; **19**. Mk 14:61; **20**. Ex 15:22.

---

[10] πιστεύετε can be either a command or a question. (In either case, the subject would be "you.") Both forms in Greek look the same. What do you think best fits this context? Remember, you can ignore the presence, or absence, of punctuation.

As you will quickly see, Greek does not always answer all your questions. But it does show the range of possible interpretations, and from there context helps you make the final decision.

[11] Why is this word in the nominative?

[12] Many proper names are not declined, but context generally clarifies their case.

Adjectives

:cause you are not parsing in context but looking at words in isolation, some inflected forms could be more
an one gender. Pick just one.

Inflected	Case	Number	Gender	Lexical form	Inflected meaning
ἀγαθῶν	G	P	M̶F̶N̶	ἀγαθός	of the good
πιστάς	A / E	P	F	πιστός	faithful
κακῷ	D	S	M	κακός	to the bad
νεκρόν	A	S	N	νεκρός	the dead (person)
ἐσχάτους	A	P	M	ἐσχάτος	the last things
κόσμου	G	S	M	κόσμος	of the world
ἐντολαῖς	D	P	F	ἐντολή	to the commandments
ἐμά	N / A	P	N	ἐμός	my
τρίτη	D	S	F	τρίτος	to the third
0. ἀλλήλας	A / G̶ / I̶S̶ / A	P̶ / I̶S̶ / P	F	ἀλλήλων	one another

ὁ πιστὸς δοῦλος   the faithful servant

τῇ τρίτῃ ἡμέρᾳ   on the third day

τὸν υἱὸν τὸν ἀγαπητόν   the good son

υἱὸν ἀγαπητόν   the good son / the son is good.

τὸν λόγον τὸν ἐμόν   my work

οἱ υἱοὶ τοῦ πονηροῦ (2x)   the sons of evil / the sons of the evil one

πιστὸς δὲ ὁ θεός.   and God is faithful

Translation

1. ὁ λόγος ... κρινεῖ (he/she/it will judge) αὐτὸν ἐν τῇ ἐσχάτῃ ἡμέρα.

   The Word will judge him on the last day.

2. [1] ἦν δὲ ὥρα τρίτη καὶ ἐσταύρωσαν (they crucified) αὐτόν.

   And it was the third hour and they crucified him.

3. ὁ πατὴρ (father) ἐγείρει (he/she/it raises) τοὺς νεκρούς.

   The Father raises the dead

4. [2] ὁ θεωρῶν (one who sees) τὸν υἱὸν καὶ πιστεύων (who believes) εἰς αὐτὸν ἔχῃ (he/she/it has) ζωὴν
   αἰώνιον, καὶ ἀναστήσω (I will raise) αὐτὸν ἐγὼ [ἐν] τῇ ἐσχάτῃ ἡμέρα.

   *The one who sees the Son and who believes in him has **eternal** life
   and I will raise him on the last day.*

5. μὴ νικῶ (Be conquered!) ὑπὸ τοῦ κακοῦ, ἀλλὰ νίκα (Conquer!) ἐν[3] τῷ ἀγαθῷ τὸ κακόν.

   Do not be conquered by evil,   but conquer evil with good.

6. ἔσονται[4] οἱ ἔσχατοι πρῶτοι καὶ οἱ πρῶτοι ἔσχατοι.[5]

   The last will be first and the first last.

---

[1]   Hint: What is the subject?

[2]   Hint: Identify the main verb and subjects.

[3]   ἐν has meanings other than "in." One of its uses is to indicate the "means" by which an action is accomplished. Wh
      used this way it can be translated as "with."

[4]   "They will be." A form of εἰμί.

[5]   Hint: The verb has been omitted from the second half of the verse.

ῥύσεταί (he/she/it will rescue) με[6] ὁ κύριος ἀπὸ παντὸς[7] ἔργου πονηροῦ καὶ σώσει (he/she/it will save) εἰς τὴν βασιλείαν αὐτοῦ τὴν[8] ἐπουράνιον.[9]

The Lord will rescue me from every evil work and will save in his heavenly kingdom

μείνατε (Remain!) ἐν τῇ ἀγάπῃ τῇ ἐμῇ. ἐὰν τὰς ἐντολάς μου τηρήσητε (you keep), μενεῖτε (you will remain) ἐν τῇ ἀγάπῃ μου, καθὼς ἐγὼ τὰς ἐντολὰς τοῦ πατρός (father) μου τετήρηκα (I have kept) καὶ μένω (I remain) αὐτοῦ[10] ἐν τῇ ἀγάπῃ. αὕτη ἐστὶν ἡ ἐντολὴ ἡ ἐμή, ἵνα ἀγαπᾶτε (you love) ἀλλήλους καθὼς ἠγάπησα (I loved) ὑμᾶς (you).

Remain in my love. If you keep my commandments, you will remain in my love, even as I have kept my father's commandments and I remain in his love.
This is my commandment, that you love each other as I loved you.

αὐτοῦ[11] γάρ ἐσμεν ποίημα (workmanship), κτισθέντες (created) ἐν Χριστῷ Ἰησοῦ ἐπὶ (for) ἔργοις ἀγαθοῖς οἷς[12] προητοίμασεν (he/she/it prepared beforehand) ὁ θεός, ἵνα ἐν αὐτοῖς περιπατήσωμεν (we might walk).

For we are his workmanship, created in Jesus Christ for good works which God prepared beforehand that we might walk in them.

). ὁ ἀγαθὸς ἄνθρωπος ἐκ τοῦ ἀγαθοῦ θησαυροῦ (treasure) ἐκβάλλει (he/she/it brings out) ἀγαθά, καὶ ὁ πονηρὸς ἄνθρωπος ἐκ τοῦ πονηροῦ θησαυροῦ ἐκβάλλει πονηρά.

The good man/person brings out the good out of the good treasure, and the evil man brings the evil out of the evil treasure.

This is the accusative form of ἐγώ.

This word is in the genitive and means "every."

Notice that the article is placing ἐπουράνιον in an attributive position, even though there is a word (αὐτοῦ) between it and the word it modifies (βασιλείαν).

"Heavenly." Even though it may not look like it, this is a feminine word, which explains the gender of the article.

Although the possessive αὐτοῦ normally follows the word it modifies, it can also precede the word it modifies.

What does Paul's placement of αὐτοῦ at the beginning of the verse tell you about the emphasis of the verse?

"Which." Do not use the key word in translating this word. We will explain why in chapter 14.

Additional

11. ὁ δὲ Ἰησοῦς ἀπεκρίθη τῷ δούλῳ· αἱ ἐντολαὶ τοῦ θεοῦ πισταὶ καὶ ἀγαθαί, οὐ κακαί.
And Jesus answered the servant; the commandments of God are faithful & good, not bad.

12. ἐν τῇ τρίτῃ ἡμέρᾳ οἱ πονηροὶ ἐξῆλθον (they went out) ἐκ τοῦ οἴκου τοῦ θεοῦ.
On the third day the evil people went out of the house of God.

13. οἱ ὀφθαλμοί[13] μου ἐπὶ τοὺς πιστούς.
My eyes are on the faithful.

14. ἐν τοῖς λόγοις Δαυὶδ[14] τοῖς ἐσχάτοις ἐστὶν ὁ ἀριθμὸς[15] υἱῶν Λευὶ[16] ἀπὸ εἰκοσαετοῦς (twenty years old) καὶ ἐπάνω (above). *In the last words of David is the number of s— of Levi twenty years old and above.*

15. νῦν γὰρ ἔγνων (I know) ὅτι φοβῇ (you fear) τὸν θεὸν σὺ καὶ οὐκ ἐφείσω[17] τοῦ υἱοῦ σου τοῦ ἀγαπητοῦ δι᾽ ἐμέ.[18] *For now I know that you fear God and you spared not your beloved from*

16. γινώσκομεν (we know) ὅτι ἐσχάτη ὥρα ἐστίν.[19]
We know that it is the last hour.

17. ἡ βασιλεία ἡ ἐμὴ οὐκ ἔστιν ἐκ τοῦ κόσμου τούτου.[20]
My kingdom is not of this world.

18. Ἐὰν ἀγαπᾶτέ (you love) με,[18] τὰς ἐντολὰς τὰς ἐμὰς τηρήσετε (you will keep).
If ye love me, ye will keep my commandments.

19. ἰδοὺ δέδωκα (I have set) πρὸ προσώπου σου σήμερον τὴν ζωὴν καὶ τὸν θάνατον, τὸ ἀγαθὸν καὶ τὸ κακόν. *Behold, I have set before your face today life and death, good and evil.*

20. ὁ πιστεύων (one who believes) εἰς τὸν υἱὸν ἔχει (he/she/it has) ζωὴν αἰώνιον· ὁ δὲ ἀπειθῶν (one who does not believe) τῷ υἱῷ οὐκ ὄψεται (he/she/it will see) ζωήν, ἀλλ᾽ ἡ ὀργὴ τοῦ θεοῦ μένει (he/she/it remains) ἐπ᾽ αὐτόν. *One who believes in the Son has eternal life. But one who does not believe the Son will not see life, but the anger of God remains in him.*

Summary

1. It is often important to identify the main subject first to give structure to the verse.

References

α. Mt 24:45; β. Mt 16:21; γ. Gen 22:2; δ. Mk 12:6; ε. Jn 8:43; ζ. Mt 13:38; η. 1 Cor 10:13; **1**. Jn 12:48; **2**. Mk 15:25; **3**. J— 5:21; **4**. Jn 6:40; **5**. Rom 12:21; **6**. Mt 20:16; **7**. 2 Tim 4:18; **8**. Jn 15:9-10, 12; **9**. Eph 2:10; **10**. Mt 12:35; **11**. —; **12**. —; **13**. Ps 101:6 [LXX 100:6]; **14**. 1 Chr 23:27; **15**. Gen 22:12; **16**. 1 Jn 2:18; **17**. Jn 18:36; **18**. Jn 14:15; **19**. Dt 30:15; **20**. J— 3:36.

---

[13] ὀφθαλμός, -οῦ, ὁ, *eye*.

[14] Hint: Δαυὶδ is a genitive.

[15] ἀριθμός, -οῦ, ὁ, *number*.

[16] Hint: Λευί is a genitive.

[17] ἐφείσω means "you spared" and takes its direct object in the genitive. There are other words that will do this as well.

[18] The accusative of ἐγώ.

[19] Hint: What is the subject of this verb?

[20] τούτου is the genitive singular masculine form of οὗτος, meaning "this." Did you notice anything different about its position? It is in a predicate position, but you cannot make sense of the sentence if you try to insert "is." It is a peculiarity o— this word that it is used in the predicate position, but we must translate it as if it were in the attributive position. We wi— discuss this word more fully in chapter 13.

Review #2

How do you identify the stem of a noun or an adjective?

Match the following grammatical functions with their proper Greek case.

Direct object   Dative case

Indirect object   Genitive case

Possession   Nominative case

Subject   Accusative case

In the following sentences write the words that correspond to the given functions.

a. ἀγαπᾷ (he/she/it loves) ὁ θεὸς τὸν κόσμον, ᾧ (to which) ἔδωκε (he/she/it gave) τὸν υἱὸν αὐτοῦ.

Subject   ὁ θεὸς

Direct object   τὸν κόσμον

Possessive   αὐτοῦ

b. οἱ προφῆται τοῦ Ἰησοῦ ἐλάλησαν (they spoke) τοῖς ἀνθρώποις τὸν λόγον.

Subject   οἱ προφῆται

Direct object   τὸν λόγον

Possessive   τοῦ Ἰησοῦ

Indirect object   τοῖς ανθρώποις

How does the form of the article or any adjective correspond to the noun it modifies?

s in gender, number & case

What is the difference between the substantival and adjectival function of an adjective?

In the substantival function it acts as a noun; in the adjectival it modifies a noun.

6. How can you tell if an adjective is in the attributive or predicate position? How do you translate an adject
   if you cannot tell its position?

7. Give examples of the two positions of an attributive adjective.

   a. ὁ ἀγαθος ανθρωπος

   b. ὁ ανθρωπος ὁ ἀγαθος

8. What is the rule that governs whether a feminine noun will exhibit the alpha to eta shift in the femin
   singular, genitive, and dative?

9. How can you tell if an adjective is used substantivally?

10. Write out the first six noun rules.

   1.

   2.

   3.

   4.

   5.

   6.

1. Write out the full paradigm of the case endings for the first and second declension.

	masc	fem	neut		masc	fem	neut
nom sg	ς	–	ν	nom pl	ι	ι	α
gen sg	ου	ς	ου	gen pl	ων	ων	ων
dat sg	ι	ι	ι	dat pl	ις	ις	ις
acc sg	ν	ν	ν	acc pl	ους	ας	α

2. Write out the full paradigm of the definite article.

	masc	fem	neut		masc	fem	neut
nom sg	ὁ	ἡ	τό	nom pl	οἱ	αἱ	τά
gen sg	τοῦ	τῆς	τοῦ	gen pl	τῶν	τῶν	τῶν
dat sg	~~τῷ~~ τῷ	τῇ	τῷ	dat pl	τοῖς	ταῖς	τοῖς
acc sg	τόν	τήν	τό	acc pl	τούς	τάς	τά

Parsing

1. λόγοις   M S D

2. ἀγάπη   F S D

3. τέκνα   N P N/A

4. ἁμαρτίας   F P A

5. ταῖς   F P D

6. κόσμου   M S G

7. καιρῶν   M P G

8. εὐαγγελίῳ   N S D

9. ἅγιον   N S N/A / M S A

10. ἀγάπης   F S G

* dative of means / instrumental dative
By this

Translation

Translate 1 John 4:1-6. Use the lexicon to find the meaning of words that you have not had as vocabulary word
Try to maintain the Greek order in your translation unless it produces very poor English.

πνεῦμα is a third declension word (chapter 10) that means "spirit." πνεύματι is dative singular, and πνεύματα
nominative or accusative plural.

[4:1] Ἀγαπητοί, μὴ παντί (every) πνεύματι πιστεύετε[1] ἀλλὰ δοκιμάζετε (test!) τὰ πνεύματα εἰ
Beloved, do not believe every spirit, but test the spirits

ἐκ τοῦ θεοῦ ἐστιν, ὅτι πολλοὶ (many) ψευδοπροφῆται ἐξεληλύθασιν (they have gone out) εἰς τὸν
are from God, for many false witnesses have gone out into the world.

κόσμον. [4:2] ἐν τούτῳ (this) γινώσκετε (you know) τὸ πνεῦμα τοῦ θεοῦ· πᾶν (Every) πνεῦμα ὃ (that)
In this you know the spirit of God. Every spirit that

ὁμολογεῖ (he/she/it confesses that) Ἰησοῦν Χριστὸν ἐν σαρκὶ (flesh) ἐληλυθότα (he/she/it has come) ἐ
confesses that Jesus Christ has come in the flesh is from God

τοῦ θεοῦ ἐστιν, [4:3] καὶ πᾶν πνεῦμα ὃ μὴ ὁμολογεῖ τὸν Ἰησοῦν ἐκ τοῦ θεοῦ οὐκ ἔστιν· καὶ τοῦτό (this
*and every spirit that does not confess ~~that~~ Jesus is ~~from G~~
not ~~from~~ from God.*

ἐστιν τὸ[2] τοῦ ἀντιχρίστου, ὃ ἀκηκόατε (you have heard) ὅτι ἔρχεται (he/she/it is coming), καὶ νῦν ἐ
the spirit of the Antichrist, which you have heard is coming, and now

τῷ κόσμῳ ἐστὶν ἤδη. *already.*   ★ *The spirit of the Antichrist is this*
is in the world ~~today~~

[4:4] Ὑμεῖς ἐκ τοῦ θεοῦ ἐστε, τεκνία (little children), καὶ νενικήκατε (you have overcome) αὐτούς
You are from God, little children, and you have overcome them,

ὅτι μείζων ἐστὶν ὁ (the one who is) ἐν ὑμῖν ἢ ὁ ἐν τῷ κόσμῳ. [4:5] αὐτοὶ ἐκ τοῦ κόσμου εἰσίν, διὰ τοῦτο
*because the one who is in you is greater than the one   They are from the world, for this
who is in the world.*   *of*

ἐκ τοῦ κόσμου λαλοῦσιν (they speak) καὶ ὁ κόσμος αὐτῶν ἀκούει.[4] [4:6] ἡμεῖς ἐκ τοῦ θεοῦ ἐσμεν, ὁ
of the world   ←they speak and the world hears ~~them~~. We are from God,

γινώσκων (one who knows) τὸν θεὸν ἀκούει ἡμῶν (us), ὃς (who) οὐκ ἔστιν ἐκ τοῦ θεοῦ οὐκ ἀκούει
*the one who knows God hears us, who ~~does~~ not from God does not hear us.
is*

ἡμῶν. ἐκ τούτου[5] γινώσκομεν (we know) τὸ πνεῦμα τῆς ἀληθείας καὶ τὸ πνεῦμα τῆς πλάνης.
By this we know the spirit of truth and the spirit of error.

---

[1]   The verb means "believe!" and can take a direct object in the dative.
[2]   What word has been omitted that τό would normally modify?
[3]   διὰ τοῦτο is an idiom that means "for this reason."
[4]   This verb means "he/she/it hears" and can take a direct object in either the genitive or accusative.
[5]   ἐκ τούτου is an idiom that here means "by this."

Third Declension

te out the master paradigm of all case endings.

	first/second declension		third declension	

first/second declension

	masc	fem	neut
m sg	ς	—	ν
n sg	υ	ς	υ
t sg	ι	ι	ι
sg	ν	ν	ν

	masc		fem	neut
m pl	ι			α
a pl	ων			
t pl	ις			
pl	ους		ας	α

third declension

	masc/fem	neut
m sg	ς	—
n sg	ος	
t sg	ι	
sg	α / ν	—

	masc/fem	neut
m pl	ες	α
a pl	ων	
t pl	σι(ν)	
pl	ας	α

rsing

Inflected	Case	Number	Gender	Lexical form	Inflected meaning
σαρκί	D	S	F	σάρξ	to the flesh
τίνος	G	S	MFN	τίς	of whom?
πάσας	A	P	F	πᾶς	all
ἑνός	G	S	N A M	εἷς	of one
σῶμα	N A	S	N	σῶμα	the body
ὀνομάτων	G	P	N	ὄνομα	of the names
ἕνα	A	P	M	εἷς εἷς	one
τινες	N	P	MF	τίς	anyone
σαρξί	D	P	F	σάρξ	to the flesh
πνεύματα	N A	P		πνεῦμα	the spirit

31

Warm-up

α.   τῷ ὀνόματί μου
    to   my   law

β.   τὴν ἀγάπην τὴν εἰς πάντας τοὺς ἁγίους
    the love (which is) into all the saints

γ.   εἰς σάρκα μίαν
    into one flesh

δ.   τινῶν ἀνθρώπων αἱ ἁμαρτίαι
    the sins of   men

ε.   ἐν τῷ σώματι τῆς σαρκὸς αὐτοῦ
    in the body of his flesh

ζ.   τίνες εἰσὶν οἱ ἀδελφοί μου;
    Who are my brothers?

η.   ἐν τῇ σαρκὶ αὐτοῦ
    in his flesh

Translation

1.   πάντες ἔρχονται (they are going) πρὸς αὐτόν.
    Everyone is going to him.

2.   Παῦλος καὶ Τιμόθεος δοῦλοι[1] Χριστοῦ Ἰησοῦ πᾶσιν τοῖς ἁγίοις ἐν Χριστῷ Ἰησοῦ τοῖς οὖσ[

    (ones who are) ἐν Φιλίπποις.
    Paul and Timothy, servants of Jesus Christ to all the saints in
    Jesus Christ to the ones who are in Philippi.

3.   τί ἀγαθὸν[2] ποιήσω (I must do) ἵνα σχῶ (I might inherit) ζωὴν αἰώνιον;
    What good must I do in order that I might inherit eternal life?

4.   καὶ ἐλάλησαν (they told) αὐτῷ τὸν λόγον τοῦ κυρίου σὺν πᾶσιν τοῖς ἐν τῇ οἰκίᾳ αὐτοῦ.
    And they told the word of the Lord to him with all those
    in his house.

---

[1]   Hint: Remember apposition (exercise 7; sentence 10)?

[2]   Was the rich young man asking what was required of him to be a follower of Jesus, or was he trying to earn his way ir
heaven? The inclusion of this word gives you a hint.

³ καὶ ἅγιον τὸ ὄνομα αὐτοῦ.

> And holy is his name.

ἔλεγεν (he/she/it was speaking) περὶ τοῦ ναοῦ (temple) τοῦ⁴ σώματος αὐτοῦ.

> He was speaking concerning the temple of his body.

> Nobody when he speaks in the spirit of God says, "Anathema."

οὐδεὶς ἐν πνεύματι θεοῦ λαλῶν (when he speaks) λέγει (he/she/it says)· Ἀνάθεμα⁵ Ἰησοῦς, καὶ

οὐδεὶς δύναται (he/she/it is able) εἰπεῖν (to say)· Κύριος Ἰησοῦς, εἰ μὴ ἐν πνεύματι ἁγίῳ.

> and nobody is able to say "Lord Jesus," except in the Holy Spirit.

τί με⁶ λέγεις (you call) ἀγαθόν;⁷ οὐδεὶς ἀγαθὸς εἰ μὴ εἷς ὁ θεός.⁸

> Why do you call me good? Nobody is good except the one God.

τίνα λέγουσιν (they say) οἱ ἄνθρωποι εἶναι (to be) τὸν υἱὸν τοῦ ἀνθρώπου;

> Who do the men say the Son of man to be?

⁹ τοῖς πᾶσιν γέγονα (I have become) πάντα.

> I have become everything to everyone.

Hint: This is a complete sentence, not a phrase. You will have to supply a verb.

Hint: What is the grammatical relationship between σώματος and ναοῦ? Cf. exercise 7, sentence 10.

If you pronounce it, you will know what it means.

με is the accusative singular of ἐγώ.

Often a verb will require two direct objects. Sometimes, one object will be personal and the other impersonal (as in this example). Other times both objects are impersonal. This is called the "double accusative."

What is the grammatical relationship between θεός and εἷς?

Hint: Think through the different possibilities of the gender of both adjectives.

Additional

11. καθαρίζομαι (I am cleansed) ἀπὸ ἁμαρτίας μου ὑπὸ τῆς σαρκὸς τοῦ Ἰησοῦ.
    I am cleansed from my sins by the flesh of Jesus.

12. τὰ γὰρ ὀνόματα τῶν ἁγίων παρὰ τῷ θεῷ ἐστιν ἐν τοῖς αἰωνίοις οὐρανοῖς.
    For the laws of the saints in the presence of God are in the eternal heavens

13. κατατριβῶσιν (they are consumed) σάρκες σώματός σου.
    The fleshes of your body are consumed.

14. ἀσπάζομαι (I send greetings) ἐν ὀνόματι Ἰησοῦ Χριστοῦ, υἱοῦ πατρός· κατὰ σάρκα καὶ πνεῦ[
    ἡνωμένοις (those who are united) πάσῃ ἐντολῇ αὐτοῦ. *I send greetings in the name of
    Jesus Christ, son of the Father;*

15. καὶ ἐκάλεσεν (he/she/it gave) Ἀδὰμ ὀνόματα πᾶσιν.
    And he gave Adam all ~~true~~ names

16. καὶ ἐδικαιώθη (he/she/it is vindicated) ἡ σοφία ἀπὸ πάντων τῶν τέκνων αὐτῆς.
    And Wisdom is vindicated by all her children.

17. Ἀγαπητοί, μὴ παντὶ πνεύματι πιστεύετε[10] ἀλλὰ δοκιμάζετε (test!) τὰ πνεύματα εἰ ἐκ τοῦ θε[
    ἐστιν. *Beloved, do not believe every spirit, but test the spirits if they are fr[
    God.*

18. πάντα ἐνώπιον αὐτοῦ εἰσίν, καὶ οὐδὲν λέληθεν (he/she/it is hidden from) τὴν βουλὴν αὐτοῦ.
    All things are before him, and nothing is hidden from his plan

19. Παῦλος ἀπόστολος Χριστοῦ Ἰησοῦ διὰ θελήματος θεοῦ καὶ Τιμόθεος ὁ ἀδελφὸς τῇ ἐκκλησ[
    τοῦ θεοῦ τῇ οὔσῃ (one that is) ἐν Κορίνθῳ σὺν τοῖς ἁγίοις πᾶσιν τοῖς οὖσιν (ones who are) ἐν ὅ[
    τῇ Ἀχαΐᾳ.

20. ἐν ἀγάπῃ προσελάβετο (he/she/it received) ἡμᾶς (us) ὁ δεσπότης.[11] διὰ τὴν ἀγάπην, ἣν (which
    ἔσχεν (he had) πρὸς ἡμᾶς, τὸ αἷμα αὐτοῦ ἔδωκεν (he/she/it gave) ὑπὲρ ἡμῶν Ἰησοῦς Χριστὸς
    κύριος ἡμῶν (our) ἐν θελήματι θεοῦ, καὶ τὴν[12] σάρκα ὑπὲρ τῆς σαρκὸς ἡμῶν καὶ τὴν ψυχὴν
    ὑπὲρ τῶν ψυχῶν ἡμῶν.
    The master received us in love. On account of the love [which] he had for us

Summary

1. Sometimes a verb requires two direct objects ("double accusative"). The two objects will be personal a[
   impersonal, or both with be impersonal. The second object will sometimes require a helping word in tra[
   lation, such as "about" in the sense of "with reference to."

References

α. Mk 9:37; β. Eph 1:15; γ. Mt 19:5; δ. 1 Tim 5:24; ε. Col 1:22; ζ. Mt 12:48; η. Eph 2:14; 1. Jn 3:26; 2. Phil 1:1; 3.
19:16; 4. Ac 16:32; 5. Lk 1:49; 6. Jn 2:21; 7. 1 Cor 12:3; 8. Mk 10:18; 9. Mt 16:13; 10. 1 Cor 9:22; 11. —; 12. —; 13. P[
5:11; 14. IRom 1:0; 15. Gen 2:20; 16. Lk 7:35; 17. 1 Jn 4:1; 18. 1 Clem 27:6; 19. 2 Cor 1:1; 20. 1 Clem 49:6.

---

[10] "Believe!" Takes a direct object in the dative.

[11] δεσπότης, -ου, ὁ, *master, lord.*

[12] Hint: Do you remember that the definite article can perform other functions as well?

First and Second Person Personal Pronouns

Parsing

Inflected	Person / Case	Number	Gender	Lexical form	Inflected meaning
1. σοι	2 D	S		σύ	to you
2. ὑμῖν	2 D	P		ὑμεῖς	to you (pl.)
3. πίστιν	A	S	F	πίστις	faith/belief
4. σε	2 A	S		σύ	you
5. πατρός	·G	S	M	πατήρ	of the father
6. ὑμεῖς	2 N	P	▪	υμεῖς	you (pl.)
7. ὕδατα	N A	P	N	ὕδωρ ~~ὕδωρ~~	waters
8. ἡμᾶς	I G	P	F	ἡμεῖς	us
9. πίστεις	N A	P	F	πίστις	faiths / beliefs
10. ἐμοῦ (3x)	I G	S	MFN	ἐγώ	my
	N/M G	S		ἐμός	

Warm-up

1. <small>MAS MAS GS IAS</small>
ἤνεγκα (I brought) τὸν υἱόν μου πρὸς σέ. I brought my son to you.

2. <small>MNS MNS IGS   MNS MNS IGS</small>
ὁ κύριός μου καὶ ὁ θεός μου   My Lord and my God.

3. <small>MNP ⬛GS MGS 2GP</small>
υἱοὶ τοῦ πατρὸς ὑμῶν   Sons of our father

4. <small>FSD FDS NGS NGS   NGS</small>
ἐπὶ τῇ πίστει τοῦ ὀνόματος αὐτοῦ   on the basis of faith of his name

5. <small>MDP MDP FGS FGS   FGS FGS FGS</small>
τοῖς λόγοις τῆς πίστεως καὶ τῆς καλῆς διδασκαλίας (teaching)   to the words of faith and of good teaching

6. <small>2AP FNP FNP FNP</small>
Ἀσπάζονται (they greet) ὑμᾶς αἱ ἐκκλησίαι πᾶσαι. All the churches greet you (pl.)

7. <small>MNP</small>
οὐκ ἔχω (I have) ἄνδρα. I do not have ~~men~~. a husband.

Translation

1. ¹ ἐγὼ ἐβάπτισα (I baptized) ὑμᾶς ὕδατι, αὐτὸς δὲ βαπτίσει (he/she/it will baptize) ὑμᾶς ἐν πνεύματι ἁγίῳ.

   I baptized you by means of water, but he will baptize you in the Holy Spirit.

2. ἐγὼ ἐλήλυθα (I have come) ἐν τῷ ὀνόματι τοῦ πατρός μου.

   I have come in the name of my Father.

3. ἰδοὺ ἡμεῖς ἀφήκαμεν (we have left) πάντα καὶ ἠκολουθήκαμεν² σοι.

   Behold, we have left everything and have followed you.

4. καὶ καυχώμεθα (we rejoice) ἐπ᾿ ἐλπίδι τῆς δόξης τοῦ θεοῦ.

   And we rejoice on the basis of hope of the glory of God.

5. ὃς (who) ἂν ἓν τῶν τοιούτων (these) παιδίων (children) δέξηται (he/she/it receives) ἐπὶ³ τῷ ὀνόματί μου, ἐμὲ δέχεται·⁴ καὶ ὃς ἂν ἐμὲ δέχηται (he/she/it receives), οὐκ ἐμὲ δέχεται ἀλλὰ τὸν ἀποστείλαντά (one who sent) με.

   Whoever receives one of these children in my name receives me; and whoever receives me does not receive me but the One who sent me.

---

1   Is there any emphasis implied in this verse by the use of the personal pronoun? As always, let context be your guide.

2   "We have followed." This verb takes a direct object in the dative, which also means you do not use a key word with σοι.

3   The meanings of many Greek words you are learning are actually more fluid than you might have guessed. In the text we are giving you nice, neat definitions so you can learn their basic significance, and yet most words have a range of meaning that you will start to grasp in later chapters.

   This is especially true of prepositions. Rarely will a preposition have just one or two meanings, and ἐπί is perhaps the most fluid of all prepositions. At times it may seem that it means almost anything it wants to. It doesn't, but its meaning is quite flexible. One of its more important meanings is to describe *the basis upon which an emotion or action is based*. Here it describes the basis upon which a child is received, and in English we say, *"in my name."*

4   Hint: What is the subject of δέχεται, which means "he/she/it receives"?

MNS   2GS MNS MNS   MNP   2NP MNP

εἷς γάρ ἐστιν ὑμῶν ὁ διδάσκαλος (teacher), πάντες δὲ ὑμεῖς ἀδελφοί ἐστε.

~~For the teacher is one of you(pl.) and all of you are brothers.~~

For your teacher is one   you are all brothers

(You have one teacher)

         MNS MNS FAS FAS MGP   MDS   MDS

καὶ ἰδὼν (after seeing) ὁ Ἰησοῦς[5] τὴν πίστιν αὐτῶν λέγει (he/she/it says) τῷ παραλυτικῷ

     NNS   2GS FNP FNP

(paralytic)· τέκνον, ἀφίενταί (they are forgiven) σου αἱ ἁμαρτίαι.

And after seeing their faith, Jesus says to the paralytic, "Child, your sins

are forgiven."

   FNS FNS 2GS   MNP MNP 2GS   FNP FNP 2GS   2AS

ἰδοὺ ἡ μήτηρ σου καὶ οἱ ἀδελφοί σου [καὶ αἱ ἀδελφαί[6] σου] ἔξω ζητοῦσίν (they seek) σε. καὶ

          MDP   MNS   FNS FNS IGS   MNP MNP IGS

ἀποκριθεὶς (answering) αὐτοῖς λέγει (he/she/it says)· τίς ἐστιν ἡ μήτηρ μου καὶ οἱ ἀδελφοί [μου];

FNS FNS IGS   MNP MNP   IGS MNS   NAS NAS MGS

... ἴδε ἡ μήτηρ μου καὶ οἱ ἀδελφοί μου. ὃς (who) [γὰρ] ἂν ποιήσῃ (he/she/it does) τὸ θέλημα τοῦ

MGS MNS MNS IGS   FNS   FNS

θεοῦ, οὗτος ἀδελφός μου καὶ ἀδελφὴ καὶ μήτηρ ἐστίν.

Behold your mother, your brothers, and your sisters - they seek you outside.

And answering them he says, "Who is my mother and my brothers?

Behold my mother and my brothers. For whoever does the will of God,

that one is my brother and my sister and my mother."

N NP IDS   MGS MGS MGS   MNS   MAS MAS

Πάντα μοι παρεδόθη (they were given) ὑπὸ τοῦ πατρός μου, καὶ οὐδεὶς ἐπιγινώσκει[7] τὸν υἱὸν εἰ

MNS MNS   MAS MAS MNS   MNS MNS

μὴ ὁ πατήρ,[8] οὐδὲ τὸν πατέρα τις ἐπιγινώσκει εἰ μὴ ὁ υἱός.

All things were given by   my father, and no one knows the son except the

father,   who knows the father except the son

Because Ἰησοῦς is nominative, it cannot be the object of the participle ἰδὼν. It is common in biblical Greek for the author to place the subject of the sentence (ὁ Ἰησοῦς) inside the participial phrase (ἰδὼν τὴν πίστιν αὐτῶν). You will always have to pull the subject out, placing it either before or after the participial phrase.

A "participle" is an "ing" word like "eating," "seeing." A "participial phrase" is the participle and its direct object and modifiers. Participial phrases are dependent phrases; they cannot contain the main subject and verb of the sentence. We will discuss them in chapter 26.

This actual word does not occur fifty or more times; but by knowing that it follows natural gender, you should be able to determine its meaning.

"He/she/it knows." ἐπιγινώσκω describes a fuller, more complete knowledge than does γινώσκω.

Hint: πατήρ is nominative because it is followed by an implied ἐπιγινώσκει.

10. Οὐκ⁹ εἰμὶ ἐλεύθερος (free); οὐκ εἰμὶ ἀπόστολος; οὐκ Ἰησοῦν τὸν κύριον ἡμῶν ἑόρακα (I have
MNS *MNS* *MAS MAS MAS IGP*

seen); οὐ τὸ ἔργον μου ὑμεῖς ἐστε ἐν κυρίῳ;¹⁰
NNS NNS IGS 2NP *MDS*

Am I not free? Am I not an apostle? Have I not seen Jesus our Lord?
Are you not my work in the Lord?

Additional *To you are the love of God and faith in Jesus.*

11. ὑμῖν δὲ ἡ ἀγάπη τοῦ θεοῦ καὶ ἡ πίστις εἰς τὸν Ἰησοῦν.
2DP *FNS FNS MGS MGS* *FNS FNS* *MAS MAS*
The will of our God is that we keep his good commandments.

12. τὸ θέλημα τοῦ θεοῦ ἡμῶν ἐστιν ἵνα τηρῶμεν (we keep) τὰς ἐντολὰς τὰς ἀγαθὰς αὐτοῦ.
NNS NNS MGS MGS IGP *FAP FAP FAP FAP MGS*
And he named the city on the basis of his son's name Enoch.

13. καὶ ἐπωνόμασεν (he/she/it named) τὴν πόλιν (city) ἐπὶ τῷ ὀνόματι τοῦ υἱοῦ αὐτοῦ Ἐνώχ.
FAS FAS *NDS NDS MGS MGS MGS*
Do we not have one God and one Christ and one spirit of hope poured out on us

14. οὐχ ἕνα θεὸν ἔχομεν (we have) καὶ ἕνα Χριστὸν καὶ ἓν πνεῦμα τῆς χάριτος τὸ ἐκχυθὲν (one th
MAS *MAS* *NAS FGS FGS NNS*
was poured out) ἐφ᾽ ἡμᾶς, καὶ μία κλῆσις (calling) ἐν Χριστῷ;
IAP *FNS* *MDS*
and one calling in Christ

15. τιμήσει (he/she/it will honor) αὐτοὺς ὁ κύριος Ἰησοῦς Χριστός, εἰς ὃν (whom) ἐλπίζουσιν (the
MAP MNS MNS MNS MNS
hope) σαρκί, ψυχῇ,¹¹ πνεύματι, πίστει, ἀγάπη, *Jesus Christ will honor them, in whom*
FDS FDS NDS FDS FDS
they hope by flesh, soul, spirit, faith, and love.

16. καὶ εἶπεν ὁ θεός· τί ἐποίησας (you did); φωνὴ αἵματος τοῦ ἀδελφοῦ σου βοᾷ (he/she/it is cryi
MNS MNS *FNS NGS MGS MGS MGS*
out) πρός με ἐκ τῆς γῆς. *And God says, "What did you do? The voice of your broth*
IAS *FNS FNS*
blood is crying out to me out of the earth."

17. ὁδοὶ δύο εἰσὶν διδαχῆς καὶ ἐξουσίας, ἡ ... τοῦ φωτὸς καὶ ἡ τοῦ σκότους· διαφορὰ¹² δὲ πολλὴ
FGS FGS FNS NGS NGS FNS NGS NGS FNS
τῶν δύο ὁδῶν.
FGP 2GP FGP

18. καὶ εἶπεν Δαυὶδ πάσῃ τῇ ἐκκλησίᾳ· εὐλογήσατε (bless!) κύριον τὸν θεὸν ὑμῶν καὶ, εὐλόγησε
MNS FDS FDS FDS *MAS MAS MAS 2GP*
(he/she/it blessed) πᾶσα ἡ ἐκκλησία κύριον τὸν θεὸν τῶν πατέρων αὐτῶν.
FNS FNS FNS MAS MAS MAS MGP MGP MGP
And David says to each congregation, "Bless the Lord our God!" and each congregation
MNS blessed the Lord God of their fathers.

19. οὗτος ἦλθεν (he/she/it came) εἰς μαρτυρίαν ἵνα μαρτυρήσῃ (he/she/it might witness) περὶ τοῦ
MNS *FAS* *NG*
φωτός, ἵνα πάντες πιστεύσωσιν (they might believe) δι᾽ αὐτοῦ. οὐκ ἦν ... τὸ φῶς, ἀλλ᾽ ἵνα
NGS MNP *MGS* *NNS NNS*
μαρτυρήσῃ περὶ τοῦ φωτός. *And this one came in testimony that he might witness*
NGS NGS
concerning the light, that all might believe through him. He was not the light, but that
MNS might witness concerning the light

20. Καὶ Ἰησοῦς προέκοπτεν (he/she/it increased) [ἐν τῇ] σοφίᾳ καὶ ἡλικίᾳ¹⁴ καὶ χάριτι παρὰ θεῷ κ
FDS FDS FDS FDS MDS
ἀνθρώποις. *And Jesus increased in wisdom and stature and hope in God and hu*
MDP
the presence of

---

9. There are several ways to ask a question in Greek. In two of the ways, the answer is implied in the question. If the s
tence begins of οὐ, the implied answer is "Yes." If it begins with μή, then the implied answer is "No."

  We do the same thing in English. "You want to learn Greek, don't you?" and "You don't want to learn Greek, do yo
  both imply an answer. This is discussed in detail at §31.19.

10. Sometimes when translating a question it is easiest to first translate it as a regular indicative sentence, and shift ove
  a question. You might also at first find it helpful to ignore the initial οὐ and οὐχ.

11. ψυχή, -ῆς, ἡ, *soul, life, self*.

12. διαφορά, -ᾶς, ἡ, *difference*.

13. Hint: πολλή is in the predicate.

14. ἡλικία, -ας, ἡ, *stature*.

English to Greek

It is against our general practice to include any English to Greek exercises because we are concentrating on recognition of Greek. But personal pronouns are important and easy. It would be a good practice to try going from English to Greek in this situation. It is especially good to confirm that you understand the different forms of the English pronouns.

1. to me   μοι

2. our   ἡμῶν

3. us   ἡμᾶς

4. you   σύ

5. my   μου

6. to you (plural)   ὑμῖν

7. I   ἐγω

8. your   σου

9. we   ἡμεῖς

10. you (plural)   ὑμεῖς

Summary

1. ἐπί can be used to describe the basis upon which an action or emotion is based. Many words, especially prepositions, are flexible in their meaning.

2. The subject of the main verb can be placed inside the participial phrase.

3. When a question begins with μή, the author is expecting a negative answer. If the question begins with οὐ, the author is expecting a positive answer.

References

α. Mk 9:17; β. Jn 20:28; γ. Mt 5:45; δ. Ac 3:16; ε. 1 Tim 4:6; ζ. Rom 16:16; η. Jn 4:17; **1.** Mk 1:8; **2.** Jn 5:43; **3.** Mk 10:28; **4.** Rom 5:2; **5.** Mk 9:37; **6.** Mt 23:8; **7.** Mk 2:5; **8.** Mk 3:32-35; **9.** Mt 11:27; **10.** (1 Cor 9:1); **11.** —; **12.** —; **13.** Gen 4:17; **14.** (1 Clem 46:6); **15.** IPhil 11:2; **16.** Gen 4:10; **17.** Barn 18:1; **18.** 1 Chr 29:20; **19.** Jn 1:7-8; **20.** Lk 2:52.

ΠΑΤΕΡ ΗΜΩΝ Ο ΕΝ ΤΟΙΣ ΟΥΡΑΝΟΙΣ
ΑΓΙΑΣΘΗΤΩ Τ᾿ΟΝΟΜΑ ΣΟΥ
ΕΛΘΕΤΩ Η ΒΑΣΙΛΕΙΑ ΣΟΥ ΓΕΝΗΘΗΤΩ
ΤΟ ΘΕΛΗΜΑ ΣΟΥ ΩΣ ΕΝ ΟΥΡΑΝΩ ΚΑΙ
ΕΠΙ ΤΗΣ ΓΗΣ ΤΟΝ ΑΡΤΟΝ ΗΜΩΝ ΤΟΝ
ΕΠΙΟΥΣΙΟΝ ΔΟΣ ΗΜΙΝ ΣΗΜΕΡΟΝ ΚΑΙ
ΑΦΕΣ ΗΜΙΝ ΤΑ ΟΦΕΙΛΗΜΑΤΑ ΗΜΩΝ
ΩΣ ΚΑΙ ΗΜΕΙΣ ΑΦΙΕΜΕΝ ΤΟΙΣ ΟΦΕΙΛΕΤΑΙΣ
ΗΜΩΝ ΚΑΙ ΜΗ ΕΙΣΕΝΕΓΚΗΣ ΗΜΑΣ ΕΙΣ
ΠΕΙΡΑΣΜΟΝ ΑΛΛΑ ΡΥΣΑΙ ΗΜΑΣ ΑΠΟ ΤΟΥ
ΠΟΝΗΡΟΥ ΟΤΙ ΣΟΥ ΕΣΤΙΝ Η ΒΑΣΙΛΕΙΑ ΚΑΙ
Η ΔΥΝΑΜΙΣ ΚΑΙ Η ΔΟΞΑ ΕΙΣ ΤΟΥΣ ΑΙΩΝΑΣ
ΑΜΗΝ

This is the Lord's Prayer inscribed on the inside of an evangelical church in Greece. It is modern Greek. Here it is in Koine, without the textually uncertain ending.

Πάτερ ἡμῶν ὁ ἐν τοῖς οὐρανοῖς·
ἁγιασθήτω τὸ ὄνομά σου·
ἐλθέτω ἡ βασιλεία σου· γενηθήτω
τὸ θέλημά σου, ὡς ἐν οὐρανῷ καὶ
ἐπὶ γῆς· τὸν ἄρτον ἡμῶν τὸν
ἐπιούσιον δὸς ἡμῖν σήμερον· καὶ
ἄφες ἡμῖν τὰ ὀφειλήματα ἡμῶν,
ὡς καὶ ἡμεῖς ἀφήκαμεν τοῖς ὀφειλέταις
ἡμῶν· καὶ μὴ εἰσενέγκῃς ἡμᾶς εἰς
πειρασμόν, ἀλλὰ ῥῦσαι ἡμᾶς ἀπὸ τοῦ
πονηροῦ.

Exercise 12 — Track 1

αὐτός

arsing

Inflected	Person / Case	Number	Gender	Lexical form	Inflected meaning
αὐτό	3 NA	S	N	αὐτός	it
σοι	2 D	S		σύ	to you
αὐταί	3 N	P	F	αὐτός	they
αὐτοῖς	3 D	P	MN	αὐτός	to them
αὐτήν	3 A	S	F	αὐτός	her
ἡμῖν	1 D	P		ἡμεῖς	to us
αὐτῷ	3 D	S	MN	αὐτός	to him /it
πόδα	A	P	~~MN~~ M	πούς	feet
αὐτῆς	3 G	S	F	αὐτός	~~s~~ of her ~~her~~
0. ὑμῶν	2 G	P		ὑμεῖς	of you all

Warm-up

MNS   F DS
αὐτός εἶπεν αὐτῇ   He says to her.

    F GS
ὑπὲρ αὐτῆς   on behalf of her

MNS   MNS   ? GP   MNS   MGS
ὁ διδάσκαλος αὐτῶν ἐστιν μαθητὴς αὐτοῦ. Their teacher is his disciple.

MNP   MNP MNP 2GP
αὐτοὶ γάρ εἰσιν οἱ πόδες ὑμῶν.   For they are your feet.

FNS FNS FNS
ἡ αὐτὴ σάρξ   the flesh itself

MNS MNS MNS,   MNS
αὐτὸς ὁ ὀφθαλμός ἐστιν καλός.   eye   is good

        NAP NAP
πιστεύω (I believe) τὸ αὐτό.   I believe (these) things the

Translation

1. φέρετε (Bring!) αὐτὸν πρός με. καὶ ἤνεγκαν (they brought) αὐτὸν πρὸς αὐτόν.
   ^{MAS} ^{IAS}   ^{MAS}   ^{MAS}

   Bring him to me! And they brought him to him.

2. πάλιν οὖν αὐτοῖς ἐλάλησεν (he/she/it spoke) ὁ Ἰησοῦς λέγων (saying)· ἐγώ εἰμι τὸ φῶς τοῦ
   ^{MDP}   ^{MNS MNS}   ^{INS}   ^{NNS NNS MGS}
   κόσμου. Therefore Jesus spoke to them again, saying, "I am the light
   ^{MGS}
   of the world."

3. ὁ δὲ παρήγγειλεν (he/she/it commanded) αὐτοῖς μηδενὶ εἰπεῖν (to speak).
   ^{MNS}   ^{MDP}
   And he commanded them to speak to no one.

4. προσηύξαντο (they prayed) περὶ αὐτῶν ὅπως λάβωσιν (they might receive) πνεῦμα ἅγιον.
                                 ^{? GP}   ^{NAS NAS}
   They prayed concerning them so that they might receive the Holy Spirit.

5. Ἰησοῦς αὐτὸς οὐκ ἐβάπτιζεν (he/she/it was baptizing) ἀλλ᾽ οἱ μαθηταὶ αὐτοῦ.
   ^{MNS MNS}   ^{MNP MNP} ^{MGS}
   Jesus himself was not baptizing, but his disciples.

6. [1] πιστεύετέ (Believe!) μοι ὅτι ἐγὼ ἐν τῷ πατρὶ καὶ ὁ πατὴρ ἐν ἐμοί· εἰ δὲ μή, διὰ τὰ ἔργα αὐτὰ
            ^{IDS}   ^{MDS MDS}   ^{MNS MNS}   ^{IDS}   ^{NAP NAP NAP}
   Believe me that I am in the Father and the Father is in me; except, believe
   πιστεύετε. on account of his works.

7. Παρακαλῶ (I urge) δὲ ὑμᾶς, ἀδελφοί, διὰ[2] τοῦ ὀνόματος τοῦ κυρίου ἡμῶν Ἰησοῦ Χριστοῦ, ἵνα
                       ^{2AS} ^{MVP}   ^{NGS NGS}   ^{MGS MGS} ^{IGP} ^{MGS} ^{MPS}
   τὸ αὐτὸ[4] λέγητε (you say) πάντες.[5]
   ^{NNS NNS}   ^{MNP}
   But I urge you, brothers, through the name of our Lord Jesus Christ

---

[1] Hint: You may need to supply a verb in the ὅτι clause.

[2] In this context, διά means "in."

[3] Did you notice that the usual translation "in order that" makes no sense in this verse. What translation does?

[4] You are going to have to add an extra word to your translation of this word. Take its number and gender from natura
gender.

[5] Hint: Since this is nominative, it must be the subject, but the subject of what?

8. πορευθέντες (having gone) οὖν μαθητεύσατε (make disciples of!) πάντα τὰ ἔθνη (nations),
NAP NAP NAP

βαπτίζοντες (baptizing) αὐτοὺς εἰς τὸ ὄνομα τοῦ πατρὸς καὶ τοῦ υἱοῦ καὶ τοῦ ἁγίου πνεύματος,
NAP NAS NAS MGS MGS MGS MGS NGS NGS NGS

διδάσκοντες (teaching) αὐτοὺς τηρεῖν (to keep) πάντα ὅσα ἐνετειλάμην (I have commanded) ὑμῖν·
MAP NAP 2DP

καὶ ἰδοὺ ἐγὼ μεθ᾽ ὑμῶν εἰμι πάσας τὰς ἡμέρας[6] ἕως τῆς συντελείας (end) τοῦ αἰῶνος.
INS 2GP FAP FAP FAP FGS FGS MGS MGS

Therefore having gone, make disciples of all nations!
baptizing them in the name of the Father and of the Son and of the Holy Spirit
teaching them to keep all that I have commanded to you.
And behold, I am with you always, even the end of the age.
(all the days) as far as

9. ἐπάραντες (raising up) δὲ τοὺς ὀφθαλμοὺς αὐτῶν οὐδένα[7] εἶδον (they saw) εἰ μὴ αὐτὸν Ἰησοῦν
MAP MAP MGP NAP MAS MAS

μόνον. And raising up their eyes, they saw noone except Jesus Christ himself.
MAS

10. [8] ἀδελφοί μου, χαίρετε (rejoice!) ἐν κυρίῳ. τὰ αὐτὰ γράφειν (to write) ὑμῖν ἐμοὶ μὲν οὐκ ὀκνηρόν
MVP IGS MDS NAP NAP 2DP IDS NNS NAS

(troublesome). My brothers, rejoice in the Lord! To write these things to you

is not troublesome to me, (indeed.)

(indeed)

Additional But the disciple is not over his lord, for he is first of all
MNS MNS MAS MAS MGS MNS MNS MNS MGP MGP

11. ὁ δὲ μαθητὴς οὐκ ἔστιν ὑπὲρ τὸν κύριον αὐτοῦ, οὗτος γὰρ ὁ πρῶτος τῶν πάντων.

And Jesus answered again. The faithful themselves will enter into life itself
MNS MNS FAS FAS FAS

12. πάλιν δὲ ὁ Ἰησοῦς ἀπεκρίθη· οἱ πιστοὶ αὐτοὶ εἰσελεύσονται (they will enter) εἰς τὴν αὐτὴν ζωήν.
MNP MNP MNP

And it gave its smoke and to her husband with her
MAS MAS MGS MDS MDS FGS FGS

13. καὶ ἔδωκεν (he/she/it gave) τὸν καρπὸν αὐτοῦ[9] καὶ τῷ ἀνδρὶ αὐτῆς μετ᾽ αὐτῆς.

14. σὺ οὖν ἐπιγνοὺς (recognizing) τὰ ἔργα αὐτοῦ ἀπόστα (stay away!) ἀπ᾽ αὐτοῦ καὶ μηδὲν αὐτῷ
2NS NNP NNP NGS NNP MGS MDS

πίστευε (believe!), ὅτι τὰ ἔργα αὐτοῦ πονηρά εἰσι καὶ ἀσύμφορα[10] τοῖς δούλοις τοῦ θεοῦ.
NNP NNP NGS NNP NAP MDP MDP MGS MGS

---

6   Time designations of *when* an action will occur are placed in the dative ("dative of time when"); time designations of *how long* an action will occur are placed in the accusative ("accusative of time how long").

7   Is οὐδένα masculine or neuter?

8   The verb has been omitted from the second sentence.

9   The antecedent of αὐτοῦ is the tree of knowledge of good and evil.

10 ἀσύμφορος, ον, harmful.

And he blessed Noah and his sons and said to them, "Be fruitful!"

15. καὶ ηὐλόγησεν (he/she/it blessed) ὁ θεὸς τὸν Νῶε καὶ τοὺς υἱοὺς αὐτοῦ καὶ εἶπεν αὐτοῖς· αὐξάνεσθε (be fruitful!).
MNS MNS MAS MAS   MAP MAP MGS   MDP

If God is glorified in him and God will glorify him in him

16. [εἰ ὁ θεὸς ἐδοξάσθη (is glorified) ἐν αὐτῷ] καὶ ὁ θεὸς δοξάσει (he/she/it will glorify) αὐτὸν ἐν αὐτῷ, καὶ εὐθὺς δοξάσει αὐτόν.
MNS MNS   MDS   MNS MNS   MAS   MDS
and he will glorify him immediately

And Jesus himself will not   entrust it to him.

17. αὐτὸς δὲ Ἰησοῦς οὐκ ἐπίστευεν (he/she/it entrust) αὐτὸν αὐτοῖς.
MNS MNS   NAS MDP

18. Διαιρέσεις (varieties) δὲ χαρισμάτων εἰσίν, τὸ δὲ αὐτὸ πνεῦμα· καὶ διαιρέσεις διακονιῶν εἰσιν, καὶ ὁ αὐτὸς κύριος· καὶ διαιρέσεις ἐνεργημάτων[11] εἰσίν, ὁ δὲ αὐτὸς θεὸς ὁ ἐνεργῶν (one who works) τὰ πάντα ἐν πᾶσιν.[12]
NP   NGP   NNS NNS NNS   NP   GP   MNS MNS MNS   NP   GP

For their fathers were doing these things to the prophets.

19. [13] τὰ αὐτὰ γὰρ ἐποίουν (they were doing) τοῖς προφήταις οἱ πατέρες αὐτῶν.
NAP NAP   MDP MDP MNP MNP MGP

20. [14] καὶ κύριον αὐτὸν καὶ Χριστὸν ἐποίησεν (he/she/it made) ὁ θεός.
MAS MAS   MAS   MNS MNS
God made both the Lord Himself and Christ.

English to Greek

Write out the Greek equivalent of these English pronouns.

1. him   αυτον
2. its   αυτοῦ
3. to them   αυτοῖς αυταῖς
4. their   αυτῶν
5. her (possessive)   αυτῆς
6. his   αυτοῦ
7. to it   αυτῳ
8. she   αυτή
9. they   αυτοι αυται α
10. he   αυτό

Summary

1. The dative is used to indicate when an action takes place, the accusative to tell how long.

References

α. —; β. —; γ. —; δ. —; ε. 1 Cor 15:39; ζ. —; η. —; **1.** Mk 9:19-20; **2.** Jn 8:12; **3.** Lk 8:56; **4.** Ac 8:15; **5.** Jn 4:2; **6.** Jn 14:11; **7.** 1 Cor 1:10; **8.** Mt 28:19-20; **9.** Mt 17:8; **10.** Phil 3:1; **11.** —; **12.** —; **13.** (Gen 3:6); **14.** Shep 36:6; **15.** Gen 9:1; **16.** Jn 13:32; **17.** Jn 2:24; **18.** 1 Cor 12:4-6; **19.** Lk 6:23; **20.** Ac 2:36.

---

[11] ἐνέργημα, -ματος, τό, *activity, working.*

[12] Is πᾶσιν masculine or neuter?

[13] Hint: What is the subject? How does the ordering of the words help you understand the point of the passage?

[14] Hint: αὐτόν is the direct object. Find the subject first. The καί ... καί construction can be translated "both ... and." We will discuss "correlative conjunctions" in exercise 22, sentence 7.

Demonstratives

~~P~~arsing

Inflected	Person / Case	Number	Gender	Lexical form	Inflected meaning
τούτων	G	P	M F N	οὗτος	of these
ἐκείνας	A	P	F	ἐκεῖνος	~~that~~ those
με	1 A	S	C	ἐγώ	me
αὐτή	3 N	S	F	αὐτός	she
ἐκεῖνο	N A	S	N	ἐκεῖνος	that
ἑνί	D	S	M/N	~~ἐν~~ εἷς	one
ταῦτα	N A	P	N	οὗτος	these
αὕτη	N	S	F	οὗτος	that
τούτου	G	S	M N	οὗτος	**of this**
ἡμᾶς	1 A	P	C	ἡμεῖς	us

~~W~~arm-up

M G S M G S M,G S　from
ἐκ τοῦ κόσμου τούτου　~~out of~~ this world　out of this world ἐξώ

FDP　FDP　FDP　and/but
Ἐν δὲ ταῖς ἡμέραις ἐκείναις　in those days

NNS
πῶς ἐστιν τοῦτο;　How is this?　How can this be?　How is this possible?

MNS 1 G P
Πάτερ ἡμῶν　our Father

MDP
καὶ ἐκείνοις εἶπεν　and ~~those people say~~　he said to those people / he said to them

MNS　　MNS MNS MGS
οὗτός ἐστιν ὁ υἱός μου.　This is my Son.　my Son is this One

FDS FDS FDS
ἐν τῇ πόλει ταύτῃ　in this city

peritaxis → ~~look~~ this up.
και peritaxis

45

Translation

FAS   FAS   FAS   MGS MGS MGS
1. ταύτην τὴν ἐντολὴν ἔλαβον (I received) παρὰ τοῦ πατρός μου.

I received this commandment from my father.

FNS   FNS FNS   FNS   FNS
2. αὕτη ἐστὶν ἡ μεγάλη[1] καὶ πρώτη ἐντολή.

This is the first and greatest commandment.

N NP   M NP   M A P
3. εἰ ταῦτα οἴδατε (you know), μακάριοί ἐστε ἐὰν ποιῆτε (you do) αὐτά.

If you know these things, you are blessed when you do them.

FGS FGS   FGS   M NP   3MS MGP MGP   MA
4. Ἐκ δὲ τῆς πόλεως ἐκείνης πολλοὶ ἐπίστευσαν (they believed) εἰς αὐτὸν τῶν Σαμαριτῶν[2] διὰ τὸ
MAS FGS   FGS
λόγον τῆς γυναικός.   *woman's*

From that city many ↑ believed in him on account of the ^ word of the
woman (of the Samaritans.)

NAP 2NP   MGS MGS
5. διὰ τοῦτο[3] ὑμεῖς οὐκ ἀκούετε (you hear), ὅτι ἐκ τοῦ θεοῦ οὐκ ἐστέ.

For this reason you do not hear, since you are not of/from God.

MNS   NGS N GS
6. οὗτος ἦλθεν (he/she/it came) . . . ἵνα μαρτυρήσῃ (he/she/it might bear witness) περὶ τοῦ φωτός, ἵνα
MNP   MGS   MNS M
πάντες πιστεύσωσιν (they might believe) δι᾽ αὐτοῦ. οὐκ ἦν ἐκεῖνος τὸ φῶς, ἀλλ᾽ ἵνα μαρτυρήσῃ
NGS NGS
περὶ τοῦ φωτός.

This one came that he might bear witness concerning the light
*   That one   the*
that all might believe through him. He was not that light, but that he
might bear witness concerning the light.

MAS FNS FNS MVS   IDS NAS NAS NAS
7. λέγει (he/she/it says) πρὸς αὐτὸν ἡ γυνή· κύριε, δός (give!) μοι τοῦτο τὸ ὕδωρ.

The woman says to him, "Lord, give me this water."

---

[1] While the Greek superlative was dying out and its function being assumed by the comparative, in this verse we hav
something a little more unusual in that the positive degree is being used as a superlative.
[2] What word does τῶν Σαμαριτῶν modify?
[3] διὰ τοῦτο means "for this reason." It is a common idiom and should be memorized.

8.   MNS   FAS FAS   FAS   MDS   MAS   MNS

    καὶ πᾶς ὁ ἔχων[4] τὴν ἐλπίδα ταύτην ἐπ' αὐτῷ ἁγνίζει (he/she/it purifies) ἑαυτόν, καθὼς ἐκεῖνος

    MNS
    ἁγνός (pure) ἐστιν.   And   everyone who has this hope one the basis of him

    purifies himself, even as that one is pure.

9.   FDS   FDS NAP   MNS 2DS   FAS   FAS   FAS

    ἐν ποίᾳ[5] ἐξουσίᾳ ταῦτα ποιεῖς (you do); ἢ τίς σοι ἔδωκεν (he/she/it gave) τὴν ἐξουσίαν ταύτην

    NAS
    ἵνα ταῦτα ποιῇς (you might do);   By what authority do you do these things?

    Or who gave you this authority that you might do these things?

10.   IGS   MVS   IAS   FGB

    Νῦν ἡ ψυχή μου τετάρακται (he/she/it is troubled), καὶ τί εἴπω;[6] πάτερ, σῶσόν (save!) με ἐκ τῆς

    FGS FGS   NAP   FAS FAS FAS MVS   MGS

    ὥρας ταύτης; ἀλλὰ διὰ τοῦτο ἦλθον (I came) εἰς τὴν ὥραν ταύτην. πάτερ, δόξασόν (glorify!) σου

    NAS, NAS   FNS   GS   GS

    τὸ ὄνομα. ἦλθεν (he/she/it came) οὖν φωνὴ ἐκ τοῦ οὐρανοῦ· καὶ ἐδόξασα (I glorified) καὶ πάλιν

                   MNS   IASFNS FNS FNS

    δοξάσω (I will glorify).... ἀπεκρίθη Ἰησοῦς καὶ εἶπεν· οὐ δι' ἐμὲ ἡ φωνὴ αὕτη γέγονεν (he/she/it

                  2AP
    came) ἀλλὰ δι' ὑμᾶς.

    Now my soul is troubled, and <u>what</u> (who) can I say? Father, save me from

    this hour? but I came into this hour ~~on account of these things~~ (for this reason).

    Father, glorify your name. Then came a voice from heaven: and I

    glorified and again I will glorify... answered Jesus and said:

    the voice came not me but you.

Additional

11.   FNP   FNP   FNP   FAS   FNP   NDS, NDS

    αἱ δὲ γυναῖκες αὗται οὐκ ἐλπίδα ἔχουσιν (they have) ὅτι αὐταῖς οὐ δικαιοσύνη ἐν τῷ ὀνόματι

    MGS, MGS MGS
    τοῦ Ἰησοῦ Χριστοῦ.

    These women have no hope since they do not   in the name of Jesus Christ.

12.   MN.P   MNP, MNP   MGS, MGS MAP   MAP   MAP , MAP

    οἱ δώδεκα μαθηταὶ οἱ μετὰ τοῦ Ἰησοῦ τοὺς πολλοὺς λόγους ἐκείνους ἤκουσαν (they heard) ἐν

    MDS NDS MGS MGS
    τῷ οἴκῳ τοῦ θεοῦ.

    The twelve disciples with Jesus heard those many words in the house of God.

---

4   ὁ ἔχων means "one who has."

5   Ἐν ποίᾳ means "by what."

6   "I can say." But this is a question, so you will have to change the word order.

16. Seek ye first the kingdom of God and his righteousness, and all these things will be added unto you.

13. καὶ εἶπεν Ἀδάμ· τοῦτο νῦν ὀστοῦν[7] ἐκ τῶν ὀστέων μου καὶ σαρξ ἐκ τῆς σαρκός μου· αὕτη κληθήσεται (he/she/it will be called) γυνή ὅτι ἐκ τοῦ ἀνδρὸς αὐτῆς ἐλήμφθη (he/she/it was taken) αὕτη.

And Adam said, "Now this bone of my bone and this flesh of my flesh. This one will be c woman since ... taken from her husband.

14. καὶ ἐκάλεσεν (he/she/it called) Ἀδάμ τὸ ὄνομα τῆς γυναικὸς αὐτοῦ Ζωὴ ὅτι αὕτη μήτηρ πάντων τῶν ζώντων.[8]

And Adam called the name of his wife "Life" since she is mother of all those who are living,

15. πολλαὶ γυναῖκες ἐκοπίασαν (they labored) διὰ τῆς χάριτος τοῦ θεοῦ αὐτῶν.

Many women labored through the grace of their God.

16. ζητεῖτε (Seek!) δὲ πρῶτον[9] τὴν βασιλείαν [τοῦ θεοῦ] καὶ τὴν δικαιοσύνην αὐτοῦ, καὶ ταῦτα πάντα προστεθήσεται (he/she/it will be added) ὑμῖν.

17. τί ποιοῦμεν (we do) ὅτι οὗτος ὁ ἄνθρωπος πολλὰ ποιεῖ (he/she/it is doing) σημεῖα;

18. Τῶν δὲ δώδεκα ἀποστόλων τὰ ὀνόματά ἐστιν ταῦτα. *And these are the names of the 12 di*

19. ἐν ἐκείνῃ τῇ ἡμέρᾳ γνώσεσθε (you will know) ὑμεῖς ὅτι ἐγὼ ἐν τῷ πατρί μου καὶ ὑμεῖς ἐν ἐμοὶ κἀγὼ ἐν ὑμῖν.

20. Περὶ δὲ τῆς ἡμέρας ἐκείνης ἢ τῆς ὥρας οὐδεὶς οἶδεν (he/she/it knows), οὐδὲ[10] οἱ ἄγγελοι ἐν οὐρανῷ οὐδὲ ὁ υἱός, εἰ μή[11] ὁ πατήρ.

Summary

1. In Koine Greek, the superlative is falling out of use and the comparative can express both the comparative ("better") and superlative ("best") idea. Even in some instances the positive is used for one of the other degrees. As always, let context be your guide.

2. διὰ τοῦτο means "for this reason."

3. Any adjective can function adverbially. Usually it will be in the accusative neuter when it does so (cf. example 16).

References

α. Jn 18:36; β. Mt 3:1; γ. (Lk 1:34); δ. Mt 6:9; ε. Mt 20:4; ζ. Mt 3:17; η. Mt 10:23; **1.** Jn 10:18; **2.** Mt 22:38; **3.** Jn 13:17; **4.** Jn 4:39; **5.** Jn 8:47; **6.** Jn 1:7-8; **7.** Jn 4:15; **8.** 1 Jn 3:3; **9.** Mk 11:28; **10.** Jn 12:27-28, 30; **11.** —; **12.** —; **13.** Gen 2:23; **14.** Gen 3:20; **15.** (1 Clem 55:3); **16.** Mt 6:33; **17.** Jn 11:47; **18.** Mt 10:2; **19.** Jn 14:20; **20.** Mk 13:32.

17. What do we do? For that man is doing many miracles.

19. And in that day you will know that I am in my father and you are ... me and I in you.

20. But nobody knows concerning that day or hour, neither the angels in heaven nor the Son, only the Father

---

[7] ὀστέον, ου, τό, with the genitive plural ὀστέων, *bone*. Also occurs in its contracted form, ὀστοῦν, οῦ, τό (i.e., the εο has contracted to ου).

[8] τῶν ζώντων means "those who are living."

[9] In this context πρῶτον is functioning adverbially. In fact, any adjective can function adverbially. When they do, they normally are in the accusative and most often in the neuter.

[10] Just as we saw with καί in the previous chapter, here the two occurrences of οὐδέ act as correlative conjunctions meaning "neither ... or."

[11] In this context, εἰ μή means "only."

Relative Pronouns

Parsing

Inflected	Person / Case	Number	Gender	Lexical form	Inflected meaning
1. ἅ	N A	P	N	ὅς	which
2. ᾧ	D	S	M N	ὅς	to which
3. ἥ	N	S	F	ἥ / ὁ	the
4. ἐκείνους	A	P	M	ἐκεῖνος	those
5. ἅς	A	P	F	ὅς	which
6. οὗτοι	N	P	M	οὗτος	these
7. ἧς	G	S	F	ὅς	which
8. ὧν	G	P	F M N	ὅς	whose
9. φωτί	D	S	N	φῶς	to light
10. ἥν	A	S	F	ὅς	which

Warm-up

α.   NNP NNP NNP
  τὰ σημεῖα ἃ ἐποίει (he/she/it was doing)   the miracles which he was doing

β.   FNS   FNS   FAS MNS   IDP
  ἡ ἐπαγγελία ἣν αὐτὸς ἐπηγγείλατο (he/she/it promised) ἡμῖν
  the promise which he promised to us

γ.   MNS   FAS FAS 2GS
  ὃς κατασκευάσει (he/she/it will prepare) τὴν ὁδόν σου   who will prepare your way

δ.   NNS N GP N GP MNS MGS
  ἓν τῶν πλοίων, ὃ ἦν Σίμωνος   one of the ships which was Simon's

ε.   MNS   IGP   IGP
  ὃς γὰρ οὐκ ἔστιν καθ᾿ ἡμῶν, ὑπὲρ ἡμῶν ἐστιν. he who for ~~that which~~ is not ~~order~~ against us is ~~over~~ with us.

ζ.   NGP   NGP   NAP   MGS MGS MGS
  [1] ἀπὸ τῶν ἑπτὰ πνευμάτων ἃ ἐνώπιον τοῦ θρόνου αὐτοῦ from the 7 spirits which are before his throne

η.   MNS MNS FGS FGS MNS   2GP
  ὁ θεὸς τῆς εἰρήνης ὃς ἔσται μεθ᾿ ὑμῶν   the God of peace who will be ~~is~~ with you

---

[1] There is no verb in this warm-up. It is made up of a phrase and a clause.

Translation

Be able to identify every relative pronoun, explain its case, number, and gender, and explain what word the relative clause modifies and what function it performs in the sentence.

1. ^{NNP} ^{NNP} ^{NAP INS} τὰ ῥήματα ἃ ἐγὼ λελάληκα (I have spoken) ^{2DP} ὑμῖν ^{NNS} πνεῦμά ἐστιν καὶ ^{FNS} ζωή ἐστιν.

    The words which I have spoken to you is both spirit and life.
                                              (are)

2. ἐπίστευσαν (they believed) ^{FDS} τῇ ^{FDS} γραφῇ καὶ ^{MDS} τῷ ^{MDS} λόγῳ ^{MAS} ὃν ^{MNS} εἶπεν ὁ ^{MNS} Ἰησοῦς.

    They believed in the writing and in the word which Jesus said.
                                   Scripture

3. ² Γνωρίζω (I make known) δὲ ^{2DP} ὑμῖν, ^{MVP} ἀδελφοί, ^{NAS} τὸ ^{NAS} εὐαγγέλιον ^{NAS} ὃ εὐηγγελισάμην (I preached) ^{2DP} ὑμῖν, ^{NA} ὃ

    καὶ παρελάβετε (you received), ἐν ^{NDS} ᾧ καὶ ἐστήκατε (you stand), δι᾽ ^{NGS} οὗ καὶ σῴζεσθε (you are saved).

    For I make known, brothers, the good news which I preached to you,
    ~~and~~ *which* ^{also} *you received* ~~and~~ *in which* ^{also} *you stand, and* ^{also} *through which you a[re]*
    saved.

4. ^{FDS} χάριτι δὲ ^{MGS} θεοῦ εἰμι ^(MNS) ^{NNS} ὃ εἰμι.

    By the grace of God I am ~~who~~ ^{what} *I am.*

5. ³ ἔρχεται (he/she/it comes) ^{FDS} ὥρα ^{MNP} ἐν ᾗ πάντες οἱ ἐν ^{MDP} τοῖς ^{MDP} μνημείοις (tombs) ἀκούσουσιν⁴ ^{FGS} τῆς ^{FGS} φωνῆς

    ^{MGS} αὐτοῦ. ^{An} ~~The~~ *hour comes in which all the ones in the tombs will hear*
    his voice.

    adverbial use of
    ↳ *και*
    also

---

² Hint: If you diagram this verse it is easier to translate.

³ If you have problems with this verse, try diagramming it. Find the subject, main verb, and the function of the relative clause.

⁴ "They will hear." This verb can take a direct object in the genitive or the accusative.

ὃς γὰρ ἐὰν[5] θέλῃ (he/she/it wishes) τὴν ψυχὴν αὐτοῦ σῶσαι (to save) ἀπολέσει[6] αὐτήν· ὃς δ' ἂν
ἀπολέσει τὴν ψυχὴν αὐτοῦ ἕνεκεν[7] ἐμοῦ καὶ τοῦ εὐαγγελίου σώσει (he/she/it will save) αὐτήν.

For whoever wishes to save his life will lose it, ~~and~~ **but** whoever loses his life
on account of me and **of** the Gospel will save it.

ἀληθεύοντες (speaking the truth) δὲ ἐν ἀγάπῃ αὐξήσωμεν (let us grow) εἰς αὐτὸν ... ὅς ἐστιν ἡ
κεφαλή, Χριστός.   And speaking the truth in love, let us grow into him
that is / namely
he who is the head, Christ.

ὥσπερ (just as) γὰρ ὁ πατὴρ ἐγείρει (he/she/it raises) τοὺς νεκροὺς καὶ ζῳοποιεῖ (he/she/it gives
life), οὕτως καὶ ὁ υἱὸς οὓς θέλει (he/she/it wishes) ζῳοποιεῖ (he/she/it gives life to).   **also**

For just as the Father raises the dead and gives life, so ∧ does the
Son give life to whom he wishes.

νῦν δὲ ζητεῖτέ (you seek) με ἀποκτεῖναι (to kill) ἄνθρωπον ὃς τὴν ἀλήθειαν ὑμῖν λελάληκα (I have
spoken) ἣν ἤκουσα (I heard) παρὰ τοῦ θεοῦ.   But now you seek me to kill the man
I have spoken the truth which I heard concerning God to you.
But now you seek to kill me, the man who has spoken the
truth which I heard concerning God to you.

. καὶ ἡμεῖς μάρτυρες (witnesses) πάντων ὧν ἐποίησεν (he/she/it did) ἔν (τε) τῇ χώρᾳ (region) τῶν
Ἰουδαίων (Judeans) καὶ [ἐν] Ἰερουσαλήμ.   **both**

And we **are** witnesses of all that he did in the region of the
∧
Judeans and in Jerusalem

Remember, γάρ is postpositive, so it can separate words that normally belong together. ἐάν makes ὅς contingent, hence "whoever."

ἀπολέσει means "he/she/it will lose." What is the subject of this verb?

ἕνεκεν is a preposition meaning "on account of"; it takes the genitive.

According to the Gospel of John
Jesus did great miracles and many things, in the city of Jerusalem which the crowds saw.

52   *Basics of Biblical Greek Workbo*

Additional

11. *NNS NNS   MGS   MGS   MNS MNS   NAP   NAP   NNP*
κατὰ τὸ εὐαγγέλιον τοῦ Ἰωάννου ὁ Ἰησοῦς ἐποίησεν (he/she/it did) σημεῖα μεγάλα καὶ πολλ
FDS FDS   MGS   FGS   MNP   MNP
ἐν τῇ πόλει τῆς Ἰερουσαλήμ, ἃ οἱ ὄχλοι εἶδον (they saw).

12. *MNS MNS   FNS FNS   MNS MNS MNS   FDS FDS   NAS NAS   MGP   FDS FDS*
ὁ ἀνὴρ καὶ ἡ γυνὴ οἷς ἐστιν ὁ οἶκος οὗτος εἰσιν ἐν τῇ ὁδῷ πρὸς τὸ πλοῖον αὐτῶν ἐπὶ τῇ θαλάσσ
And she gave food which she made into the hands of her son Jacob.

13. *NAP NAP   NAP   FAP FAP*
καὶ ἔδωκεν (he/she/it gave) τὰ ἐδέσματα[8] ... ἃ ἐποίησεν (he/she/it made) εἰς τὰς χεῖρας Ἰακὼ
MGS MGS FGS
τοῦ υἱοῦ αὐτῆς. *The grace of our Lord Jesus Christ is with you and with all*

14. *FNS FNS MGS MGS 3GP   MGS   MGS   2GP   GP   GP*
Ἡ χάρις τοῦ κυρίου ἡμῶν Ἰησοῦ Χριστοῦ μεθ' ὑμῶν καὶ μετὰ πάντων ... τῶν κεκλημένων (one
MGS MGS   MDS MDS   MNS MNS   MG
who have been called) ὑπὸ τοῦ θεοῦ καὶ δι' αὐτοῦ, δι' οὗ αὐτῷ δόξα, ... θρόνος αἰώνιος ἀπὸ τῶ
MGP   MAP   MAP   MGP   MGP
αἰώνων εἰς τοὺς αἰῶνας τῶν αἰώνων. ἀμήν.

15. *NNP*
σῴζεσθε,[9] *NGS* ἀγάπης τέκνα καὶ εἰρήνης. *MNS MNS FGS FGS   FGS   FGS   NGS* ὁ κύριος τῆς δόξης καὶ πάσης χάριτος μετὰ τοῦ
πνεύματος ὑμῶν. *The Lord of glory and all grace is with your spirit*
Farewell, children of love and peace

16. Ἰγνάτιος, ὁ καὶ Θεοφόρος, τῇ εὐλογημένῃ (one who is blessed) *in the grace of God the Father in* *FDS   MGS   MGS   MDS* ἐν χάριτι θεοῦ πατρὸς ἐν Χριστῷ
MDS   MDS   MGP   MDS   FAS   FAS
Ἰησοῦ τῷ σωτῆρι[10] ἡμῶν, ἐν ᾧ ἀσπάζομαι (I greet) τὴν ἐκκλησίαν.
Christ Jesus Our Savior, in whom I greet the church.

17. *MNS   MAS   NAS   NAS   the Spirit descending   and remaini*
ἐκεῖνός[11] μοι εἶπεν· ἐφ' ὃν ἂν ἴδῃς (you see) *MAS MAS   MNS   MNS* τὸ πνεῦμα καταβαῖνον (descending) καὶ μένον
MDS MDS
(remaining) ἐπ' αὐτόν, οὗτός ἐστιν ὁ βαπτίζων (one who baptizes) ἐν πνεύματι ἁγίῳ. κἀγὼ ἑώρακ
MNS MNS MAS MGS
(I have seen), καὶ μεμαρτύρηκα (I have witnessed) ὅτι οὗτός ἐστιν ὁ υἱὸς τοῦ θεοῦ.

18. *MNS MNS FGS   FGS   FGS*
ἤγγιζεν (he/she/it has drawn near) ὁ χρόνος τῆς ἐπαγγελίας ἧς[12] ὡμολόγησεν (he/she/it promised
MNS MNS MDS   MDS
ὁ θεὸς τῷ Ἀβραάμ. *The time of the promise which God promised to Abraham has drawn*
near.

19. *MAS   MAS   MAS   MNS MNS MAS MAS MAS MAS 2NP*
καὶ κύριον αὐτὸν καὶ Χριστὸν ἐποίησεν (he/she/it made) ὁ θεός, τοῦτον τὸν Ἰησοῦν ὃν ὑμεῖς
ἐσταυρώσατε (crucified). *And God made him Lord and Christ, this Jesus whom you crucified.*

20. *NAS   2DP   MGS MGS*
ἃ δὲ γράφω (I write) ὑμῖν, ἰδοὺ ἐνώπιον τοῦ θεοῦ ὅτι οὐ ψεύδομαι (I lie).
And that which I write to you, behold before God that I do not lie.

Summary

14. The grace of our Lord Jesus Christ with you and with all
of the ones who have been called by God and through Him
1. σῴζεσθε, οἱ μαθηταί.   *eternal throne from age to age of the ages. Amen.*
Farewell, disciples.

References

α. Jn 2:23; β. 1 Jn 2:25; γ. Mk 1:2; δ. Lk 5:3; ε. Mk 9:40; ζ. Rev 1:4; η. (Phil 4:9); **1.** Jn 6:63; **2.** Jn 2:22; **3.** 1 Cor 15:1–
4. 1 Cor 15:10; **5.** Jn 5:28; **6.** Mk 8:35; **7.** Eph. 4:15; **8.** Jn 5:21; **9.** Jn 8:40; **10.** Ac 10:39; **11.** —; **12.** —; **13.** Gen 27:1
14. 1 Clem 65:2; **15.** Barn 21:9; **16.** Mag 1:0; **17.** Jn 1:33–34; **18.** Ac 7:17; **19.** Ac 2:36; **20.** Gal 1:20.

17. He said to me: on whomever you see the Spirit descending and remaining on him
this one is the one who baptizes in the Holy Spirit. And I have seen and I have wit

[8] ἔδεσμα, -ματος, τό, *food.* *that he is the Son of God.*

[9] While this sentence does not have a relative pronoun, it is just too cool a verse not to include, and it does use a vocabular
word for this chapter. σῴζεσθε is a plural imperative meaning *Be saved!* It is a way of saying *Farewell.* Be sure to use
when saying goodbye to your teacher and fellow students after class.

[10] σωτήρ, -ῆρος, ὁ, *savior, deliverer.*

[11] Here is an example of what we discussed earlier, that the demonstrative pronoun can "weaken" to the point that it func
tions as a personal pronoun.

[12] ἧς has been "attracted" to the case of the preceding word. See Advanced Information for the explanation.

Review #3 — Track 1

Grammar

1. Explain how the stem was modified in the following inflected forms. Start by writing out the word's stem, add the case ending, show the final form, and explain the changes.

   a. σάρξ   σάρκ

   b. ὄνομα   ὀνοματο

   c. χάρισιν   χαριτο

   d. πίστεως   πίστι

   e. πᾶς   παντ

2. Write out the seventh and eighth noun rules.

   7.

   8.

3. Describe what happens when you add a sigma to the following stops.

   a. τ + σ ▸   σ   d. π + σ ▸ ψ

   b. β + σ ▸ ψ   e. γ + σ ▸ ξ

   c. δ + σ ▸   σ   f. κ + σ ▸ ξ

4. List the case endings

	first/second declension			third declension	
	masc	*fem*	*neut*	*masc/fem*	*neut*
nom sg	ς	—	ν	ς	—
gen sg	οῦ	ης /ας	οῦ	ος	
dat sg	ι			ι	
acc sg	ν			α	—

53

	masc	fem	neut	masc/fem	neut
nom pl	ι	ι	α	ες	~~ο~~ α
gen pl	ὧν			ὧν	
dat pl	ις			σι	
acc pl	υς	ας	α	ας	~~ο~~ α

5. What determines the case, number, and gender of a personal pronoun?

   a. Case   *function in sentence*

   b. Number/gender   *antecedent*

6. Write out the paradigm of the English personal pronouns

	first person	second person		first person	second person
subjective sg	I	you	subjective pl	we	you
possessive sg	my	your	possessive pl	our	your
objective sg	me	you	objective pl	us	you

7. What are the three uses of αὐτός?

   a. *3rd person singular personal pronoun*

   b. *intensive*

   c. *"same"*

8. How do you distinguish the form of the feminine personal pronoun from the feminine demonstrative?
   τ appears in the forms of the demonstrative

9. In what adjectival position will you find the demonstratives when they are modifying nouns?
   attributive

10. What are the four basic rules of the vocative?

    a.

    b.

    c.

    d.

What determines the case, number, and gender of a relative pronoun?

a. Case *its use within the clause BUT watch for attraction*

b. Number/gender *antecedent*

How do you distinguish the form of the relative pronoun from the article?

Relative pronouns are accented as well as having a rough breathing.

rsing

πόλεσιν

ὀνόματι *N DS*   *to the name*   ὄνομα

ἡμάς   *3 A P*   *we*   ἡμεῖς

αὕτη   *F N S*   *this*   αὐτός

ὅν   *M A S*   *which*   ὅ

πᾶσαν *F A S*   *each*   πᾶς

ἐκκλησίαις *F D P*   *to the churches* ἐκκλησία

ἐμοί   *I D S*   *to me* *my/mine* ἐμός

τούτους *M A P*   *these*   αὐτός

ἡ   *F N S*   *the*   ὁ ἡ τό

οἷς   *N/M D P*   *to which*   ὅς

πολλοῖς *M D P*   *to many*   πολ

ποδί   *N D S*   *to the foot* πούς

ἐκεῖνα *N N/A P*   *those*   ἐκεῖνος

ὕδωρ   *N N S*   *water*   ὕδωρ

Translation: 1 John 1:5-2:5

^{1:5} Καὶ ἔστιν αὕτη ἡ ἀγγελία[1] ἣν ἀκηκόαμεν (we have heard) ἀπ᾽ αὐτοῦ καὶ ἀναγγέλλομεν
And this is the message which we have heard from him and which we proclaim to you

(we proclaim) ὑμῖν, ὅτι ὁ θεὸς φῶς ἐστιν καὶ σκοτία ἐν αὐτῷ οὐκ ἔστιν οὐδεμία. ^{1:6} Ἐὰν εἴπωμεν (we
That God is light and darkness is nothing to him.   If we say

say) ὅτι κοινωνίαν ἔχομεν (we have) μετ᾽ αὐτοῦ καὶ ἐν τῷ σκότει περιπατῶμεν (we are walking),
we have community with him and we are walking in darkness,

ψευδόμεθα (we lie) καὶ οὐ ποιοῦμεν (we do) τὴν ἀλήθειαν· ^{1:7} ἐὰν δὲ ἐν τῷ φωτὶ περιπατῶμεν (we
we lie and we do not do the truth.   But if we walk in the light

walk) ὡς αὐτός ἐστιν ἐν τῷ φωτί, κοινωνίαν ἔχομεν (we have) μετ᾽ ἀλλήλων καὶ τὸ αἷμα Ἰησοῦ το
as He is in the light   we have community with each other and the blood of Jes

υἱοῦ αὐτοῦ καθαρίζει (he/she/it cleanses) ἡμᾶς ἀπὸ πάσης ἁμαρτίας. ^{1:8} ἐὰν εἴπωμεν (we say) ὅτι
his Son cleanses us from all sin.   If we say that we

ἁμαρτίαν οὐκ ἔχομεν (we have), ἑαυτοὺς πλανῶμεν (we deceive) καὶ ἡ ἀλήθεια οὐκ ἔστιν ἐν ἡμῖν
we have no sin, we deceive ourselves   and the truth is not in us.

^{1:9} ἐὰν ὁμολογῶμεν (we confess) τὰς ἁμαρτίας ἡμῶν, πιστός ἐστιν καὶ δίκαιος, ἵνα ἀφῇ (he/she/it
If we confess our sins   that he might

might forgive) ἡμῖν τὰς ἁμαρτίας καὶ καθαρίσῃ (he/she/it will cleanse) ἡμᾶς ἀπὸ πάσης ἀδικίας.
forgive us our sins and He will cleanse us from all unrighteousness.

^{1:10} ἐὰν εἴπωμεν (we say) ὅτι οὐχ ἡμαρτήκαμεν (we have sinned), ψεύστην ποιοῦμεν[2] αὐτὸν καὶ ὁ
If we say that we have not sinned, we make

λόγος αὐτοῦ οὐκ ἔστιν ἐν ἡμῖν.
and His word is not in us.

^{2:1} Τεκνία[3] μου, ταῦτα γράφω (I write) ὑμῖν ἵνα μὴ ἁμάρτητε (you might sin). καὶ ἐάν τις
My little children, I write these things to you that you might not sin. And if anyone

ἁμάρτῃ (he/she/it sins), παράκλητον[4] ἔχομεν (we have) πρὸς τὸν πατέρα Ἰησοῦν Χριστὸν δίκαιον
sins, we have an advocate with the Father, Jesus Christ the righteous

^{2:2} καὶ αὐτὸς ἱλασμός[5] ἐστιν περὶ τῶν ἁμαρτιῶν ἡμῶν, οὐ περὶ τῶν ἡμετέρων[6] δὲ μόνον ἀλλὰ κα
And He is an atoning sacrifice for our sins, not for our sins only but for

περὶ ὅλου τοῦ κόσμου.
the world.

^{2:3} Καὶ ἐν τούτῳ γινώσκομεν (we know) ὅτι ἐγνώκαμεν (we have known) αὐτόν, ἐὰν τὰς
And in this we know that we have known him, if we keep his command

ἐντολὰς αὐτοῦ τηρῶμεν (we keep). ^{2:4} ὁ λέγων (one who says) ὅτι ἔγνωκα (I have known) αὐτὸν καὶ τὸ
The one who says that I have known him and does

ἐντολὰς αὐτοῦ μὴ τηρῶν (is keeping), ψεύστης ἐστιν καὶ ἐν τούτῳ ἡ ἀλήθεια οὐκ ἔστιν· ^{2:5} ὃς δ᾽ ὁ
keep his commandments   and the truth is not in him

τηρῇ (he/she/it is keeping) αὐτοῦ τὸν λόγον, ἀληθῶς ἐν τούτῳ ἡ ἀγάπη τοῦ θεοῦ τετελείωται (he/
Whoever is keeping his word   in this the love of God has been perfe

she/it has been perfected), ἐν τούτῳ γινώσκομεν (we know) ὅτι ἐν αὐτῷ ἐσμεν.
in this we know that we are in Him.

---

[1] ἀγγελία, -ας, ἡ, *message.*

[2] "We make." This verb can take a "double accusative," which means it requires two objects to make a complete thoug

[3] τεκνίον, -ου, τό, *little child.*

[4] παράκλητος, -ου, ὁ, *advocate.*

[5] ἱλασμός, -οῦ, ὁ, *atoning sacrifice.*

[6] ἡμέτερος, -α, -ον, *our.*

Present Active Indicative

Parsing

Inflected	Person / Case	Number	Tense / Gender	Voice	Mood	Lexical form	Inflected meaning
λέγουσιν	3	P	P	A	I	λέγω	they say
ἔχει	3	S	P	A	I	ἔχω	he/she/it has
πιστεύομεν	1	P	P	A	I	πιστεύω	we believe
λύεις	2	S	P	A	I	λύω	you loose/destroy
ἀκούω	1	S	P	A	I	ἀκούω	I hear
βλέπουσι	3	P	P	A	I	βλέπω	they see
ἔργοις	D	P	N			ἔργον	to works
λέγετε	2	P	P	A	I	λέγω	you say
ὧν	C	P	G			ὅ	of whom/which ~~that which who~~
πιστεύεις	2	S	P	A	I	πιστεύω	you believe

Warm-up

πιστεύω. I believe

τὴν φωνὴν αὐτοῦ ἀκούεις. You hear his voice

ἐξουσίαν ἔχει ὁ υἱὸς τοῦ ἀνθρώπου. The son of man has authority

τὸ φῶς τοῦ κόσμου τούτου βλέπουσιν. They see the light of this world

τότε ἀκούομεν τὸν νόμον μετὰ χαρᾶς. Then we hear the law with joy.

τὸν δὲ νόμον τοῦ κυρίου οὐ λύετε. And you do not loose/destroy the law of the lord.

καὶ ἀκούει ὁ τυφλὸς τὴν φωνήν. And the blind man hears the voice

Translation

1. τούτῳ ὑμεῖς οὐ πιστεύετε.

   You do not believe this

2. ἀπεκρίθη ὁ ὄχλος· δαιμόνιον ἔχεις.

   The crowd answered, " You have a demon."

3. οὐκ ἔχω ἄνδρα.

   I do not have a husband

4. τί δὲ βλέπεις τὸ κάρφος (splinter) τὸ ἐν τῷ ὀφθαλμῷ τοῦ ἀδελφοῦ σου;

   But how do you see the splinter in your brother's eye?

5. ὁ ὢν (one who is) ἐκ τοῦ θεοῦ τὰ ῥήματα τοῦ θεοῦ ἀκούει· διὰ τοῦτο ὑμεῖς οὐκ ἀκούετε, ὅτι ἐ
   The one who is from God hears God's **words** *; for this reason you do not hear*
   τοῦ θεοῦ οὐκ ἐστέ.
   for you are not of God.

6. πάντοτε (always) γὰρ τοὺς πτωχοὺς (poor) ἔχετε μεθ᾽ ἑαυτῶν,[1] ἐμὲ δὲ οὐ πάντοτε ἔχετε.

   For you always have the poor with you(rselves), but you do not always have me.

7. σὺ πιστεύεις εἰς τὸν υἱὸν τοῦ ἀνθρώπου;

   Do you believe in the Son of man?

8. λέγω γὰρ ὑμῖν ὅτι οἱ ἄγγελοι αὐτῶν[2] ἐν οὐρανοῖς διὰ παντὸς[3] βλέπουσι τὸ πρόσωπον τοῦ
   For I say to you that his angels in heaven always see the face of my Fat
   πατρός μου τοῦ ἐν οὐρανοῖς.
   who is in heaven.

---

[1] Here is a good example of how ἑαυτοῦ is not always third person.

[2] What is the antecedent of this word? You will have to rely on your general Bible knowledge because the antecedent
not in this verse.

[3] διὰ παντός is an idiom meaning "always."

4. ὑμῶν[5] δὲ μακάριοι οἱ ὀφθαλμοὶ ὅτι βλέπουσιν καὶ τὰ ὦτα (ears) ὑμῶν ὅτι ἀκούουσιν.

And blessed are your eyes which see and your ears which hear.

0. λέγουσιν οὖν τῷ τυφλῷ πάλιν· τί σὺ λέγεις περὶ αὐτοῦ, ὅτι ἠνέῳξέν (he/she/it opened) σου τοὺς

ὀφθαλμούς; ὁ δὲ εἶπεν ὅτι προφήτης ἐστίν....

οὗτός ἐστιν ὁ υἱὸς ὑμῶν, ὃν ὑμεῖς λέγετε ὅτι τυφλὸς ἐγεννήθη (he/she/it was born); πῶς οὖν

βλέπει ἄρτι (now); ....

ἀπεκρίθη οὖν ἐκεῖνος· εἰ ἁμαρτωλός (sinner) ἐστιν οὐκ οἶδα (I know)· ἓν οἶδα ὅτι τυφλὸς ὢν[6]

ἄρτι βλέπω.

Then they said to the blind man , " Why do you say about him, that he opened your eyes? And he said that he is a prophet....

This one is your son, whom you say was born blind? Then how does he now see?

Then he/that one answered, " If he is a sinner, I do not know. One thing I know — that even though I was blind, now I see.

Additional

1. πιστὸν τὸ ῥῆμα τοῦτο· διὰ τὴν πίστιν ὑμῶν ἐν τῷ υἱῷ τοῦ θεοῦ εἰρήνην τε καὶ χαρὰν ἐν τῷ
πνεύματι τῷ ἁγίῳ ἔχετε.

on account of your faith in the Son of God you have peace and joy in the Holy Spirit

2. ὅτε δὲ τῶν λόγων τῶν καλῶν τοῦ θεοῦ ἀκούομεν, ταῦτα πάντα πιστεύομεν, ἔχουσιν γὰρ ἡμῖν
τὴν ἐπαγγελίαν τῆς αἰωνίας ζωῆς.

3. καὶ εἶπεν κύριος πρὸς Μωϋσῆν· τί οὐ πιστεύουσίν μοι ἐν πᾶσιν τοῖς σημείοις οἷς βλέπουσιν ἐν
αὐτοῖς; *And the Lord said to Moses: why do they not believe me in all the signs which they see in them?*

4. σὺ γὰρ ζωῆς καὶ θανάτου ἐξουσίαν ἔχεις. *For you have authority over life and death.*

This verse is two sentences, with the main verb omitted from both. Split the verse in half before translating.

What word does ὑμῶν modify?

This word means "being," but in this context you can translate, "even though I was."

15. καὶ νῦν οὐ πιστεύετέ μοι; οὐ μέγας ὁ βασιλεὺς[7] τῇ ἐξουσίᾳ αὐτοῦ;

16. τὴν ἀγάπην τοῦ θεοῦ οὐκ ἔχετε ἐν ἑαυτοῖς.

17. [8] ἐγὼ δὲ ὅτι τὴν ἀλήθειαν λέγω, οὐ πιστεύετέ μοι.

18. ἀλλὰ διὰ τῆς χάριτος τοῦ κυρίου Ἰησοῦ πιστεύομεν σωθῆναι (that we are saved).

19. νῦν δὲ ὑπὸ ἀγγέλου βλέπεις, διὰ τοῦ αὐτοῦ μὲν πνεύματος.

20. Ἰησοῦς δὲ ἔκραξεν (he/she/it cried out) καὶ εἶπεν· ὁ πιστεύων (one who believes) εἰς ἐμὲ οὐ πιστεύει εἰς ἐμὲ ἀλλὰ εἰς τὸν πέμψαντά (one who sent) με.

English to Greek

1. they say λέγουσι

2. you (plural) have ἔχετε

3. we believe πιστευομεν πιστεύομεν

4. he sees βλέπει

5. you (singular) hear ακούεις

Summary

1. διὰ παντός is an idiom meaning "always."

References

α. Mk 9:24; β. Jn 3:8; γ. Mk 2:10; δ. (Jn 11:9); ε. —; ζ. —; η. —; **1.** Jn 5:38; **2.** Jn 7:20; **3.** Jn 4:17; **4.** Mt 7:3; **5.** Jn 8:4
6. Mt 26:11; **7.** Jn 9:35; **8.** Mt 18:10; **9.** Mt 13:16; **10.** Jn 9:17,19,25; **11.** —; **12.** —; **13.** (Num 14:11); **14.** Wsd 16:1
15. (1 Esdr 4:28); **16.** Jn 5:42; **17.** Jn 8:45; **18.** Ac 15:11; **19.** Shep 78:2; **20.** Jn 12:44.

17. But that I tell you the truth, you do not believe me

18. But through the grace of Lord Jesus we believe that we are saved.

20. And Jesus cried out and said," The one who believes in me believes not i but in the One who sent Me."

---

[7] βασιλεύς, -έως, ὁ, *king.*

[8] Hint: Find the subject and the main verb. Remember, the main verb cannot occur in a dependent clause.
Hint: ἐγώ should technically be inside the ὅτι clause.

Contract Verbs

Parsing

	Inflected	Person / Case	Number	Tense / Gender	Voice	Mood	Lexical form	Inflected meaning
1.	λαλοῦμεν	1	P	P	A	I	λαλέω	we speak
2.	ἀγαπῶσι	3	P	P	A	I	ἀγαπάω	they love
3.	τηρῶ	1	S	P	A	I	τηρῶ	I keep
4.	πληροῦτε	2	P	P	A	I	πληρόω	you fill
5.	ζητοῦσιν	3	P	P	A	I	ζητέω	they seek
6.	ἀγαπᾷ	3	S	P	A	I	ἀγαπάω	he she it loves
7.	καλεῖς	2	S	P	A	I	καλέω	you call
8.	πληροῖ	3	S	P	A	I	πληρόω	he/she/it fills
9.	λαλεῖτε	2	P	P	A	I	λαλέω	you speak
10.	ποιεῖ	3	S	P	A	I	ποιέω	he/she/it does

Warm-up

2. τὰς ἐντολὰς αὐτοῦ τηροῦμεν. We keep his commandments

 οὐ ποιῶ τὰ ἔργα τοῦ πατρός μου. I do not do the works of my Father

ζητοῦσίν σε. They seek you.

ἀγαπᾷς με; Do you love me?

τὸ σάββατον οὐ τηρεῖ. He does not keep the Sabbath

τί λαλεῖς μετ᾽ αὐτῆς; Why do you speak with them?

ἀγαπῶμεν τὰ τέκνα τοῦ θεοῦ. We love the children of God.

Translation

1. Τί δέ με καλεῖτε· κύριε, κύριε, καὶ οὐ ποιεῖτε ἃ λέγω;
   And why do you call me, "Lord, Lord" but do not do that which I say?

2. οἱ μαθηταὶ εἶπαν (they said) αὐτῷ· διὰ τί[1] ἐν παραβολαῖς λαλεῖς αὐτοῖς;
   The disciples said, "Why do you speak to them in parables?"

3. ἡμεῖς οἴδαμεν ὅτι μεταβεβήκαμεν (we have passed) ἐκ τοῦ θανάτου εἰς τὴν ζωήν, ὅτι ἀγαπῶμεν
   τοὺς ἀδελφούς. We hear that we have passed from death into life, that we
   love the brothers.

4. ὁ πατὴρ ἀγαπᾷ τὸν υἱὸν καὶ πάντα δέδωκεν (he/she/it has given) ἐν τῇ χειρὶ αὐτοῦ.
   The Father loves the son and has given all things into his hand.

5. αὐτοὶ ἐκ τοῦ κόσμου εἰσίν, διὰ τοῦτο ἐκ τοῦ κόσμου λαλοῦσιν καὶ ὁ κόσμος αὐτῶν ἀκούει.
   They are of the world, for this reason they speak from the world and the world
   hears them.

6. σὺ πιστεύεις ὅτι εἷς ἐστιν ὁ θεός, καλῶς (well) ποιεῖς· καὶ τὰ δαιμόνια πιστεύουσιν καὶ
   φρίσσουσιν (they shudder).
   You believe that God is One, you do well; and the demons believe and
   shudder.

7. ὁ μὴ ἀγαπῶν (one who loves) με τοὺς λόγους μου οὐ τηρεῖ· καὶ ὁ λόγος ὃν ἀκούετε οὐκ ἔστιν ἐμὸ
   The one who does not love me does not keep my words; and the word which
   you hear is not mine.

---

[1] διὰ τί is an idiom meaning "Why?" You may want to make a vocabulary flash card for the phrase.
[2] What is the theological significance of the aspect of this verbal form?

8. τί[3] ποιοῦμεν ὅτι οὗτος ὁ ἄνθρωπος πολλὰ ποιεῖ σημεῖα;

What do we do since this man does many signs?

9. λέγει οὖν αὐτῷ ὁ Πιλᾶτος· ἐμοὶ οὐ λαλεῖς; οὐκ οἶδας ὅτι ἐξουσίαν ἔχω ἀπολῦσαί (to free) σε καὶ

Then Pilate says to him, "Do you not speak to me? Don't you know that I have the authority to free you

ἐξουσίαν ἔχω σταυρῶσαί (to crucify) σε;

and I have the authority to crucify you?"

10. ἰδοὺ οἱ μαθηταί σου ποιοῦσιν ὃ οὐκ ἔξεστιν[4] ποιεῖν (to do) ἐν σαββάτῳ.

Behold, your disciples do that which is not lawful to do on the Sabbath

Additional

1. εἰ οὖν τὰς ἐντολὰς καὶ τοὺς νόμους τοῦ θεοῦ τηροῦμεν, οἴδαμεν ὅτι ἔχομεν τὴν ἀγάπην τὴν μεγάλην αὐτοῦ ἐν ταῖς καρδίαις ἡμῶν.

Then if we keep God's commandments and laws, we know that we have his great love in our hearts.

2. πῶς ὁ Ἰησοῦς τὰ πολλὰ σημεῖα ποιεῖ ἃ βλέπετε; ἐπὶ τῇ ἐξουσίᾳ τοῦ πνεύματος τοῦ ἁγίου.

How does Jesus do the many signs which you see? By the authority of the Holy Spirit.

3. ἐν ταῖς ἡμέραις ἐκείναις οὐκ ἦν βασιλεὺς[5] ἐν Ἰσραήλ· ἀνὴρ τὸ ἀγαθὸν ἐν ὀφθαλμοῖς αὐτοῦ ποιεῖ.

In those days there was no king in Israel; man does that which is good in his (own) eyes.

4. ἀκούεις μου, Ἰακώβ, καὶ Ἰσραήλ, ὃν ἐγὼ καλῶ· ἐγώ εἰμι πρῶτος καὶ ἐγώ εἰμι εἰς τὸν αἰῶνα.[6]

You hear me, Jacob, and Israel, that which I say, "I am first and I am forever."

5. οὐ λαλεῖ περὶ ἐμοῦ καλὰ ἀλλὰ ... κακά.

You do not speak good concerning me but... evil.

6. εἰ οὖν Δαυὶδ καλεῖ αὐτὸν κύριον, πῶς υἱὸς αὐτοῦ ἐστιν;

Then if David calls him Lord, how is he his son?

7. τί οὗτος οὕτως λαλεῖ; *Why does this man speak in this manner?*

8. [7] οἱ πάντες γὰρ τὰ ἑαυτῶν ζητοῦσιν, οὐ τὰ Ἰησοῦ Χριστοῦ.

For all seek the things of themselves, not the things of Jesus Christ.

Hint: τί does not always mean "why?"

ἔξεστιν is a special type of verb. It technically is third person singular and means "it is lawful." It always has a neuter subject.

βασιλεύς, -έως, ὁ, *king*.

εἰς τὸν αἰῶνα is an idiom meaning "forever."

Hint: τά is functioning substantivally in both instances.

19. [8] ἃ ἐγὼ ἑώρακα (I have seen) παρὰ τῷ πατρὶ λαλῶ· καὶ ὑμεῖς οὖν ἃ ἠκούσατε (you heard) παρα τοῦ πατρὸς ποιεῖτε.... ὑμεῖς ποιεῖτε τὰ ἔργα τοῦ πατρὸς ὑμῶν. *I speak that which I have seen in the presence of the Father's and then you do what you heard from the Father. You do the works of your Father.*

20. καὶ κατεδίωξεν[9] αὐτὸν Σίμων καὶ οἱ μετ᾽ αὐτοῦ, καὶ εὗρον (they found) αὐτὸν καὶ λέγουσιν αὐτῷ ὅτι πάντες ζητοῦσίν σε. *And Simons and those with him sought him intently, and they found him and tell him that the ones all seek you.*

Summary

1. διὰ τί means "Why?"

2. Sometimes a preposition is used to form a compound word, and the function of the preposition is to inter sify the force of the simple word. This is the "perfective" use of a preposition. But you cannot assume th perfective force is always present. You will need to check the meaning of the word elsewhere and you immediate context (sentence 20).

References

α. 1 Jn 3:22; β. Jn 10:37; γ. Mk 3:32; δ. Jn 21:15; ε. Jn 9:16; ζ. Jn 4:27; η. 1 Jn 5:2; **1.** Lk 6:46; **2.** Mt 13:10; **3.** 1 Jn 3:1 **4.** Jn 3:35; **5.** 1 Jn 4:5; **6.** Jas 2:19; **7.** Jn 14:24; **8.** Jn 11:47; **9.** Jn 19:10; **10.** Mt 12:2; **11.** —; **12.** —; **13.** (Judg 17:6); **14.** (48:12); **15.** 1 Kgs 22:8; **16.** Mt 22:45; **17.** Mk 2:7; **18.** Phil 2:21; **19.** Jn 8:38, 41; **20.** Mk 1:36-37.

---

[8] Hint: What is the direct object of λαλῶ?

[9] κατεδίωξεν means "he/she/it sought intently." It describes a searching done in earnest. How does knowing this help yo better understand the passage?

κατά is often used to form a compound verb, and carries with it an intensifying force. It is called the "perfective" use the preposition. For example, ἐργάζομαι means "I work" while κατεργάζομαι means "I work out thoroughly, I accor plish." ἐσθίω means "I eat" while κατεσθίω means "I eat up thoroughly, I devour." Likewise, διώκω means "I search fo while καταδιώκω means "I search for thoroughly, I seek intently." (For other examples of the perfective use of prepo tions see *Metzger*, 81-85.) There is a danger here, though. You cannot always assume that a compound word carries th meaning of its parts. That is called the "Root Fallacy" (see Carson, *Exegetical Fallacies*). Sometimes a compound verb the same meaning as the simple form of the verb. As always, let context be your guide.

Present Middle/Passive Indicative

arsing

Inflected	Person / Case	Number	Tense / Gender	Voice	Mood	Lexical form	Inflected meaning
ἀκούεται	3	S	P	P	I	ἀκούω	he/she/it is heard
λύεσθε	2	P	P	P	I	λύω	you are destroyed
συνάγει	3	S	P	A	I	συνάγω	he/she/it gathers
δύναται	3	S	P	M	I	δύναμαι	he/she/it is able
πορευόμεθα	1	P	P	M	I	πορεύομαι	we go
ἔρχεσθε	2	P	P	M	I	ἔρχομαι	you go, come
ἀποκρίνῃ	3	S	P	M	I	ἀποκρίνομαι	he/she/it answers
νυξίν	D	S	F			νύξ	to night
ἀγαπώμεθα	1	P	P	P	I	ἀγαπάω	we are loved
δύνανται	3	P	P	M	I	δύναμαι	they are able

Warm-up

ἀκούεται ἐν ὑμῖν. He/she/it is heard by you.

οἱ τόποι τοῦ κακοῦ λύονται. The place of the bad/evil (people) is destroyed.

ἔρχεται εἰς οἶκον. He goes into the house.

αὐτοὶ πιστεύονται ὑπὸ τῶν δαιμονίων. They were believed by the demons

τίς δύναται σωθῆναι (to be saved); What ~~is necessary~~ can (one) do to be saved?

ἔρχομαι ὡς κλέπτης.[1] I come as a thief.

καὶ οὐδενὶ οὐδὲν ἀποκρίνεται. And noone answered anyone.

κλέπτης, -ου, ὁ, *thief.* You may have guessed this from the English cognate "kleptomaniac."

Translation

The non-deponent verbs we know occur rarely in the middle or passive in the New Testament (and even the LXX), and hence the paucity of examples below. δύναμαι and ἔρχομαι are common deponents.

1. οὐ ἀκούονται αἱ φωναὶ αὐτῶν.
    Their voices are not heard.

2. οὐχ ἡ μήτηρ αὐτοῦ λέγεται[2] Μαριὰμ καὶ οἱ ἀδελφοὶ αὐτοῦ Ἰάκωβος καὶ Ἰωσὴφ καὶ Σίμων καὶ
                                                      Mariam
    Ἰούδας; *Is his mother not called Mary and his brothers Jacob,*
    Joseph, Simon, and Judas?

3. ἐγὼ πρὸς τὸν πατέρα πορεύομαι.
    I go to the Father.

4. [3] ὅπου εἰμὶ ἐγὼ ὑμεῖς οὐ δύνασθε ἐλθεῖν (to go).
    Where I am you cannot go.

5. ὁ δὲ Πιλᾶτος πάλιν ἐπηρώτα (he/she/it began asking) αὐτὸν λέγων (saying)· οὐκ ἀποκρίνῃ οὐδέν;
    And Pilate began asking him again, saying, "Do you answer nothi...

6. [4] Καὶ συνάγονται οἱ ἀπόστολοι πρὸς τὸν Ἰησοῦν καὶ ἀπήγγειλαν (they told) αὐτῷ πάντα ὅσα[5]

    ἐποίησαν (they did) καὶ ὅσα ἐδίδαξαν (they taught).
    And the apostles ~~were~~ are gathered to Jesus and they told him
    all that they did and that they taught.

---

[2] λέγω has a wide range of meaning. It can describe the "calling" of someone as it does here. Jn 20:16 gives another example. ραββουνι (ὃ λέγεται διδάσκαλε). Here it is translated "is called" in the sense of "is translated."

[3] Note the emphatic use of the personal pronouns.

[4] It would greatly help to diagram this verse.

[5] You have to be pretty free with your translation of this word.

λέγουσιν αὐτῷ· ἐρχόμεθα καὶ ἡμεῖς σὺν σοί.

They say to him, " And we come to you."

ὁ δὲ Ἰησοῦς ἀποκρίνεται αὐτοῖς λέγων (saying)· ἐλήλυθεν (he/she/it has come) ἡ ὥρα ἵνα

δοξασθῇ (he/she/it might be glorified) ὁ υἱὸς τοῦ ἀνθρώπου.

And Jesus answered them saying, " The hour has come that the
Son of man might be glorified."

οὐδεὶς γὰρ δύναται ταῦτα τὰ σημεῖα ποιεῖν (to do) ἃ σὺ ποιεῖς, ἐὰν μὴ ᾖ (he/she/it is) ὁ θεὸς μετ'

αὐτοῦ. For noone can do these signs which you do, if God is not with

him.

0. Καὶ οἱ μαθηταὶ Ἰωάννου καὶ οἱ Φαρισαῖοι ἔρχονται καὶ λέγουσιν αὐτῷ· διὰ τί οἱ μαθηταὶ

Ἰωάννου καὶ οἱ μαθηταὶ τῶν Φαρισαίων νηστεύουσιν (they fast), οἱ δὲ σοὶ μαθηταὶ οὐ

νηστεύουσιν; And John's disciples and the Pharisees come and ~~ask~~ say to him:
why do John's disciples and the Pharisees' fast, but yours do not fast?

Additional

1. οἱ πόδες μου πορεύονται πρὸς τὸν τόπον ἐφ' ᾧ ὁ Ἰησοῦς λαλεῖ καὶ οἱ ὀφθαλμοί μου βλέπουσιν
   τὰ σημεῖα αὐτοῦ καὶ τὰ ὦτα[6] μου ἀκούει τῶν παραβολῶν αὐτοῦ. My feet go to the place ~~of~~ which
   speaks and my eyes see his signs and my ears hear his parables.

2. ἡμέρα καὶ νυκτὶ οἱ ὄχλοι συνάγουσιν περὶ τὸν Ἰησοῦν, οἴδασιν γὰρ ἐκεῖνοι ὅτι ἔρχεται αὐτοῖς
   λαλεῖν (to speak) τινὰς λόγους τῆς ἐλπίδος καὶ τῆς ζωῆς. Day and night the crowds gathered around
   Jesus   words of hope and life

3. καὶ ἔρχονται οἱ ἄγγελοι εἰς τὸν τόπον ἐκεῖνον καὶ λαλοῦσιν τοὺς λόγους εἰς τὰ ὦτα τοῦ ὄχλου.
   And the angels come into that place and say the words into the ears of the crowd.

4. καὶ εἶπεν αὐτῇ ὁ ἄγγελος κυρίου, Ἀγάρ, ποῦ (where) πορεύῃ; And the angel of the Lord
   said to her, " Hagar, where are you going?"

 οὖς, ὠτός, τό, *ear*.

15. τέλος[7] λόγου· τὸ πᾶν ἀκούεται· τὸν θεὸν φοβοῦ (fear!) καὶ τὰς ἐντολὰς αὐτοῦ φύλασσε (keep!) ὅτι τοῦτο τὸ ὅλον ἔργον τοῦ ἀνθρώπου.

16. καὶ εἶπεν Νωεμίν· ἐπιστράφητε (turn back!) ... θυγατέρες μου.... τί πορεύεσθε μετ' ἐμοῦ; μὴ ἔτι μοι υἱοὶ ἐν τῇ κοιλίᾳ μου καὶ ἔσονται (they will be) ὑμῖν εἰς ἄνδρας;

17. λέγει αὐτοῖς ὁ Ἰησοῦς· πιστεύετε ὅτι δύναμαι τοῦτο ποιῆσαι (to do); λέγουσιν αὐτῷ· ναί, κύριε

18. καὶ εἶπεν αὐτῷ Ναθαναήλ· ἐκ Ναζαρὲτ δύναταί τι ἀγαθὸν εἶναι (to come);

19. Ἀνέβη (he/she/it went up) δὲ καὶ Ἰωσὴφ ἀπὸ τῆς Γαλιλαίας ἐκ πόλεως Ναζαρὲθ εἰς τὴν Ἰουδαίαν εἰς πόλιν Δαυὶδ ἥτις καλεῖται Βηθλέεμ.

20. τί οὗτος οὕτως λαλεῖ; βλασφημεῖ· τίς δύναται ἀφιέναι (to forgive) ἁμαρτίας εἰ μὴ εἷς ὁ θεός;

References

α. 1 Cor 5:1; β. —; γ. Mk 3:20; δ. —; ε. Mk 10:26; ζ. Rev 16:15; η. Shep 43:8; **1.** (Ps 19:3 [LXX 18:4]); **2.** Mt 13:55; **3.** Jr 14:12; **4.** Jn 7:34; **5.** Mk 15:4; **6.** Mk 6:30; **7.** Jn 21:3; **8.** Jn 12:23; **9.** Jn 3:2; **10.** (Mk 2:18); **11.** —; **12.** —; **13.** (1 Sam 11:4) **14.** Gen 16:8; **15.** (Eccl 12:13); **16.** Ruth 1:11; **17.** Mt 9:28; **18.** Jn 1:46; **19.** Lk 2:4; **20.** Mk 2:7.

15. An end of the word; it is heard by all; fear God and his commandments *keep* since this whole work of man.

16. And Naomi said, "Turn back... my daughters... why do you come with me? are there ~~are not~~ *still* sons in my womb ~~anymore~~, and they will be husbands to you?"

17. Jesus ~~said~~ *says* to them, "Do you believe that I can do this?"; they said to him, "Yes, Lord."

18. And Nathaniel said to him, "Can any good come from Nazareth?"

19. And Joseph went up to Galilee from the city of Nazareth in Judea into the city of David which is called Bethlehem

20. "You blaspheme" Who can forgive sins if not the one God?

---

[7] τέλος, -ους, τό, end.

Exercise 19 — Track 1

Future Active/Middle Indicative

Parsing

	Inflected	Person / Case	Number	Tense / Gender	Voice	Mood	Lexical form	Inflected meaning
1.	λύσει	3	S	F	A	I	λύω	he/she/it will destroy
2.	ἀκούσεις	2	S	F	A	I	ἀκούω	you will listen
3.	γεννήσομεν	1	P	F	M	I	γεννάω	we will give birth
4.	ζήσουσι	3	P	F	A	I	ζητέω	they will seek
5.	πορεύσεται	3	S	M	M	I	πορεύομαι	he/she/it will
6.	βλέψεις	2	S	F	A	I	βλέπω	you will see
7.	ἕξετε	2	P	F	A	I	ἔχω	you will have
8.	καλέσομεν	1	P	F	A	I	καλέω	we will call
9.	ὅλους	A	P	M			ὅλος	the whole (thing)
10.	συνάξουσιν	3	P	F	A	I	συνάγω	they will gather

Warm-up

α. πάντες πιστεύσουσιν εἰς αὐτόν.   All will believe in him.

β. αὐτὸς περὶ ἑαυτοῦ λαλήσει.   He will speak concerning himself

γ. συνάξω τοὺς καρπούς μου.   I will gather my fruit.

δ. ἕξει τὸ φῶς τῆς ζωῆς.   He shall have the light of life.

ε. σὺν ἐμοὶ πορεύσονται.   Then he/she/it will come to me

ϛ. βλέψετε καὶ οὐ λαλήσει.   You will see and not speak.

η. ἀκούσει τις ... τὴν φωνὴν αὐτοῦ.   He/she/it will hear anyone... his voice

Translation

1. κύριον τὸν θεόν σου προσκυνήσεις.[1]

    You will worship the Lord your God.

2. [2]βασιλεὺς Ἰσραήλ ἐστιν, καταβάτω (let him come down!) νῦν ἀπὸ τοῦ σταυροῦ (cross) καὶ

    πιστεύσομεν ἐπ᾽ αὐτόν. He is the King of Israel; now let him come

    down from the cross & we will believe in him.

3. ἡ γυνή σου Ἐλισάβετ γεννήσει υἱόν σοι καὶ καλέσεις τὸ ὄνομα αὐτοῦ Ἰωάννην.

    His wife Elizabeth will give birth   his name John.
    to his son   and will call his

4. ὁ δὲ θεός μου πληρώσει πᾶσαν χρείαν (need) ὑμῶν κατὰ τὸ πλοῦτος (riches) αὐτοῦ ἐν δόξῃ ἐν

    Χριστῷ Ἰησοῦ. And/But my God will fulfill all your needs   according to

    his riches in glory in Jesus Christ.

5. ἀμὴν ἀμὴν λέγω ὑμῖν ὅτι ἔρχεται ὥρα καὶ νῦν ἐστιν ὅτε οἱ νεκροὶ ἀκούσουσιν τῆς φωνῆς τοῦ

    υἱοῦ τοῦ θεοῦ καὶ οἱ ἀκούσαντες (ones who hear it) ζήσουσιν.

    Amen, amen I say to you that the hour comes and now is when
    the dead will hear the voice of the Son of God and the
    ones who hear it will seek (him).

6. καὶ ἔσεσθε μισούμενοι (hated) ὑπὸ πάντων διὰ τὸ ὄνομά μου.

    And you will be hated by all on account of my name.

---

[1] Notice that although this is a future verb, it is being used as an imperative to state a command. This is a common use of
     the future in both Greek and English. See the *Exegetical Insight* to this chapter.

[2] Hint: The people are probably taunting Jesus and being sarcastic. Interestingly, some manuscripts (A, 𝔐, Latin, Syriac,
     et al.) insert εἰ before βασιλεύς.

. ³ ἀμὴν ἀμὴν λέγω ὑμῖν, ὁ πιστεύων (one who believes) εἰς ἐμὲ τὰ ἔργα ἃ ἐγὼ ποιῶ κἀκεῖνος (that one) ποιήσει καὶ μείζονα τούτων⁴ ποιήσει, ὅτι ἐγὼ πρὸς τὸν πατέρα πορεύομαι.

Amen, amen I say to you, the one who believes in me the works which
I do that one will do better than this one, which I go to the Father.

. ὑμεῖς προσκυνεῖτε ὃ οὐκ οἴδατε· ἡμεῖς προσκυνοῦμεν ὃ οἴδαμεν, ὅτι ἡ σωτηρία (salvation) ἐκ τῶν Ἰουδαίων ἐστίν. ἀλλὰ ἔρχεται ὥρα καὶ νῦν ἐστιν, ὅτε οἱ ἀληθινοὶ (true) προσκυνηταὶ (worshipers) προσκυνήσουσιν τῷ πατρὶ ἐν πνεύματι καὶ ἀληθείᾳ.

You worship that which you do not know. We worship what we know —
that salvation is from the Jews. But the hour comes and now is,
when the true worshippers will worship the Father in Spirit and truth.

. ζητήσετέ με, καὶ καθὼς εἶπον (I said) τοῖς Ἰουδαίοις ὅτι ὅπου ἐγὼ ὑπάγω (I go) ὑμεῖς οὐ δύνασθε ἐλθεῖν (to go), καὶ ὑμῖν λέγω. You will seek me, but as I said to the Jews
that I where I go you will not be able to go, I say to you.

0. ἄκουε (Listen!), Ἰσραήλ, κύριος ὁ θεὸς ἡμῶν κύριος εἷς ἐστιν, καὶ ἀγαπήσεις κύριον τὸν θεόν σου ἐξ ὅλης τῆς καρδίας σου καὶ ἐξ ὅλης τῆς ψυχῆς σου καὶ ἐξ ὅλης τῆς διανοίας (mind) σου καὶ ἐξ ὅλης τῆς ἰσχύος (strength) σου. Hear, O Israel, the Lord our God is One,
and you will love the Lord your God with your whole heart and your
whole soul and your whole mind and your whole strength.

---

³ This verse is a good example of Jn's repetitive style. He often describes the subject of the sentence with a clause, and then repeats the subject with a pronoun or some other word.

⁴ τούτων is an example of the "genitive of comparison." A comparative adjective such as μείζων is almost always followed by a word in the genitive to indicate comparison, and you can use the key word "than."

Additional

11. τίνι ἡμέρᾳ ἡ μητὴρ καὶ ὁ πατήρ σου πορεύσονται ὧδε ἀπὸ τοῦ οἴκου αὐτῶν παρὰ τῇ θαλάσσῃ; *Will your mother and father go someday* *from their house to the sea?*
τῇ τρίτῃ ἡμέρᾳ μετὰ τὸ σάββατον. *the third day after the Sabbath.*

12. προσκυνήσομεν τὸν κύριον τὸν βασιλέα ἡμῶν διὰ τὴν μεγαλὴν ἀγάπην αὐτοῦ ἡμῖν καὶ τὰς
ἐπαγγελίας αὐτοῦ τῆς εἰρήνης καὶ τῆς δικαιοσύνης. *We will worship the Lord our King*
according to his great love for us and his of peace and righteousness.

13. υἱοὺς καὶ θυγατέρας[5] γεννήσεις καὶ οὐκ ἔσονταί σοι.
You will give birth to sons and daughters, but they will not be yours.

14. οὐ προσκυνήσεις τοῖς θεοῖς αὐτῶν οὐδὲ ποιήσεις κατὰ τὰ ἔργα αὐτῶν.
You will not worship their gods, neither will you do according to their works.

15. καὶ εἶπεν κύριος τῷ Ἀβράμ· ἔξελθε (go out!) ἐκ τῆς γῆς[6] σου ... καὶ ἐκ τοῦ οἴκου τοῦ πατρός σου
εἰς τὴν γῆν ἣν ἄν σοι δείξω (I will show) καὶ ποιήσω σε εἰς ἔθνος[7] μέγα καὶ εὐλογήσω[8] σε ... καὶ
ἔσῃ εὐλογητός.[9] *And the Lord said to Abraham: Go out into your land... and out of*
your father's house and into the land which I will show you and I will make a great nation
you and bless you and you shall be blessed.

16. ἔσεσθε οὖν ὑμεῖς τέλειοι ὡς ὁ πατὴρ ὑμῶν ὁ οὐράνιος[10] τέλειός ἐστιν.
And you will be ~~holy~~ perfect as your Father, heavenly father is ~~holy~~ perfect.

17. δικαιοσύνη γὰρ θεοῦ ἐν αὐτῷ ἀποκαλύπτεται ἐκ πίστεως εἰς πίστιν, καθὼς γέγραπται (it is
written)· ὁ δὲ δίκαιος ἐκ πίστεως ζήσεται.

18. Ἐὰν ἀγαπᾶτέ με, τὰς ἐντολὰς τὰς ἐμὰς τηρήσετε.
If ye love me, ye will keep my commandments

19. εἴ τις θέλει πρῶτος εἶναι,[11] ἔσται πάντων ἔσχατος.
If anyone wishes to be first, he will be last.

20. εὗρον (I have found) Δαυὶδ τὸν[12] τοῦ Ἰεσσαί, ἄνδρα κατὰ τὴν καρδίαν μου, ὃς ποιήσει πάντα τὰ
θελήματά μου. *I have found David, Jesse's son, a man ———— my heart*
who will do all my wishes

Summary

1. The future can be used to make a command.
2. A comparative adjective such as μείζων is almost always followed by a word in the genitive to indicate comparison. You can use the key word "than" in your translation.

References

α. Jn 11:48; β. Jn 9:21; γ. Lk 12:17; δ. Jn 8:12; ε. 1 Cor 16:4; ζ. —; η. Mt 12:19; **1**. Mt 4:10; **2**. Mt 27:42; **3**. Lk 1:13; **4**. Phil 4:19; **5**. Jn 5:25; **6**. Mk 13:13; **7**. Jn 14:12; **8**. Jn 4:22-23; **9**. Jn 13:33; **10**. Mk 12:29-31; **11**. —; **12**. —; **13**. Dt 28:41; **14**. (Ex 23:24); **15**. Gen 12:1-2; **16**. Mt 5:48; **17**. Rom 1:17; **18**. Jn 14:15; **19**. Mk 9:35; **20**. Ac 13:22.

---

[5] θυγάτηρ, -τρός, ἡ, *daughter.*

[6] γῆ, γῆς, ἡ, *earth, land, region.*

[7] ἔθνος, -ους, τό, *nation.*

[8] εὐλογέω, *I bless.*

[9] εὐλογητός, -ή, -όν, *blessed, praised.*

[10] οὐράνιος, -ον, *heavenly.*

[11] "To be." Takes a predicate nominative.

[12] The word τόν is modifying is often dropped out of this type of construction. What is the word?

Verbal Roots, and Other Forms of the Future

the verb is future, try to see what it would be in the present, and vice versa.

arsing

Inflected	Person / Case	Number	Tense / Gender	Voice	Mood	Lexical form	Inflected meaning
ἀρεῖς	2	S	P	A	I	ἄρω	you raise / take up
ὄψεται	3	S	F	M	I	ὁράω ὄψομαι	she/he/it will see
ἐκβαλοῦμεν	1	P	▪F	A	I	ἐκβάλλω	we will cast out
ἐγεροῦσιν	3	P	P	A	I	ἐγείρω	They raise up / wake
ἀποκτενεῖτε	2	P	P	A	I	ἀποκτείνω	you kill
σώσει	3	S	F	A	I	σώζω	he/she/it will save
ἀποστελεῖ	3	S	P	A	I	ἀποστέλλω	he/she/it sends
βαπτίσεις	2	S	F	A	I	βαπτίζω	you will baptize
ποιοῦσι	3	P	P	A	I	ποιέω	they do / make
0. κρινεῖτε	2	P	⁄F	A	I	κρίνομαι	you will judge

Warm-up

ἐκεῖνος κρινεῖ αὐτὸν ἐν τῇ ἐσχάτῃ ἡμέρᾳ. That man   him on the last day

πολλοὶ γὰρ ἐλεύσονται ἐπὶ τῷ ὀνόματί μου. For many   on my name

ἐν τῷ ὀνόματί μου δαιμόνια ἐκβαλοῦσιν. They will cast out demons in my name.

γνωσόμεθα τὴν ἀλήθειαν. We will know the truth.

ἐρῶ τῇ ψυχῇ μου.   I will speak to my soul.

αὐτὸς μένει ἐπὶ τὸν κόσμον ἀλλὰ σὺ μενεῖς εἰς τοὺς αἰῶνας. He remains in the word by
you remain forever.

πῶς πάσας τὰς παραβολὰς γνώσεσθε;
How do will you know all the parables?

73

Translation

1. ἐγὼ ἐβάπτισα (I baptized) ὑμᾶς ὕδατι, αὐτὸς δὲ βαπτίσει ὑμᾶς ἐν πνεύματι ἁγίῳ.
   I baptized you with water, but he will baptize you in the
   Holy Spirit.

2. ἀποστελεῖ ὁ υἱὸς τοῦ ἀνθρώπου τοὺς ἀγγέλους αὐτοῦ.
   The Son of Man will send   his   angels.

3. ἐκεῖ αὐτὸν ὄψεσθε, καθὼς εἶπεν ὑμῖν.
   There you will see him, even as   he told you / said to you

4. ἀπεκρίθη Ἰησοῦς καὶ εἶπεν αὐτῷ· ἐάν τις ἀγαπᾷ[1] με τὸν λόγον μου τηρήσει καὶ ὁ πατήρ μου
   ἀγαπήσει αὐτὸν καὶ πρὸς αὐτὸν ἐλευσόμεθα.
   Jesus answers and said to them, "Whoever loves me will keep my word
   and my father will love him and we will come after/to him

5. τέξεται (he/she/it will bear) δὲ υἱόν, καὶ καλέσεις τὸ ὄνομα αὐτοῦ Ἰησοῦν. αὐτὸς γὰρ σώσει τὸ
   λαὸν αὐτοῦ ἀπὸ τῶν ἁμαρτιῶν αὐτῶν. For she will bear a son, and you will
   call his name Jesus. For he will save his people from their sins.

6. ἢ οὐκ οἴδατε ὅτι οἱ ἅγιοι τὸν κόσμον κρινοῦσιν; ... οὐκ οἴδατε ὅτι ἀγγέλους κρινοῦμεν;
   Or do you not know that the holy judge   do you not know that we will judge
   the world?   the messengers?

7. πάντες πιστεύσουσιν εἰς αὐτόν, καὶ ἐλεύσονται οἱ Ῥωμαῖοι καὶ ἀροῦσιν τὸν τόπον ἡμῶν.
   All will believe in him, and the Romans will come and take away our place.

---

[1] This form is actually in the subjunctive mood (chapter 31), but in this case it is identical in form to the indicative and is translated the same way.

Ἀλλὰ ἐρεῖ τις· πῶς ἐγείρονται οἱ νεκροί; ποίῳ (in what sort of) δὲ σώματι ἔρχονται;

But he will say something: how are the dead raised? in what sort of body does he come?

λέγει αὐτῷ· ἐκ τοῦ στόματός σου κρινῶ σε, πονηρὲ δοῦλε.

He says to him, " out of your mouth will I judge you, evil servant."

. διὰ τοῦτο καὶ ἡ σοφία τοῦ θεοῦ εἶπεν· ἀποστελῶ εἰς αὐτοὺς προφήτας καὶ ἀποστόλους, καὶ ἐξ αὐτῶν[2] ἀποκτενοῦσιν. *For this reason he ~~speaks~~ spoke the wisdom of God: I will send ~~them~~ prophets and apostles, and they will kill some of them.*

dditional

. τί οἱ κακοὶ ἀποκτείνουσιν τοὺς ἀγαθούς, οἳ τηροῦσιν τὸν νόμον τοῦ θεοῦ καὶ ἀγαπῶσι πάντας;
Why do the evil kill the good, which keep the name of God and love all?

. ἐν τῷ στόματί μου μεγάλην σοφίαν λαλήσω καὶ κατὰ τὴν ὅλην ζωὴν ἐρῶ περὶ τῆς δικαιοσύνης τε καὶ τῆς ὁδοῦ τῆς ἀληθείας. *In my mouth I will speak great wisdom*

. καὶ καλέσεις τὰ σάββατα ἅγια τῷ θεῷ σου καὶ οὐκ ἀρεῖς τὸν πόδα σου ἐπ᾽ ἔργῳ οὐδὲ λαλήσεις λόγον ἐν ὀργῇ[3] ἐκ τοῦ στόματός σου. *And you will call the sabbaths holy unto the Lord and will not raise up your feet in work nor speak a word of anger from your mouth.*

. ὁ θεός ἐστιν κύριος, καὶ αὐτὸς οἶδεν, καὶ Ἰσραὴλ αὐτὸς γνώσεται.
God is Lord, and he knows, he will know Israel.

. τὸ ὕδωρ αὐτοῦ πιστόν· βασιλέα μετὰ δόξης ὄψεσθε, καὶ ἡ ψυχὴ ὑμῶν μελετήσει[4] φόβον[5] κυρίου.
and your soul will cultivate a fear of the Lord

. καὶ τὰ τέκνα αὐτῆς ἀποκτενῶ ἐν θανάτῳ. καὶ γνώσονται πᾶσαι αἱ ἐκκλησίαι ὅτι ἐγώ εἰμι ὁ ἐραυνῶν (one who searches) νεφροὺς[6] καὶ καρδίας, καὶ δώσω (I will give) ὑμῖν ἑκάστῳ κατὰ τὰ ἔργα ὑμῶν. *And her children will kill ~~kill~~ in death, and all the churches will know that I am the one who searches minds and hearts, and I will give you to each of according to your works*

. Μὴ μόνον οὖν αὐτὸν καλῶμεν (let us call) κύριον, οὐ γὰρ τοῦτο σώσει ἡμᾶς.
Then let us not call him only Lord, for he will not save us

αὐτῶν is called the "partitive genitive," where the word in the genitive indicates a larger group (αὐτῶν) and the word it is modifying represents a part of the smaller group. The problem here is that the noun it is modifying is unexpressed. Supply "some" in your translation for the smaller group.

ὀργή, -ῆς, ἡ, *wrath, anger.*

μελετάω, *I practice, cultivate.*

φόβος, -ου, ὁ, *fear, reverence.*

νεφρός, -οῦ, ὁ, *mind.*

18. [7]μακάριοι οἱ καθαροὶ τῇ καρδίᾳ, ὅτι αὐτοὶ τὸν θεὸν ὄψονται.
    Blessed are the   in heart, for they shall see God.

19. Ἀλλ᾽ ἐρεῖ τις· σὺ πίστιν ἔχεις, κἀγὼ ἔργα ἔχω. δεῖξόν (Show!) μοι τὴν πίστιν σου χωρὶς τῶν ἔργων, κἀγώ σοι δείξω (I will show) ἐκ τῶν ἔργων μου τὴν πίστιν. σὺ πιστεύεις ὅτι εἷς ἐστιν ὁ θεός, καλῶς ποιεῖς. καὶ τὰ δαιμόνια πιστεύουσιν καὶ φρίσσουσιν.[8]

20. ἐὰν τὰς ἐντολάς μου τηρήσητε (you keep), μενεῖτε ἐν τῇ ἀγάπῃ μου, καθὼς ἐγὼ τὰς ἐντολὰς το πατρός μου τετήρηκα (I have kept) καὶ μένω αὐτοῦ[9] ἐν τῇ ἀγάπῃ.

Summary

1. The partitive genitive indicates the larger group, and the word it modifies indicates the smaller group.

References

α. Jn 12:48; β. Mt 24:5; γ. Mk 16:17; δ. (Jn 8:32); ε. Lk 12:19; ζ. —; η. Mk 4:13; **1.** Mk 1:8; **2.** Mt 13:41; **3.** Mk 16:7; Jn 14:23; **5.** Mt 1:21; **6.** 1 Cor 6:2-3; **7.** (Jn 11:48); **8.** 1 Cor 15:35; **9.** Lk 19:22; **10.** Lk 11:49; **11.** —; **12.** —; **13.** (Is 58:13 **14.** (Josh 22:22); **15.** Barn 11:5; **16.** Rev 2:23; **17.** 2 Clem 4:1; **18.** Mt 5:8; **19.** Jas 2:18-19; **20.** Jn 15:10.

19. But someone will say: You have faith and I have works. Show me your faith apart from works, and I will show faith from my works. You believe that God is One; you do well. And the demons believe and tremble

20. If you keep my commandments, you will remain in my love, as I have kept the commandments of my father and remain in his love.

---

[7] You have to assume the verb in the first half of the sentence.

[8] φρίσσω, I *tremble*.

[9] Normally αὐτοῦ follows the word it modifies, but not always. How do you know what word it modifies?

Review #4 — Track 1

rammar

Define the following three aspects, clearly differentiating among them.

a. Continuous

b. Undefined

c. Punctiliar

Write out the twelve forms of λύω, present active and passive.

active

1st sg   1st pl

2nd sg   2nd pl

3rd sg   3rd pl

passive

1st sg   1st pl

2nd sg   2nd pl

3rd sg   3rd pl

Write out the Master Verb Chart

Tense	Aug/Redup	Tense stem	Tense formative	Conn. vowel	Personal endings	First singular
Pres act						
Pres mid/pas						
Future act						
Liquid future act						
Future mid						

4. What are "The Big Five" contraction rules?

    a.

    b.

    c.

    d.

    e.

5. What vowels form the following contractions?

    a. ει

    b. ει

    c. α

    d. ου

    e. ου

    f. ου

    g. ω

6. How do you form the following English tenses with the verb "eat"?

    a. present active continuous

    b. present passive punctiliar

7. Define what a "deponent" verb is and give one example.

8. Write out the "Square of Stops," and what happens to each class of stop when followed by a sigma.

    a. labials:

    b. velars:

    c. dentals:

What is the difference between a verbal "root" and "stem"?

a. Root

b. Stem

. What are the three basic ways in which tense stems are formed from verbal roots?

a.

b.

c.

ɪrsing

ἀκούετε

ἀκούσεις

πορεύεται

οὕστινας

ζήσουσιν

τηροῦμαι

γνώσεται

ἔσονται

ἀγαπῶμεν

. βλέψεται

. λαλῶ

. ὄψῃ

. πληροῖ

. σώσω

Translation: John 12:27-36

^{12:27} Νῦν ἡ ψυχή μου τετάρακται (he/she/it has been troubled), καὶ τί εἴπω (I can say); πάτερ,

σῶσόν (save!) με ἐκ τῆς ὥρας ταύτης; ἀλλὰ διὰ τοῦτο ἦλθον (I came) εἰς τὴν ὥραν ταύτην. ^{12:28} πάτερ

δόξασόν (glorify!) σου τὸ ὄνομα. ἦλθεν (he/she/it came) οὖν φωνὴ ἐκ τοῦ οὐρανοῦ· καὶ ἐδόξασα (I

glorified) καὶ πάλιν δοξάσω. ^{12:29} ὁ οὖν ὄχλος ὁ ἑστὼς (one that was standing) καὶ ἀκούσας (hearing)

ἔλεγεν (he/she/it was saying) βροντὴν γεγονέναι,[1] ἄλλοι ἔλεγον (they were saying)· ἄγγελος αὐτῷ

λελάληκεν (he/she/it has spoken). ^{12:30} ἀπεκρίθη Ἰησοῦς καὶ εἶπεν· οὐ δι᾽ ἐμὲ ἡ φωνὴ αὕτη γέγονεν

(he/she/it came) ἀλλὰ δι᾽ ὑμᾶς. ^{12:31} νῦν κρίσις ἐστὶν τοῦ κόσμου τούτου, νῦν ὁ ἄρχων τοῦ κόσμου

τούτου ἐκβληθήσεται (he/she/it will be cast out) ἔξω· ^{12:32} κἀγὼ ἐὰν ὑψωθῶ (I am lifted up) ἐκ τῆς γῆς

πάντας ἑλκύσω (I will draw) πρὸς ἐμαυτόν. ^{12:33} τοῦτο δὲ ἔλεγεν (he/she/it was saying) σημαίνων

(signifying) ποίῳ θανάτῳ ἤμελλεν (he/she/it was about) ἀποθνῄσκειν (to die).

^{12:34} Ἀπεκρίθη οὖν αὐτῷ ὁ ὄχλος· ἡμεῖς ἠκούσαμεν (we heard) ἐκ τοῦ νόμου ὅτι ὁ Χριστὸς

μένει εἰς τὸν αἰῶνα, καὶ πῶς λέγεις σὺ ὅτι δεῖ ὑψωθῆναι (to be lifted up) τὸν υἱὸν τοῦ ἀνθρώπου;[2]

τίς ἐστιν οὗτος ὁ υἱὸς τοῦ ἀνθρώπου; ^{12:35} εἶπεν οὖν αὐτοῖς ὁ Ἰησοῦς· ἔτι μικρὸν χρόνον τὸ φῶς ἐν

ὑμῖν ἐστιν. περιπατεῖτε (walk!) ὡς τὸ φῶς ἔχετε, ἵνα μὴ σκοτία ὑμᾶς καταλάβῃ (he/she/it might

overtake)· καὶ ὁ περιπατῶν (one walking) ἐν τῇ σκοτίᾳ οὐκ οἶδεν ποῦ ὑπάγει. ^{12:36} ὡς τὸ φῶς ἔχετε,

πιστεύετε (believe!) εἰς τὸ φῶς, ἵνα υἱοὶ φωτὸς γένησθε (you might be).

---

[1] βροντὴν γεγονέναι means "that it was thunder."
[2] τὸν υἱὸν τοῦ ἀνθρώπου is acting as the subject of ὑψωθῆναι.

Imperfect Indicative

Parsing

Inflected	Person / Case	Number	Tense / Gender	Voice	Mood	Lexical form	Inflected meaning	
ἐβάπτιζες	2	S	I	A	I	βαπτίζω	you were baptizing	
ἤκουον	1 3	S P	I	A	I	ἀκούω	I was listening They were listening	hearing
ἠθέλετε	2	P	I	A	I	θέλω	you all were wanting	willing
ἐσῴζεσθε	2	P	I	■ P	I	σῴζω	you all were being saved	
ἐποίει	3	S	I	A	I	ποιε	he she it was doing	
ἐξέβαλλον	1 3	S P	I	A	I	εκβάλλω	I was they were casting out	
ἦσαν	3	P	I	A	I	εἰμί	they were	
ἐπορευόμην	1	P	I	■ P	I	πορεύομαι	~~we were~~ going I was	
ἔξουσι	3	P	F	A	I	ἔχω	they will have	
ἐπηρώτων	3	P	I	A	I	Ἐπηρωτάω	they were asking	

Warm-up

ἐβάπτιζεν αὐτούς. He baptized *was baptizing* them.

δαιμόνια πολλὰ ἐξέβαλλον. They cast out *were casting out* many demons. I was...

ἐβαπτίζοντο ὑπ᾽ αὐτοῦ. They were being baptized by him

ἤρχοντο πρὸς αὐτόν. They came to him. *were coming* middle deponent

οὐκ ... ἐκρινόμεθα. We are not being judged *were* We were not judging for ourselves

εἰ γὰρ ἐπιστεύετε Μωϋσεῖ, πιστεύσετε ἐμοί. For if you were believing Moses, you will *would* believe me.

ἐλάλει αὐτοῖς τὸν λόγον. He was speaking the word to them.

Translation

1. ἐκεῖνος[1] δὲ ἔλεγεν περὶ τοῦ ναοῦ (temple) τοῦ σώματος αὐτοῦ.

   But he was speaking concerning the temple of his body.

2.   *was coming*

   καὶ πᾶς ὁ ὄχλος ἤρχετο πρὸς αὐτόν, καὶ ἐδίδασκεν αὐτούς.

   And all the mob came to him and he taught them.
            crowd   *was teaching*
       the whole crowd

3. ἤκουον δὲ ταῦτα πάντα οἱ Φαρισαῖοι.

   And the Pharisees were hearing all these things.

4. ἦσαν γὰρ πολλοὶ καὶ ἠκολούθουν αὐτῷ.

   For they were many and they followed him.
                         were following

5. ἠγάπα[2] δὲ ὁ Ἰησοῦς τὴν Μάρθαν καὶ τὴν ἀδελφὴν[3] αὐτῆς καὶ τὸν Λάζαρον.

   And Jesus loved Martha and her sister and Lazarus.

6. καὶ ἐπηρώτα αὐτόν· τί ὄνομά σοι;[4] καὶ λέγει αὐτῷ· Λεγιὼν ὄνομά μοι, ὅτι πολλοί ἐσμεν.

   And he asked him, "What is your name?" And he said to him, "Legion is my name
   for we are many."

---

[1] Did you notice that the demonstrative is functioning as a personal pronoun? It is more apparent if you can rememb
the context.

[2] Why is this verb in this tense?

[3] Note the gender. ἀδελφή occurs twenty-six times in the New Testament but it is easy to remember.

[4] This expression is slightly idiomatic, somewhat common in the New Testament, and you should be able to figure o
what it means.

αὐτὸς γὰρ ἐγίνωσκεν[5] τί ἦν ἐν τῷ ἀνθρώπῳ.   *humanity*

For he knew what was in ~~mankind/human beings.~~
the man.

ἐπηρώτων αὐτὸν οἱ μαθηταὶ αὐτοῦ τὴν παραβολήν.[6]   *his disciples*

His disciples asked him ~~for a parable~~ / questioned him about the parable?
His disciples were asking him

Καὶ μετὰ ταῦτα περιεπάτει ὁ Ἰησοῦς ἐν τῇ Γαλιλαίᾳ· οὐ γὰρ ἤθελεν ἐν τῇ Ἰουδαίᾳ περιπατεῖν

(to walk), ὅτι ἐζήτουν αὐτὸν οἱ Ἰουδαῖοι ἀποκτεῖναι (to kill).   *was unwilling*

And after these things Jesus was walking in Galilee: for he did not want to walk

in Judea for the Jews sought/were seeking to kill him.   *complementary*
↓ *Judeans (there were Jews in Galilee, too.)* *infinitive*

Then indeed...

Οἱ μὲν οὖν συνελθόντες (when they had come together) ἠρώτων αὐτὸν λέγοντες (saying)· κύριε, εἰ[7]

ἐν τῷ χρόνῳ τούτῳ ἀποκαθιστάνεις (are you restoring) τὴν βασιλείαν τῷ Ἰσραήλ;

When they had come together, they asked him, saying,
"Lord, are you restoring the kingdom ~~of~~ *to* Israel ~~in~~ *at* this time/age?"

kingdom = right of rule
political power

dditional

ὅτε ὁ Ἰησοῦς ἐν ταῖς συναγωγαῖς τῶν Ἰουδαίων ἐδίδασκεν ἐπὶ παντὶ τῷ σαββάτῳ, οἱ
Φαρισαῖοι ἐπηρώτων τίνι ἐξουσίᾳ ἐκείνους τοὺς λόγους λαλεῖ. When Jesus was teaching in the Jews'
synagogues on every Sabbath, the Pharisees asked/demanded by what authority he spoke those words. ~~the~~

οἱ ἄνθρωποι οἱ διδάσκουσιν τὸν λόγον τοῦ θεοῦ αὐτοὶ ἐδιδάσκοντο μὴ κηρύσσειν (to preach) ἐν
πολλῷ χρόνῳ; The men who teach the   were taught not to preach in much time?
word of God   ?

ὁ δὲ οὐκ ἤθελεν,[8] εἶπεν δὲ τῇ γυναικὶ τοῦ κυρίου αὐτοῦ· ὁ κύριός μου οὐ γινώσκει[9] δι' ἐμὲ οὐδὲν
ἐν τῷ οἴκῳ αὐτοῦ καὶ πάντα ὅσα ἐστὶν αὐτῷ ἔδωκεν (he/she/it has given) εἰς τὰς χεῖράς μου....
τότε πῶς ποιήσω τὸ ῥῆμα[10] τὸ πονηρὸν τοῦτο; But he was not willing, and he said to his lord's
wife, "My lord is ~~unaware of~~ anything in his house ~~through~~ *because of* me and *all/as many which*
not concerned about
is his he has given into my hands... then ~~why will~~ you do this evil thing?"
how could I

Did you notice that the usual translation of the imperfect does not make a lot of sense in this verse? Think of the basic significance of the imperfect, and then you should see why it is in the imperfect.

What is the name we gave to this type of accusative construction?   *everything that he has*

εἰ is used here to introduce a question and does not need to be translated.

Hint: This verb not only describes a wish but also a person's willingness to do something.

In this context γίνωσκω means "I am aware," "I am concerned."

ῥῆμα can be translated as "thing" in this context.

12. The people who are teaching the word of God, were they taught not to preach for a long time?

14. καὶ ἠρώτα αὐτὸν ὁ βασιλεὺς κρυφαίως[11] εἰπεῖν (to say) εἰ ἔστιν λόγος παρὰ κυρίου, καὶ εἶπε
    ἔστιν. *And the king secretly asked him to say if ~~the word was~~ from the Lord, and*
    was asking   *there   is a word*
    he said, "~~It~~ is." There is.

15. καὶ αὐτὴ ἐλάλει ἐν τῇ καρδίᾳ αὐτῆς ... καὶ φωνὴ αὐτῆς οὐκ ἠκούετο.
    was speaking
    And she spoke in her heart... and her voice was not heard.

16. ἠρώτων αὐτὸν οἱ περὶ αὐτὸν σὺν τοῖς δώδεκα τὰς παραβολάς.
    being
    The ones around him with the twelve asked him parables.

17. ἀληθῶς οὗτος ὁ ἄνθρωπος υἱὸς[12] θεοῦ ἦν.
    for about the
    Truly, this man was the Son of God.

18. παραβολαῖς πολλαῖς ἐλάλει αὐτοῖς ⟨τὸν λόγον⟩ καθὼς ἠδύναντο ἀκούειν (to listen).
    He spoke many parables ~~to them~~   just as they were able to listen.
    the word to them in

19. Ἀγαπητοί, οὐκ ἐντολὴν καινὴν γράφω ὑμῖν ἀλλ' ἐντολὴν παλαιὰν ἣν εἴχετε[13] ἀπ' ἀρχῆς.
    Beloved, I do not write a new ~~commandment~~ to you, but an old commandment which you had from
    have   *the beginn*

20. ἐδίδασκεν γὰρ τοὺς μαθητὰς αὐτοῦ καὶ ἔλεγεν αὐτοῖς ὅτι ὁ υἱὸς τοῦ ἀνθρώπου παραδίδοτο
    (he/she/it will be betrayed)[14] εἰς χεῖρας ἀνθρώπων, καὶ ἀποκτενοῦσιν αὐτόν.
    For he was teaching his disciples and telling them that the Son of Man will be
    betrayed into the hands of men and they will kill him.

References

α. —; β. Mk 6:13; γ. Mk 1:5; δ. Mk 1:45; ε. (1 Cor 11:31); ζ. (Jn 5:46); η. Mk 2:2; **1.** Jn 2:21; **2.** Mk 2:13; **3.** Lk 16:
4. Mk 2:15; **5.** Jn 11:5; **6.** Mk 5:9; **7.** Jn 2:25; **8.** Mk 7:17; **9.** Jn 7:1; **10.** Ac 1:6; **11.** —; **12.** —; **13.** (Gen 39:8, 9); **14.**
44:17; **15.** 1 Sam 1:13; **16.** Mk 4:10; **17.** Mk 15:39; **18.** Mk 4:33; **19.** 1 Jn 2:7; **20.** Mk 9:31.

★ 18. *He spoke the word to them (in) many parables, as they were able to*
       listen.

---

[11] κρυφαίως, *secretly.*

[12] The Roman centurion is speaking. Are you going to put "the" in front of this word?

[13] What is the significance of the tense of this verb?

[14] Actually, this verb is a present: "is betrayed." But in this case Jesus is using the present tense to denote the certainty w
which this event will occur.

Exercise 22

Second Aorist Active/Middle Indicative

Inflected	Person / Case	Number	Tense / Gender	Voice	Mood	Lexical form	Inflected meaning
ἤλθομεν	1	P	A	A	I	ἔρχομαι	we went
ἐγενόμεθα	1	P	A	M	I	γίνομαι	we became
ἀπεθάνετε	2	P	A	A	I	ἀποθνῄσκω	you all died
εἰσῆλθες	2	S	A	A	I	εἰσέρχομαι	you entered
ἔβαλεν	3	S	A	A	I	~~Βάλλω~~ βάλλω	he she it threw
ἔσχον	1 / 3	S / P	A	A	I	ἔχω	I had / they had
ἔγνων	1	S	A	A	I	γινώσκω	I knew
εὗρον	1 / 3	S / P	A	A	I	εὑρίσκω	I found / They found
ἀπεθάνομεν	1	P	A	A	I	ἀποθνῄσκω	we died
ἐγινόμην	~~3~~ 1	S	~~A~~ I	M	I	γίνομαι	I was becoming

ἦλθεν πρὸς τὸν Ἰησοῦν. ~~They came~~ He went to Jesus.

προσῆλθον αὐτῷ οἱ μαθηταί. The disciples came went to him.

ἔβαλεν αὐτοὺς εἰς τὴν γῆν. He cast them into the earth / threw them to the ground. threw them on the ground

πνεῦμα ἅγιον ἐλάβετε; Did you receive the Holy Spirit?

οἱ προφῆται ἀπέθανον. The prophets died.

εἰσῆλθεν εἰς γῆν Ἰσραήλ. ~~They~~ He went into the land of Israel

εὗρες γὰρ χάριν παρὰ τῷ θεῷ. For You found grace in the presence of God.

Translation

1. Χριστὸς ἀπέθανεν ὑπὲρ τῶν ἁμαρτιῶν ἡμῶν κατὰ τὰς γραφάς.

   Christ died for our sins according to the scriptures.

2. καὶ ἐξῆλθον οἱ μαθηταὶ καὶ ἦλθον εἰς τὴν πόλιν καὶ εὖρον καθὼς εἶπεν αὐτοῖς.

   And the disciples left and went into the   just as he told them city and found things

   ("And there was a voice from the heavens")

3. καὶ φωνὴ ἐγένετο ἐκ τῶν οὐρανῶν· σὺ εἶ ὁ υἱός μου ὁ ἀγαπητός.

   And a voice came from heaven: you are my beloved son.

4. διδάσκαλε, εἴδομέν τινα ἐν τῷ ὀνόματί σου ἐκβάλλοντα (who was casting out) δαιμόνια.

                     someone
   Teacher, we saw who was casting out demons in your name.

5. ὁ δὲ Ἰησοῦς εἶπεν αὐτῷ· τί με λέγεις ἀγαθόν; οὐδεὶς ἀγαθὸς εἰ μὴ εἷς ὁ θεός.[1]

   Jesus said to him, "Why do you call me good? No one
   is good except God."
                    one, namely

6. Καὶ ἐζήτουν αὐτὸν κρατῆσαι (to arrest) ... ἔγνωσαν (they knew) γὰρ ὅτι πρὸς[2] αὐτοὺς τὴν

   παραβολὴν εἶπεν. And they sought to arrest him... for they knew that he
             were seeking
   spoke the parable against them.

7. καὶ πολλάκις (often) καὶ[3] εἰς πῦρ αὐτὸν ἔβαλεν καὶ εἰς ὕδατα.

   And often ~~he~~ threw ~~himself~~ both into fire and into water.
           it   him

---

[1]   Why is ὁ θεός in the nominative?

[2]   In this context, πρός means "against."

[3]   "Correlative conjunctions" are conjunctions that work in pairs. καί ... καί can mean "both ... and." οὔτε ... οὔτε can me "neither ... nor."

οὔτε οἶδα οὔτε ἐπίσταμαι (I understand) σὺ τί λέγεις. καὶ ἐξῆλθεν ἔξω.

I neither ~~believe~~ (Know) nor understand what you say. And he went outside.

οἵτινες[4] ἀπεθάνομεν[5] τῇ ἁμαρτίᾳ, πῶς ἔτι ζήσομεν ἐν αὐτῇ;

we, died to sin, how will we still live in it?
who

ἀπεκρίθη αὐτοῖς ὁ Ἰησοῦς καὶ εἶπεν· ἀμὴν ἀμὴν λέγω ὑμῖν, ζητεῖτέ με οὐχ ὅτι εἴδετε σημεῖα,

ἀλλ᾽ ὅτι ἐφάγετε (you ate) ἐκ τῶν ἄρτων καὶ ἐχορτάσθητε (you were satisfied).

Jesus answered them and said, " Amen, amen, I say to you you are seeking me not because you saw signs, but because you ate of the bread and were satisfied.

lditional

ἐν τῷ οἴκῳ ἐν ᾧ οἱ μαθηταὶ τὸν ἄρτον ἀπὸ τῆς χειρὸς τοῦ Ἰησοῦ ἔλαβον, εἶπον σὺν ἀλλήλοις
καὶ τῷ κυρίῳ αὐτῶν. *In the house in which the disciples received the bread from Jesus' nds, they spoke with one another and with their Lord.*

οἱ ὄχλοι προσῆλθον τὴν πόλιν καὶ ἐν τῇ συναγωγῇ συνήγαγον ὅτι ὁ Παῦλος ἐδίδασκε τὴν
ἀλήθειαν περὶ Ἰησοῦ τοῦ Χριστοῦ τε καὶ τοῦ κυρίου. *The crowd ~~came~~ went to the city and gathered e synagogue because Paul taught them the truth about Jesus as Christ and Lord.*

καὶ ἀπέθανεν Σαούλ καὶ τρεῖς (three) υἱοὶ αὐτοῦ ἐν τῇ ἡμέρᾳ ἐκείνῃ καὶ πᾶς ὁ οἶκος αὐτοῦ ἐπὶ
τὸ αὐτὸ ἀπέθανεν. *Both Saul and his 3 sons died that day and his whole house belonging to him? died.   and his entire house died at the same time.*

εἰσῆλθεν δὲ Νῶε καὶ οἱ υἱοὶ αὐτοῦ καὶ ἡ γυνὴ αὐτοῦ καὶ αἱ γυναῖκες τῶν υἱῶν αὐτοῦ μετ᾽
αὐτοῦ εἰς τὴν κιβωτὸν[6] διὰ τὸ ὕδωρ. *And Noah and his sons and his wife and his son's wives went into the ark with him on account of the water.*

ἐν ἀγάπῃ προσελάβετο[7] ἡμᾶς ὁ δεσπότης[8]· διὰ τὴν ἀγάπην, ἣν ἔσχεν πρὸς ἡμᾶς, τὸ αἷμα[9] αὐτοῦ
ἔδωκεν (he/she/it gave) ὑπὲρ ἡμῶν Ἰησοῦς Χριστὸς ὁ κύριος ἡμῶν ἐν θελήματι θεοῦ, καὶ τὴν[10]
σάρκα ὑπὲρ τῆς σαρκὸς ἡμῶν καὶ τὴν ψυχὴν ὑπὲρ τῶν ψυχῶν ἡμῶν.

We learned ὅστις as "whoever." And yet the verb cannot allow this translation. Alter your translation so the person of the verb comes through. Remember, translation must be fluid, allowing for the needs of the context.

Notice the agreement between the personal ending and the subject. Can you explain it?

κιβωτός, -οῦ, ἡ, *ark.*

προσλαμβάνω, *I receive.*

δεσπότης, -ου, ὁ, *master, lord.*

αἷμα, -ματος, τό, *blood.*

Hint: The article is performing one of its other functions in this context and is parallel to ἡμῶν.

16. Ὁ οὖν Ἰησοῦς ... ἦλθεν εἰς Βηθανίαν, ὅπου ἦν Λάζαρος, ὃν ἤγειρεν (he/she/it raised) ἐκ νεκρῶ
    Ἰησοῦς. *Then Jesus went to Bethany, where Lazarus was, ~~the one~~ Jesus*
    raised from the dead.   *whom*
                                              was made

17. ἐν τῷ κόσμῳ ἦν, καὶ ὁ κόσμος δι᾽ αὐτοῦ ἐγένετο, καὶ ὁ κόσμος αὐτὸν οὐκ ἔγνω.
    And he was in the world, and the world became through him and the world did not kn

18. Μετὰ ταῦτα ἦλθεν ὁ Ἰησοῦς καὶ οἱ μαθηταὶ αὐτοῦ εἰς τὴν Ἰουδαίαν γῆν καὶ ἐκεῖ διέτριβεν (h
    she/it was spending time) μετ᾽ αὐτῶν καὶ ἐβάπτιζεν. *After these things, Jesus and his*
    disciples went to Judea and there he was spending time with them and baptizing
                                                                        was

19. πέντε γὰρ ἄνδρας ἔσχες καὶ νῦν ὃν ἔχεις οὐκ ἔστιν σου ἀνήρ.
    For you had five husbands and now the one you have is not your husba

20. εἶπον [οὖν] αὐτῷ οἱ Ἰουδαῖοι· νῦν ἐγνώκαμεν (we know) ὅτι δαιμόνιον ἔχεις. Ἀβραὰμ ἀπέθαν
    καὶ οἱ προφῆται, καὶ σὺ λέγεις· ἐάν τις τὸν λόγον μου τηρήσῃ (he/she/it might keep), οὐ μὴ[11]
    γεύσηται[12] θανάτου εἰς τὸν αἰῶνα.
    Then the Jews said to him, "Now we know that you have a demon. Abraham di
    and the prophets, and you say, 'Whoever might keep my word will NOT taste

Summary *death forever.'"*

1. "Correlative conjunctions" are a pair of conjunctions that connect two grammatically equal clauses. κα
   καί can mean "both ... and." μέν ... δέ can mean "on the one hand ... but on the other."

2. If a verb has a compound subject, the verb agrees in number with the subject that is closest to it in wo
   order (sentence 18).

References

α. Mt 14:29; β. Mt 14:15; γ. Rev 12:4; δ. Ac 19:2; ε. Jn 8:53; ζ. Mt 2:21; η. Lk 1:30; **1.** 1 Cor 15:3; **2.** Mk 14:16; **3.** M
1:11; **4.** Mk 9:38; **5.** Mk 10:18; **6.** Mk 12:12; **7.** Mk 9:22; **8.** Mk 14:68; **9.** Rom 6:2; **10.** Jn 6:26; **11.** —; **12.** —; **13.** 1 C
10:6; **14.** Gen 7:7; **15.**1 Clem. 49:6; **16.** Jn 12:1; **17.** Jn 1:10; **18.** Jn 3:22; **19.** Jn 4:18; **20.** Jn 8:52.

---

[11] Two consecutive negations do not cancel each other out as in English. οὐ μή forms a strong negation.

[12] "He/she/it will taste." It takes a direct object in the genitive.

First Aorist Active/Middle Indicative

Parsing

Inflected	Person / Case	Number	Tense / Gender	Voice	Mood	Lexical form	Inflected meaning
ἐπιστεύσαμεν	1	1P	A	A	I	we believed	πιστεύω
ἠκούσατε	2	P	A	A	I	you all heard	ἀκούω
ἐζήτησε	3	BS	A	A	I	he she it sought	ζητέω
ἐπλήρωσαν	3	P	A	A	I	They filled / fulfilled	πληρόω
ἐλεύσεται	3	S	F	M	I	he she it will go	ἔρχομαι
ἔσχομεν	1	P	A	A	I	we had	ἔχω
ἐγράψατο	3	S	A	M	I	he she it wrote for self	γράφω
ἐβάπτισας	2	S	A	A	I	you baptized	βαπτίζω
ἦλθαν	1 / 3	S / P	A	A	I	I went / They went	ἔρχομαι
ἠρξάμεθα	1	P	A	M	I	we began	ἄρχω

it is
☆
ἀπεκρίνατο
deponent

Warm-up

πολλοὶ ἐπίστευσαν εἰς τὸ ὄνομα αὐτοῦ. Many believed in his name.

ἔγραψεν ὑμῖν τὴν ἐντολὴν ταύτην. He wrote this commandment to you.

καὶ εὐθὺς ἐκάλεσεν αὐτούς. And immediately he called them.

ἐκήρυξαν ... καὶ δαιμόνια πολλὰ ἐξέβαλλον. THey preached and were casting out many demons

ἤγειρεν αὐτήν. He raised her up / woke her

ὁ δὲ ... ἀπεκρίνατο οὐδέν. But he answered nothing ~~And nobody answered~~

ἦλθεν οὖν καὶ ἦρεν τὸ σῶμα αὐτοῦ. Therefore he went and ~~raised~~ took his body

Translation

1. ἐπίστευσα, διὸ ἐλάλησα, καὶ ἡμεῖς πιστεύομεν, διὸ καὶ λαλοῦμεν.

I believed, therefore I spoke, and we believed, therefore we ~~spoke~~. *are speaking*

2. ἐγὼ ἐβάπτισα ὑμᾶς ὕδατι, αὐτὸς δὲ βαπτίσει ὑμᾶς ἐν πνεύματι ἁγίῳ.

I baptized you with water, but he will baptize you in the Holy Spirit.

3. καθὼς ἐμὲ ἀπέστειλας εἰς τὸν κόσμον, κἀγὼ ἀπέστειλα αὐτοὺς εἰς τὸν κόσμον.

Even Just as you sent me into the world, ~~and~~ I sent them into the world. *also*

4. Ἤκουσεν Ἰησοῦς ὅτι ἐξέβαλον αὐτὸν ἔξω καὶ εὑρὼν (after finding) αὐτὸν εἶπεν· σὺ πιστεύεις ε̣

τὸν υἱὸν τοῦ ἀνθρώπου;   *Jesus* He heard that they threw him out and after finding him, said,

"Do you believe in the Son of man?"

5. λέγει αὐτοῖς ὅτι ἦραν τὸν κύριόν μου, καὶ οὐκ οἶδα ποῦ (where) ἔθηκαν (they laid) αὐτόν.

He says to them that he raised my Lord and I do not know where *they took* they laid him.

6. καὶ ἀπῆλθεν καὶ ἤρξατο κηρύσσειν (to preach) ἐν τῇ Δεκαπόλει[1] ὅσα[2] ἐποίησεν αὐτῷ ὁ Ἰησοῖ

And he departed and began to preach in Decapolis (about) how much Jesus did (for) to him.

---

[1] The "Decapolis" is the region of the "ten cities" to the east of the Jordan. It was a Gentile area as you may have guess from the fact that it is a Greek name.

[2] This word is used in many different contexts. Sometimes you cannot stick to the "as great as"/"as many as" definit too closely. The NIV translates, "how much."

λέγει αὐτοῖς· ἔρχεσθε (come!) καὶ ὄψεσθε. ἦλθαν οὖν καὶ εἶδαν ποῦ (where) μένει καὶ παρ' αὐτῷ
ἔμειναν τὴν ἡμέραν ἐκείνην.

remained that day

says to them, "Come and see. Then ~~I~~ [They] went and saw where he was staying and they spent that day with him.

ἐξῆλθεν καὶ ἀπῆλθεν εἰς ἔρημον (lonely) τόπον κἀκεῖ (and there) προσηύχετο. καὶ εὗρον αὐτὸν
καὶ λέγουσιν αὐτῷ ὅτι πάντες ζητοῦσίν σε.

He departed and went away to a lonely place and there he prayed. And they found him and said to him, "Everyone is looking for you."

are ~~gather~~ gathered

Καὶ συνάγονται οἱ ἀπόστολοι πρὸς τὸν Ἰησοῦν καὶ ἀπήγγειλαν[3] αὐτῷ πάντα ὅσα ἐποίησαν καὶ
ὅσα ἐδίδαξαν.

And the apostles gathered to Jesus and reported to him all things as much as they did and taught.

all that they did and all that they taught

Many will say to me in that day

. πολλοὶ ἐροῦσίν μοι ἐν ἐκείνῃ τῇ ἡμέρᾳ· κύριε κύριε, οὐ τῷ σῷ[4] ὀνόματι ἐπροφητεύσαμεν,[5] καὶ
τῷ σῷ ὀνόματι δαιμόνια ἐξεβάλομεν, καὶ τῷ σῷ ὀνόματι δυνάμεις πολλὰς ἐποιήσαμεν; καὶ τότε
ὁμολογήσω (I will say) αὐτοῖς ὅτι οὐδέποτε (never) ἔγνων ὑμᾶς.

Many found me on that day

"Lord, Lord, didn't we prophesy in your name? and cast out demons in your name? and do many miracles in your name?"

And then I will say to them, "I never knew you."

The evil ones killed 7 men and 1 woman

The seven evil men and one woman died, but the people of God remained in the church

. οἱ πονηροὶ ἑπτὰ ἄνδρας καὶ μίαν γυναῖκα ἀπέκτειναν, ὁ δὲ λαὸς τοῦ θεοῦ ἐν τῇ ἐκκλησίᾳ
ἔμενεν ὅτι ἐκεῖ ἤκουσαν τὸ εὐαγγέλιον τῆς ζωῆς.

because there they heard the good news of life

. ὁ γὰρ Πέτρος ἔγραψε τοῖς ἐν Ἰερουσαλὴμ ὅτι δυνάμεις πολλὰς καὶ μεγάλας ποιεῖ ἐν τῷ ἁγίῳ
πνεύματι· δόξα τῷ θεῷ.

For Peter wrote to those in Jerusalem that he was doing many great miracles in the Holy Spirit: glory to God!

ἀπαγγέλλω, I report.

The adjective σός, σή, σόν means "your" in all its forms, much like ἐμός always means "my." σός occurs 27 times in the New Testament. The word occurs repeatedly throughout this passage.

προφητεύω, I prophesy.

13. καὶ ἐποίησεν αὐτὸν ἕνα τῶν φίλων[6] αὐτοῦ καὶ ἐδόξασεν αὐτὸν δόξῃ μεγάλῃ.
    one
    And he made him one of his beloved and glorified him in great glory.

14. καὶ οὐκ ἠκούσατε τῆς φωνῆς κυρίου ἧς[7] ἀπέστειλέν με πρὸς ὑμᾶς.
    obey
    But you did not hear the voice of the Lord by which he sent me to you.

15. καὶ ἔγραψεν Μωϋσῆς τὴν ᾠδὴν[8] ταύτην ἐν ἐκείνῃ τῇ ἡμέρᾳ καὶ ἐδίδαξεν αὐτὴν τοὺς υἱοὺς Ἰσραήλ. And Moses wrote this song that day and taught it to the sons of Israel.

16. καὶ ἐλάλησαν αὐτῷ τὸν λόγον τοῦ κυρίου σὺν πᾶσιν τοῖς ἐν τῇ οἰκίᾳ αὐτοῦ.
    And they spoke the word of the Lord to him, with all those in his house.

17. ἄλλους ἔσωσεν, ἑαυτὸν οὐ δύναται σῶσαι (to save). *along*
    He saved others; he cannot save himself.

18. πάντες γὰρ αὐτὸν εἶδον καὶ ἐταράχθησαν (they were troubled). ὁ δὲ εὐθὺς ἐλάλησεν μετ᾽ αὐτῶ
    For all saw him and were troubled. And immediately he spoke with them.

19. πάτερ δίκαιε, καὶ ὁ κόσμος σε οὐκ ἔγνω, ἐγὼ δέ σε ἔγνων, καὶ οὗτοι ἔγνωσαν ὅτι σύ με ἀπέστειλας. Righteous father, the world did not know you, but I knew you, and these (people) knew that you sent me.

20. νῦν δὲ ζητεῖτέ με ἀποκτεῖναι (to kill) ἄνθρωπον ὃς τὴν ἀλήθειαν ὑμῖν λελάληκα (I have spoken ἣν ἤκουσα παρὰ τοῦ θεοῦ· τοῦτο Ἀβραὰμ οὐκ ἐποίησεν. ὑμεῖς ποιεῖτε τὰ ἔργα τοῦ πατρὸς ὑμῶν. εἶπαν [οὖν] αὐτῷ· ἡμεῖς ἐκ πορνείας οὐ γεγεννήμεθα (we have been born)· ἕνα πατέρα ἔχομεν τὸν θεόν. εἶπεν αὐτοῖς ὁ Ἰησοῦς· εἰ ὁ θεὸς πατὴρ ὑμῶν ἦν ἠγαπᾶτε ἂν[9] ἐμέ, ἐγὼ γὰρ ἐ τοῦ θεοῦ ἐξῆλθον.

References

α. Jn 2:23; β. Mk 10:5; γ. Mk 1:20; δ. Mk 6:12-13; ε. Mk 1:31; ζ. Mk 14:61; η. Jn 19:38; **1.** 2 Cor 4:13; **2.** Mk 1:8; **3.** 17:18; **4.** Jn 9:35; **5.** Jn 20:13; **6.** Mk 5:20; **7.** Jn 1:39; **8.** Mk 1:35,37; **9.** Mk 6:30; **10.** Mt 7:22-23; **11.** —; **12.** —; **13.** (1 M 14:39); **14.** Jer 42:21 [LXX 49:21]; **15.** Dt 31:22; **16.** Ac 16:32; **17.** Mt 27:42; **18.** Mk 6:50; **19.** Jn 17:25; **20.** Jn 8:40-42

And now you seek to kill *me, a* man who has spoken *to you* the truth which I heard from God *to you*. Abraham did not do this. You *are doing* the works of your father. Now I said to him, "We *were not* born from *evil* *fornication* We have one father, God," Jesus said to them, "If God *were* your Father, you would love me, for I came from God."

---

[6] φίλος, -η, -ον, *beloved, friend.*

[7] ἧς has been attracted to the case of κυρίου. It "should" have been dative since it is instrumental.

[8] ᾠδή, -ῆς, ἡ, *song*

[9] ἠγαπᾶτε ἂν means "you would love."

Aorist and Future Passive Indicative

Parsing

Inflected	Person / Case	Number	Tense / Gender	Voice	Mood	Lexical form	Inflected meaning
1. ἐπιστεύθημεν	1	P	A	P	I	πιστεύω	we were believed
2. ἐβλήθητε	2	P	A	P	I	βλέπω	you were seen
3. τηρηθήσεται	3	S	F	P	I	τηρέω	she/it was kept
4. κριθήσεσθε	2	P	F	P	I	κρίνομαι	you will be judged
5. ἠκούσθητε	2	P	A	P	I	ακούω	you were heard
6. συνήχθη	3	S	A	P	I	συνάγω	s/he/it ~~will be~~ was gathered
7. ἀπεκρίθησαν	3	P	A	P	I	αποκρίνομαι	they were answered
8. βλέψεις	2	S	F	A	I	βλέπω	you will see
9. ἐγράφη	3	S	A	P	I	γράφω	it was written
10. σωθήσεσθε	2	P	F	P	I	σώζω	you will be saved

Warm-up

They were entrusted with God's words   acc. of reference (with)

They trusted

1. ἐπιστεύθησαν τοὺς λόγους τοῦ θεοῦ.   acc.?

They were believed the words of God / The words of God were believed.

2. ἐκεῖ σοι λαληθήσεται περὶ πάντων.

...it to you will be called concerning/about all

3. κηρυχθήσεται τοῦτο τὸ εὐαγγέλιον. The gospel will be preached

brought near by

4. ἐγενήθητε ἐγγὺς (near) ἐν τῷ αἵματι τοῦ Χριστοῦ. You were ~~created (near) in~~ the blood of Christ

γίνομαι

5. ἐν τούτῳ ἐδοξάσθη ὁ πατήρ μου. In this my father was glorified.

6. ὁ οἶκός μου οἶκος προσευχῆς (prayer) κληθήσεται.[1]

My house will be called a house of prayer.

7. ἐχάρησαν χαρὰν μεγάλην. They rejoiced ~~greatly~~ with great joy.

(because of their great joy, they "were caused to rejoice"

---

[1] Verbs like καλέω in the passive become virtually synonymous with εἰμί; therefore, the second οἶκος functions as a predicate nominative.

Translation

1. καὶ συνήχθησαν πολλοὶ ... καὶ ἐλάλει αὐτοῖς τὸν λόγον.
   And many were gathered... and he spoke the word to them.
                                        <u>was speaking</u>

2. ὁ δὲ ἀγαπῶν (one who loves) με ἀγαπηθήσεται ὑπὸ τοῦ πατρός μου, κἀγὼ ἀγαπήσω αὐτόν.
   But the one who loves me will be loved by my father, and I will love him.

3. Καὶ ἐγένετο ἐν ἐκείναις ταῖς ἡμέραις ἦλθεν Ἰησοῦς ἀπὸ Ναζαρὲτ τῆς Γαλιλαίας καὶ
   ἐβαπτίσθη εἰς τὸν Ἰορδάνην ὑπὸ Ἰωάννου. And it came to pass in those days
   (that) Jesus came from Nazareth to Galilee and was baptized in the Jordan
                                            of
   by John.

4. ἤγαγεν αὐτὸν πρὸς τὸν Ἰησοῦν.... ὁ Ἰησοῦς εἶπεν· σὺ εἶ Σίμων ὁ υἱὸς Ἰωάννου, σὺ κληθήσῃ
   Κηφᾶς, ὃ ἑρμηνεύεται (is translated as) Πέτρος.
   He brought him to Jesus... Jesus said," You are Simon, the son of John.
      led
   You will be called Cephas, which is translated as Peter/Petros."

5. οὐκ ἔστιν ὧδε, ἠγέρθη γὰρ καθὼς εἶπεν.
   He is not here, for he was raised just   as he said.

6.   in his house
   Καὶ ἐπορεύθησαν ἕκαστος εἰς τὸν οἶκον αὐτοῦ, Ἰησοῦς δὲ ἐπορεύθη εἰς τὸ ὄρος τῶν ἐλαιῶν
   (olives). And they went each one into his house, ~~but~~ Jesus went into the Mount of
   Olives.

7. ἔλεγεν[2] γὰρ ὅτι ἐὰν ἅψωμαι[3] κἂν (even) τῶν ἱματίων αὐτοῦ σωθήσομαι.
   For she was saying ~~that~~   " If I touch even   of his garments
   I will be saved."

---

[2] Did the woman act impulsively when she touched Jesus' clothes, or was the action thought out? The tense of the ve
     helps with the answer.

[3] ἅψωμαι means *I touch* and takes its direct object in the genitive.

ὁ μὲν υἱὸς τοῦ ἀνθρώπου ὑπάγει καθὼς γέγραπται (he/she/it is written) περὶ αὐτοῦ, οὐαὶ (woe) δὲ τῷ ἀνθρώπῳ ἐκείνῳ δι᾽ οὗ ὁ υἱὸς τοῦ ἀνθρώπου παραδίδοται (he/she/it is betrayed)· καλὸν[4] αὐτῷ εἰ οὐκ ἐγεννήθη ὁ ἄνθρωπος ἐκεῖνος.

Indeed the Son of man departs just as it is written ~~about~~ concerning him, but woe to that man ~~by~~ through whom the Son of Man is betrayed. (It is) better to him if that man was not born

distributive
the heart of each one of you

πάλιν δὲ ὄψομαι ὑμᾶς, καὶ χαρήσεται ὑμῶν ἡ καρδία, καὶ τὴν χαρὰν ὑμῶν οὐδεὶς αἴρει ἀφ᾽ ὑμῶν. *But I will see you again, and your heart will rejoice, and ~~nothing~~ noone takes away your joy from you. (in the meantime)*

0. Καὶ ἐζήτουν αὐτὸν κρατῆσαι (to arrest), καὶ[5] ἐφοβήθησαν τὸν ὄχλον, ἔγνωσαν γὰρ ὅτι πρὸς αὐτοὺς τὴν παραβολὴν εἶπεν. *And they were seeking to arrest him, but they feared the crowd, for they knew that he spoke the parable against them.*

Additional

on the mountains

1. ἐχάρημεν γὰρ ἐγὼ καὶ ἡ γυνή μου ὅτι μετὰ ἑπτὰ ἡμέρας ἕξομεν οἰκίαν ἐπὶ τοῖς ὄρεσιν τοῖς περὶ ταύτην τὴν πόλιν. *For my wife and I were rejoiced ~~for~~ after seven days we will have a house in the hills around this city.*

2. ὅτε οἱ δοῦλοι τοῦ θεοῦ ἐν ταῖς συναγώγαις τὸ εὐαγγέλιον ἐκήρυξαν, τινὲς ἐκ τῆς πόλεως ἐβλήθησαν ὑπὸ τῶν Φαρισαίων καὶ ἄλλοι ἀπεκτάνθησαν. *When God's servants preached the odd news in the synagogues, they were seen by the Pharisees and others were killed.*

3. εἶδεν δὲ Ἰσραὴλ τὴν χεῖρα τὴν μεγάλην ἃ ἐποίησεν κύριος τοῖς Αἰγυπτίοις,[6] ἐφοβήθη δὲ ὁ λαὸς τὸν κύριον καὶ (ἐπίστευσαν) τῷ θεῷ καὶ Μωϋσῇ τῷ θεράποντι[7] αὐτοῦ. *For Israel saw the great hand which was made lord of the Egyptians, but the people was seized with fear (of) the Lord and believed in God and Moses his servant.*

4. καὶ φοβηθήσονται τὰ ἔθνη τὸ ὄνομα κυρίου καὶ πάντες οἱ βασιλεῖς τῆς γῆς τὴν δόξαν σου. *And the nations ~~feared~~ will fear the name of the Lord and all the kings of the earth your glory*

Although καλός generally means "good," that obviously cannot be its meaning here. It can also be used in the comparative sense of "better."

Although καί normally means "and," you can see in this verse that it can carry an adversative force ("but") just like δέ.

Αἰγύπτιος, -ία, -ιον, *Egyptian.*

θεράπων, -οντος, ὁ, *servant.*

And Israel saw the great hand which the Lord used against the Egyptians

15. And Adam said, "Now this is bone of my bone and flesh of
flesh, (and) she will be called woman for

15. καὶ εἶπεν Ἀδάμ· τοῦτο νῦν ὀστοῦν[8] ἐκ τῶν ὀστέων μου καὶ σὰρξ ἐκ τῆς σαρκός μου, αὕτη
κληθήσεται γυνή ὅτι ἐκ τοῦ ἀνδρὸς αὐτῆς ἐλήμφθη αὕτη.

16. καὶ ἐφοβήθησαν φόβον μέγαν καὶ ἔλεγον πρὸς ἀλλήλους· τίς ἄρα οὗτός ἐστιν;
And they were seized with a great fear and were saying to each other "Who, then, is this?"

17. ὅσοι δὲ ἔλαβον αὐτόν, ἔδωκεν (he/she/it gave) αὐτοῖς ἐξουσίαν τέκνα θεοῦ γενέσθαι (to be), τοῖ
πιστεύουσιν (those who believe) εἰς τὸ ὄνομα αὐτοῦ, οἳ οὐκ ἐξ αἱμάτων[9] οὐδὲ ἐκ θελήματος
σαρκὸς οὐδὲ ἐκ θελήματος ἀνδρὸς ἀλλ᾽ ἐκ θεοῦ ἐγεννήθησαν.

18. Μακάριοι οἱ πτωχοὶ τῷ πνεύματι   Blessed are the poor in spirit
    ὅτι αὐτῶν ἐστιν ἡ βασιλεία τῶν οὐρανῶν. for theirs is the kingdom of heaven.
    μακάριοι οἱ καθαροὶ τῇ καρδίᾳ,   Blessed are the pure in heart
    ὅτι αὐτοὶ τὸν θεὸν ὄψονται. for they will see God.
    μακάριοι οἱ εἰρηνοποιοί (peacemakers),   Blessed are the peacemakers.
    ὅτι αὐτοὶ υἱοὶ θεοῦ κληθήσονται. for they will be called sons of God.

19. οἱ δὲ υἱοὶ τῆς βασιλείας ἐκβληθήσονται εἰς τὸ σκότος.
    But the kingdoms sons will be cast into darkness/into the dark.

20. οὔπω γὰρ ἦν πνεῦμα, ὅτι Ἰησοῦς οὐδέπω (not yet) ἐδοξάσθη.
For not yet was the spirit, ~~that~~ Jesus was not yet glorified.
    the Spirit was not yet   since

Summary

1. Verbs like καλέω in the passive become virtually synonymous with εἰμί and are therefore followed by
   predicate nominative.

2. καί also has an adversative function and in context can mean "but."

References

α. (Rom 3:2); β. Ac 22:10; γ. Mt 24:14; δ. Eph 2:13; ε. Jn 15:8; ζ. Mt 21:13; η. Mt 2:10; **1**. Mk 2:2; **2**. Jn 14:21; **3**. Mk 1:
4. Jn 1:42; **5**. Mt 28:6; **6**. Jn 7:53-8:1; **7**. Mk 5:28; **8**. Mk 14:21; **9**. Jn 16:22; **10**. Mk 12:10; **11**. —; **12**. —; **13**. Ex 14:3
14. Ps 102:15 [LXX 101:16]; **15**. Gen 2:23; **16**. Mk 4:41; **17**. Jn 1:12-13; **18**. Mt 5:3, 8-9; **19**. Mt 8:12; **20**. Jn 7:39.

17. But as many as received him, he gave the authority to be
    children of God

---

[8] ὀστέον, -ου, τό, *bone*. (Can contract to ὀστοῦν in the nominative and accusative singular.)

[9] The NIV translates, "natural descent."

Perfect Indicative

Parsing

Inflected	Person / Case	Number	Tense / Gender	Voice	Mood	Lexical form	Inflected meaning
πεπιστεύμεθα	1	P	P	M/P	I	πιστευω	we have been believed
ἠγάπηκα	1	S	P	A	I	αγαπάω	I have loved
γεγέννησαι	2	S	P	P	I	γεννάω	you have become
κέκλησθε	2	P	P	P	I	καλέω	you have been called
ἠκολούθηκεν	3	S P	A	P	I	ἀκολουθέω ~~ἀκούω~~	he she it has followed
ἔγνωκαν	3	S P	P	A	I	γινώσκω	They have come to know / I have known
ἀπέθανεν	3	S	A	A	I	αποθνήσκω	he/she/it died
ἀκηκόαμεν	1	P	P	A	I	ακούω	we have heard
σεσώκατε	2	P	P	A	I	σώζω	you have saved
γέγραφας	2	S	P	A	I	γράφω	you have written

Warm-up

πεπίστευκεν εἰς τὸ ὄνομα. He/She has believed in the name.

θεὸν οὐδεὶς ἑώρακεν. Noone has seen God.

πεπλήρωται ὁ καιρός. The Time has been fulfilled.

ἐγὼ εἰς τοῦτο γεγέννημαι καὶ εἰς τοῦτο ἐλήλυθα. I have been born into this & into this I have come. for this purpose

βέβληται εἰς τὴν θάλασσαν. He/she/it has been ~~seen~~ thrown into the sea. βάλλω not βλέπω

ἔχομεν ταῦτα ἃ ᾐτήκαμεν ἀπ᾽ αὐτοῦ. We have these things which we have asked of him.

ὁ διδάσκαλος τοῦ κόσμου τούτου κέκριται. The teacher of this world has been judged.

Translation

As you do these verses, be sure to keep in mind the significance of the perfect tense. Theologically it will make them come alive.

1. ἐγὼ πεπίστευκα ὅτι σὺ εἶ ὁ χριστὸς ὁ υἱὸς τοῦ θεοῦ.

    I have believed that you are the Christ, the Son of God.

2. ἀπάγγειλον (Tell!) αὐτοῖς ὅσα ὁ κύριός σοι πεποίηκεν.

    Tell them as much as the Lord has done for you.

    ὅσα = relative pronoun

3. οὐ δύναται ἁμαρτάνειν (to sin), ὅτι ἐκ τοῦ θεοῦ γεγέννηται.[1]

    He is not able to sin, for he has been born of God.

4. κἀγὼ ἑώρακα, καὶ μεμαρτύρηκα ὅτι οὗτός ἐστιν ὁ υἱὸς τοῦ θεοῦ.

    And I have both seen and witnessed that this is the Son of God.

5. ἡ πίστις σου σέσωκέν σε. καὶ ἐσώθη ἡ γυνὴ ἀπὸ τῆς ὥρας ἐκείνης.

    Your faith has saved you. And the woman was saved from that hour.
    healed   healed
              made whole (physically)   saved (spiritually)
    σώζω - to redeem, make whole, deliver from kidnap, restore

6. ὁ πιστεύων (one who believes) εἰς αὐτὸν οὐ κρίνεται· ὁ δὲ μὴ πιστεύων (one who believes) ἤδη

    κέκριται, ὅτι μὴ πεπίστευκεν εἰς τὸ ὄνομα τοῦ μονογενοῦς (only) υἱοῦ τοῦ θεοῦ.

    The one who believes in him is not judged   but the one who does
    not believed has already been judged, since/because he has
    not believed in the name of the only (begotten) son of God.

---

[1] How does the verse spell out the theological significance of this tense? ἁμαρτάνειν is a continuous verbal form.

² τοῖς πᾶσιν γέγονα πάντα.

He has become all to all.
things   men

αὕτη δέ ἐστιν ἡ κρίσις ὅτι τὸ φῶς ἐλήλυθεν εἰς τὸν κόσμον καὶ ἠγάπησαν οἱ ἄνθρωποι μᾶλλον τὸ σκότος (darkness) ἢ τὸ φῶς· ἦν γὰρ αὐτῶν πονηρὰ τὰ ἔργα.

But this is the judgement, that the light was called into the world and the humans preferred darkness to the light For their works were evil.

ἀλλὰ λέγω ὑμῖν ὅτι καὶ Ἡλίας ἐλήλυθεν, καὶ ἐποίησαν αὐτῷ ὅσα ἤθελον, καθὼς γέγραπται ἐπ᾽ αὐτόν.

But I say to you, "Elias has spoken and he did to him as much as they wanted, just as it has been written concerning him."

ₒ. ἀλλὰ ἔγνωκα ὑμᾶς ὅτι τὴν ἀγάπην τοῦ θεοῦ οὐκ ἔχετε ἐν ἑαυτοῖς. ἐγὼ ἐλήλυθα ἐν τῷ ὀνόματι τοῦ πατρός μου, καὶ οὐ λαμβάνετέ με.

But I have known you, that you do not have the love of God in yourselves. I have come in the name of my Father, and you do not receive me.

dditional

1. ὅτι πεπιστεύκαμεν τὴν ἀληθείαν περὶ τοῦ Ἰησοῦ, βαπτισθησόμεθα ἐν τοῖς ὕδασιν τῆς θαλάσσης ὑπὸ τοῦ Ἰωάννου τοῦ ἀποστόλου.

Since we have believed the truth concerning Jesus, we re baptized in the sea's water by John the apostle.
lakes

2. αἱ οὖν γλῶσσαι τῶν στομάτων ἡμῶν μεμαρτύρηκαν περὶ τοῦ κυρίου τῶν οὐρανῶν ὅτι ἡμᾶς σέσωκεν ἀπὸ τῶν ἁμαρτιῶν ἡμῶν διὰ τοῦ αἵματος τοῦ υἱοῦ αὐτοῦ.

Then the tongues of our mouths witnessed concerning the Lord of heaven that he has saved us from our sins by the blood of his Son.

3. καὶ εἶπεν Ἰσραὴλ πρὸς Ἰωσήφ· ἀποθανοῦμαι ἀπὸ τοῦ νῦν, ἐπεὶ (because) ἑώρακα τὸ πρόσωπόν σου ἔτι γὰρ σὺ ζῇς.

And Israel said to Joseph, "I will die because I have seen your face, for you still live."

4. καὶ εἶπεν Μωϋσῆς πρὸς τὸν θεόν· ἰδοὺ ἐγὼ ἐλεύσομαι πρὸς τοὺς υἱοὺς Ἰσραὴλ καὶ ἐρῶ πρὸς αὐτούς· ὁ θεὸς τῶν πατέρων ὑμῶν ἀπέσταλκέν με πρὸς ὑμᾶς· ἐρωτήσουσίν με· τί ὄνομα αὐτῷ, τί ἐρῶ πρὸς αὐτούς;

And Moses said to God, "Behold, I will go to the sons of Israel and I say to them, 'The God of your fathers has sent me to you.'" "They will ask me, 'What is his name?' "What will I say to them?"

5. καὶ εἶπεν κύριος πρὸς Μωϋσήν· καὶ τοῦτόν σοι τὸν λόγον ὃν εἴρηκας ποιήσω, εὕρηκας γὰρ χάριν ἐνώπιόν μου καὶ οἶδά σε παρὰ πάντας.

And the Lord said to Moses, "And I will do for you the word which you have spoken, for you have found grace before me and I know you alongside of all."
above

Hint: The first πᾶς is masculine and the second is neuter.

οἶδά ᵈᵉ *I have known you*

16. τὰ ῥήματα ἃ ἐγὼ λελάληκα ὑμῖν πνεῦμά ἐστιν καὶ ζωή ἐστιν.
    words
    The ~~things~~ which I have spoken to ~~you~~ the spirit and life.

17. καὶ ἡμεῖς πεπιστεύκαμεν καὶ ἐγνώκαμεν ὅτι σὺ εἶ ὁ ἅγιος τοῦ θεοῦ.
    And we have believed and we have known that you are the holy one of God.

18. ἀμὴν ἀμὴν λέγω σοι ὅτι ὃ οἴδαμεν λαλοῦμεν καὶ ὃ ἑωράκαμεν μαρτυροῦμεν, καὶ τὴν μαρτυρίαν
    ἡμῶν οὐ λαμβάνετε. Amen, amen, I say to you that we ~~know~~ speak that which we
    know and we are testifying about what we have seen, but you are not accepting our testimony

19. ὑμεῖς ἀπεστάλκατε πρὸς Ἰωάννην, καὶ μεμαρτύρηκεν τῇ ἀληθείᾳ· ἐγὼ δὲ οὐ παρὰ ἀνθρώπου
    τὴν μαρτυρίαν λαμβάνω, ἀλλὰ ταῦτα λέγω ἵνα ὑμεῖς σωθῆτε (you might be saved).
    You have sent to John   and he has borne witness to the truth
    The testimony that I receive is not from ~~that~~ man   but I say these things that you might
                                                                                                          sa

20. τότε λέγει αὐτῷ ὁ Ἰησοῦς· ὕπαγε (Depart!), σατανᾶ· γέγραπται γάρ· κύριον τὸν θεόν σου
    προσκυνήσεις. Then Jesus said to him, "Depart, Satan! For it has been
    written: You will worship the Lord your God."

References

α. Jn 3:18; β. Jn 1:18; γ. Mk 1:15; δ. Jn 18:37; ε. Mk 9:42; ζ. (1 Jn 5:15); η. (Jn 16:11); **1.** Jn 11:27; **2.** Mk 5:19; **3.** 1 Jn 3:9
4. Jn 1:34; **5.** Mt 9:22; **6.** Jn 3:18; **7.** 1 Cor 9:22; **8.** Jn 3:19; **9.** Mk 9:13; **10.** Jn 5:42-43; **11.** —; **12.** —; **13.** Gen 46:30
14. Ex 3:13; **15.** Ex 33:17; **16.** Jn 6:63; **17.** Jn 6:69; **18.** Jn 3:11; **19.** Jn 5:33-34; **20.** Mt 4:10.

Review #5

Grammar

Write out the Master Verb Chart

Tense	Aug/Redup	Tense stem	Tense formative	Conn. vowel	Personal endings	First singular
Imperfect active	ε	present		ο/ε	secondary	ἔλυον
2nd future passive	—	present	θησ	ο/ε	primary middle/passive	
1st aorist active	ε	aorist active	σα	~~ε~~	secondary active	
Liquid aorist active	ε	aorist active	α	—	secondary active	
2nd aorist middle	ε	aorist passive	—	—	secondary middle	
1st aorist passive	ε	aorist passive	θη	—	secondary passive	
1st perfect active	redup	perfect active	κα	—	primary active	
2nd perfect active	redup	perfect active	α	—	primary active	
Perfect middle/passive	redup	perfect passive	—	—	primary middle/passive	

Write out the twelve forms of λύω, imperfect active and passive.

active

1st sg	ελυον	1st pl	ελυομεν
2nd sg	ελυες	2nd pl	ελυετε
3rd sg	ελυε(ν)	3rd pl	ελυον

passive

1st sg	ελυομην	1st pl	ελυομεθα
2nd sg	ελυου	2nd pl	ελυεσθε
3rd sg	ελυετο	3rd pl	ελυονται

3. When are primary and secondary endings used?

    a. Primary: unaugmented forms - present/future/perfect

    b. Secondary: forms w/ augment

4. What are the three basic rules of augmentation?

    a. Verbs beginning with a consonant: ε

    b. Verbs beginning with a vowel: lengthen vowel

    c. Verbs beginning with a diphthong: η

5. What are three clues as to the difference between the present and second aorist forms of the same verb?

    a. augment

    b. stem

    c. secondary personal endings

6. What is the primary significance of the following tenses?

    a. Imperfect: continual habitual past action

    b. Aorist: undefined past action

    c. Perfect: action started in past continuing into present
                           or whose effects continue into present.

7. Give three different uses of the middle voice.

    a. deponent (active meaning)

    b. performing an action in one's own interest

    c. one meaning in active, one in middle: ἄρχω / ἄρχομαι

Parsing

1. ἠκολούθουν first person singular aorist passive indicative ἀκολουθέω

2. εἰσῆλθεν third person singular aorist active indicative εἰσέρχομαι

3. ἐκήρυξας second person singular aorist active indicative κηρύσσω

4. ζητηθήσεται third person singular future passive indicative ζητέω

. ἔλαβον *first person singular aorist active indicative* λαμβάνω

. πεπιστεύκατε *second person plural perfect active indicative* πιστεύω

. ἐπιστεύετο *third person singular imperfect passive indicative* πιστεύω

. ἐγράφη *third person singular aorist passive indicative* γράφω

. ἐγένου *second person singular aorist middle indicative* γίνομαι

0. ἠγάπων *1st singular / 3rd plural imperfect active indicative* ἀγαπάω

1. ἤχθησαν *third person plural aorist passive indicative* ἄγω

2. ἐμείναμεν *first person plural aorist active indicative* μένω

3. ἐλήλυθα *first person singular perfect active indicative* ἔρχομαι

ranslation: John 9:18-34

⁹ᐟ¹⁸ Οὐκ ἐπίστευσαν οὖν οἱ Ἰουδαῖοι περὶ αὐτοῦ ὅτι ἦν τυφλὸς καὶ ἀνέβλεψεν, ἕως ὅτου[1]
n the Jews did not believe concerning him that he was blind and ~~was~~ saw again,   until

φώνησαν τοὺς γονεῖς αὐτοῦ τοῦ ἀναβλέψαντος[2] ⁹ᐟ¹⁹ καὶ ἠρώτησαν αὐτοὺς λέγοντες (saying), οὗτός
y spoke to the parents of the one who had received sight.   And they asked them saying, is this

στιν ὁ υἱὸς ὑμῶν, ὃν ὑμεῖς λέγετε ὅτι τυφλὸς ἐγεννήθη; πῶς οὖν βλέπει ἄρτι; ⁹ᐟ²⁰ ἀπεκρίθησαν οὖν
  your son, which you say was born blind? Then how does he see now? Then his

ἱ γονεῖς αὐτοῦ καὶ εἶπαν· οἴδαμεν ὅτι οὗτός ἐστιν ὁ υἱὸς ἡμῶν καὶ ὅτι τυφλὸς ἐγεννήθη· ⁹ᐟ²¹ πῶς
parents answered and said," We know that this is our son and that he was born blind." ~~How~~ But

ὲ νῦν βλέπει οὐκ οἴδαμεν, ἢ τίς ἤνοιξεν αὐτοῦ τοὺς ὀφθαλμοὺς ἡμεῖς οὐκ οἴδαμεν· αὐτὸν
how he how sees we do not know, nor how his eyes were opened   we do not know. Ask

ρωτήσατε (ask!), ἡλικίαν[3] ἔχει, αὐτὸς περὶ ἑαυτοῦ λαλήσει. ⁹ᐟ²² ταῦτα εἶπαν οἱ γονεῖς αὐτοῦ ὅτι
im! He is of age; he will speak about (for) himself.   His parents said these things because they

φοβοῦντο τοὺς Ἰουδαίους, ἤδη γὰρ συνετέθειντο (they had decided) οἱ Ἰουδαῖοι ἵνα ἐάν τις αὐτὸν
feared the Jews, for the Jews had already decided that if anyone might confess him Christ,

---

ἀνοίγω

ἕως ὅτου is an idiom meaning "until."

τοῦ ἀναβλέψαντος means "the one who had received sight."

ἡλικία, -ας, ἡ, *age*.

ὁμολογήσῃ (he/she/it might confess) Χριστόν, ἀποσυνάγωγος (expelled from the synagogue) γένηται

he might be expelled from the synagogue.

(he/she/it might be). 9:23 διὰ τοῦτο οἱ γονεῖς αὐτοῦ εἶπαν ὅτι ἡλικίαν ἔχει, αὐτὸν ἐπερωτήσατε (ask!

For this reason, his parents said "He is of age, ask him!"

9:24 Ἐφώνησαν οὖν τὸν ἄνθρωπον ἐκ δευτέρου ὃς ἦν τυφλὸς καὶ εἶπαν αὐτῷ· δὸς (Give!)

Then they summoned the man which was blind a second time and said to him,

δόξαν τῷ θεῷ· ἡμεῖς οἴδαμεν ὅτι οὗτος ὁ ἄνθρωπος ἁμαρτωλός ἐστιν. 9:25 ἀπεκρίθη οὖν ἐκεῖνος· εἰ

"Give glory to God: we know that this man is a sinner."   Then he answered,"

ἁμαρτωλός ἐστιν οὐκ οἶδα· ἓν οἶδα, ὅτι τυφλὸς ὢν (being) ἄρτι βλέπω. 9:26 εἶπον οὖν αὐτῷ· τί

If he is a sinner I do not know. One thing I know, that being blind, now I see."

ἐποίησέν σοι; πῶς ἤνοιξέν σου τοὺς ὀφθαλμούς; 9:27 ἀπεκρίθη αὐτοῖς· εἶπον ὑμῖν ἤδη καὶ οὐκ

Then they said to him, "How were your eyes opened?"   He answered them," I already said to you an

ἠκούσατε· τί πάλιν θέλετε ἀκούειν (to hear); μὴ καὶ ὑμεῖς θέλετε αὐτοῦ μαθηταὶ γενέσθαι (to

you did not listen. Why will you hear it again? Do you not want to become his disciples?

become); 9:28 καὶ ἐλοιδόρησαν[4] αὐτὸν καὶ εἶπον· σὺ μαθητὴς εἶ ἐκείνου, ἡμεῖς δὲ τοῦ Μωϋσέως

And they hurled insults at him and said," You are a disciple of that one, but we are

ἐσμὲν μαθηταί· 9:29 ἡμεῖς οἴδαμεν ὅτι Μωϋσεῖ λελάληκεν ὁ θεός, τοῦτον δὲ οὐκ οἴδαμεν πόθεν ἐστίν.

disciples of Moses   We know that God has spoken to Moses,   we do not know where it thi

9:30 ἀπεκρίθη ὁ ἄνθρωπος καὶ εἶπεν αὐτοῖς· ἐν τούτῳ γὰρ τὸ θαυμαστόν[5] ἐστιν ὅτι ὑμεῖς οὐκ οἴδατε

The man answered and said to them, "For in this the remarkable thing is that you do not

πόθεν ἐστίν, καὶ ἤνοιξέν μου τοὺς ὀφθαλμούς. 9:31 οἴδαμεν ὅτι ἁμαρτωλῶν ὁ θεὸς οὐκ ἀκούει, ἀλλ'

know from whom it is, but my eyes were opened.   We know that God does not hear a sinner

ἐάν τις θεοσεβὴς[6] (godly person) ᾖ (he/she/it might be) καὶ τὸ θέλημα αὐτοῦ ποιῇ (he/she/it might do)

but whoever might be a godly person and might do his will, he hears this one.

τούτου ἀκούει. 9:32 ἐκ τοῦ αἰῶνος οὐκ ἠκούσθη ὅτι ἠνέῳξέν τις ὀφθαλμοὺς τυφλοῦ γεγεννημένου

From the ages it was not heard that the eyes of one who has been born

(who has been born)· 9:33 εἰ μὴ ἦν οὗτος παρὰ θεοῦ, οὐκ ἠδύνατο ποιεῖν (to do) οὐδέν. 9:34 ἀπεκρίθησαν

blind were opened.   If this was not from God, nothing could be done.   They answer

καὶ εἶπαν αὐτῷ· ἐν ἁμαρτίαις σὺ ἐγεννήθης ὅλος, καὶ σὺ διδάσκεις ἡμᾶς; καὶ ἐξέβαλον αὐτὸν ἔξω

and said to him, "In sins you were born entirely, and you teach us?" And they threw him o

(You were entirely born in sin)

---

4   λοιδορέω, *I hurl insults at.*

5   θαυμαστός, -ή, -όν, *wonderful, marvelous, remarkable.*

6   θεοσεβής, -ές, *god-fearing, devout.*

Present (Continuous) Adverbial Participles

Parsing

Inflected	Person / Case	Number	Tense / Gender	Voice	Mood	Lexical form	Inflected meaning
1. ἀκουόντων	N	S	M	A	P	ἀκούω	hearing
2. ζητοῦντι	D	S	MN	A	P	ζητέω	seeking
3. ἀναβαῖνον	N A	S	N	A	P	ἀναβαίνω	going up
4. πιστευομένην	A	S	F	A	P	πιστεύω	believing
5. φωνῆς	G	S	F	⬛	P	φωνή	of a voice
6. ποιοῦντας	A	⬛P	M	A	P	ποιέω	doing / making
7. καταβαίνοντα	A N A	S P	M N	A	P	καταβαίνω	going down
8. ἐμαρτύρησαν	3 ⬛	P ⬛	A ⬛	A	I	μαρτυρέω	they bore witness
9. οὔσας	A	P	F	A	P	εἰμί	being
10. προσευχομένους	A	P	M	M	P	προσεύχομαι	praying

Warm-up

1. ἀναβαίνοντες εἰς Ἱεροσόλυμα — while going up to Jerusalem

2. εἶδον αὐτοὺς ὑπάγοντας. — he/she saw them departing

3. ἀπέστειλαν πρὸς αὐτὸν καλοῦντες αὐτόν. — he/she sent to him while calling him

4. προσῆλθον αὐτῷ διδάσκοντι οἱ ἀρχιερεῖς. — the high priest went to him while teaching

5. καὶ καθήμενοι ἐτήρουν αὐτόν. — And sitting they were keeping guarding observing

6. μὴ ὁρῶντες ἀλλὰ πιστεύοντες — not seeing but believing

7. βλέποντες οὐ βλέπουσιν καὶ ἀκούοντες οὐκ ἀκούουσιν. — seeing, they do not see and hearing, they do not hear.

Translation

Be sure you can parse each participle and identify the word it is modifying.

1. Ταῦτα εἶπεν ἐν συναγωγῇ διδάσκων ἐν Καφαρναούμ.

    He said these things, teaching in the synagogue in Capernaum.
                                          while

2. ἦλθεν ὁ Ἰησοῦς εἰς τὴν Γαλιλαίαν κηρύσσων τὸ εὐαγγέλιον τοῦ θεοῦ.

    Jesus went into Galilee preaching the goodnews/ Gospel of God.

3. πολλοὶ ἐλεύσονται ἐπὶ τῷ ὀνόματί μου λέγοντες ὅτι ἐγώ εἰμι.[1]

    Many will come on the basis of my name saying that I am.

4. ἐπορεύετο γὰρ τὴν ὁδὸν αὐτοῦ χαίρων.

    For he will travel his way rejoicing.

5. Παῦλος δὲ καὶ Βαρναβᾶς διέτριβον (they stayed) ἐν Ἀντιοχείᾳ διδάσκοντες καὶ

    εὐαγγελιζόμενοι μετὰ καὶ ἑτέρων πολλῶν τὸν λόγον τοῦ κυρίου.

    But Paul and Barnabas stayed in Antioch teaching and preaching
    the word of God with many others.

6. [2] Καὶ ἀναβαίνων ὁ Ἰησοῦς εἰς Ἱεροσόλυμα παρέλαβεν (he/she/it took) τοὺς δώδεκα.

    And going down up to Jerusalem Jesus took the twelve.

---

[1] What appears to be omitted from this final phrase?

[2] On the placement of the main verb's subject inside a participial phrase, see exercise 11, sentence 7.

καὶ ἦλθεν κηρύσσων εἰς τὰς συναγωγὰς αὐτῶν εἰς ὅλην τὴν Γαλιλαίαν καὶ τὰ δαιμόνια

ἐκβάλλων. Καὶ ἔρχεται πρὸς αὐτὸν λεπρὸς (leper) παρακαλῶν αὐτόν.

And he went preaching in their synagogues In the hills of Galilee and

casting out demons. And a leper comes to him calling him.

Ὡς δὲ ἦν ἐν τοῖς Ἱεροσολύμοις ἐν τῷ πάσχα (Passover) ἐν τῇ ἑορτῇ (feast), πολλοὶ ἐπίστευσαν εἰς

τὸ ὄνομα αὐτοῦ, θεωροῦντες αὐτοῦ τὰ σημεῖα ἃ ἐποίει. But   was in Jerusalem

in the Passover feast, many believed in his name, beholding his miracles which

he did.

Τότε προσῆλθεν αὐτῷ ἡ μήτηρ τῶν υἱῶν Ζεβεδαίου μετὰ τῶν υἱῶν αὐτῆς προσκυνοῦσα καὶ

αἰτοῦσά τι ἀπ᾽ αὐτοῦ. Then the mother of Zebedee's sons went to him with her sons,

worshipping and asking anything of him.

0. δικαιοσύνη θεοῦ πεφανέρωται (he/she/it has been revealed) μαρτυρουμένη ὑπὸ τοῦ νόμου καὶ
God's righteousness has been revealed bearing witness by the law and the
τῶν προφητῶν. prophets.

Preaching to the people in Jerusalem, the disciples were glorifying Jesus
Additional an account of his miracles and powers.

1. εὐαγγελίζοντες τὸν λαὸν ἐν τῇ Ἱεροσόλυμα οἱ μαθηταὶ ἐδόξαζον τὸν Ἰησοῦν διὰ πάντα τὰ
σημεῖα καὶ τὰς δυναμεῖς αὐτοῦ.

2. καθήμενος σὺν τοῖς δυσὶν ἐν τῇ ἐκκλησίᾳ οὗτος παρεκάλησεν τὸν ἄνδρα καὶ τὴν γυναῖκα
ἀλλήλοις λαλεῖν (to speak) ἐν τοῖς λόγοις τῆς ἀγάπης. Sitting with the two in the church
they urged the man and the woman to speak to each other in the words of love.

3. ᾔδει γὰρ ὁ θεὸς ὅτι ἐν ᾗ ἂν ἡμέρᾳ φάγητε (you might eat) ἀπ᾽ αὐτοῦ διανοιχθήσονται[3] ὑμῶν οἱ
ὀφθαλμοί καὶ ἔσεσθε ὡς θεοὶ γινώσκοντες καλὸν καὶ πονηρόν.

4. καὶ εἶπεν[4] πρὸς τοὺς ἄνδρας· γινώσκουσα γινώσκω ἐγὼ ὅτι ὁ θεὸς ὑμῶν
παραδίδωσιν (he/she/it is handing over) ὑμῖν τὴν γῆν ταύτην. And she said to the men,"
Knowing I know that your God is handing over this land to you."

διανοίγω, *I open.*

Hint: Is the person speaking male or female?

you might eat of it, your eyes will be opened and you will
be like God, knowing good and evil

15. ποιοῦντες γὰρ τὸ θέλημα τοῦ Χριστοῦ εὑρήσομεν ἀνάπαυσιν.[5]
    For doing the will of Christ we will find rest.

16. καὶ ἀπεκρίθη αὐτῷ εἷς ἐκ τοῦ ὄχλου· διδάσκαλε, ἤνεγκα[6] τὸν υἱόν μου πρὸς σέ, ἔχοντα πνεῦμα
    ἄλαλον.[7] And one from the crowd answered him, "Teacher, I have brought my son
    to you, having a mute spirit."

17. ὀφθαλμοὺς ἔχοντες οὐ βλέπετε καὶ ὦτα[8] ἔχοντες οὐκ ἀκούετε;
    Having eyes, do you not see, and having ears, do you not hear?

18. πολλὰ μὲν οὖν καὶ ἕτερα παρακαλῶν εὐηγγελίζετο τὸν λαόν.
                                        he preached the good news to the people

19. αὐτὸς διώδευεν[9] κατὰ[10] πόλιν καὶ κώμην κηρύσσων καὶ εὐαγγελιζόμενος τὴν βασιλείαν τοῦ
    θεοῦ, καὶ οἱ δώδεκα σὺν αὐτῷ. He traveled through each city and village preaching
    and bringing good news (of) the kingdom of God, and the twelve with him.

20. Εἰσελθὼν (after entering) δὲ εἰς τὴν συναγωγὴν ἐπαρρησιάζετο[11] ἐπὶ μῆνας τρεῖς διαλεγόμενος
    καὶ πείθων [τὰ] περὶ τῆς βασιλείας τοῦ θεοῦ. But after entering the synagogue
    he spoke boldly for three months arguing and persuading for the kingdom of
    God.

Summary

1. It is common for the biblical writers to place the subject of the main verb inside a participial phrase. Be sur
    to distinguish between the two.

2. Greek negates a word by adding the alpha privative to the beginning of a word (sentence 16).

3. You will see the distributive function of κατά, so be sure to remember it (sentence 19).

References

α. Mk 10:32; β. Mk 6:33; γ. Mk 3:31; δ. Mt 21:23; ε. Mt 27:36; ζ. (1 Pt 1:8); η. Mt 13:13; **1**. Jn 6:59; **2**. Mk 1:14; **3**. M
13:6; **4**. Ac 8:39; **5**. Ac 15:35; **6**. Mt. 20:17; **7**. Mk 1:39-40; **8**. Jn 2:23; **9**. Mt 20:20; **10**. Rom 3:21; **11**. —; **12**. —; **13**. Ge
3:5; **14**. 1 Clem 12:5; **15**. 2 Clem 6:7; **16**. Mk 9:17; **17**. Mk 8:18; **18**. Lk 3:18; **19**. Lk 8:1; **20**. Ac 19:8.

---

[5] ἀνάπαυσις, -εως, ἡ, *rest, relief.*

[6] This is an unusual aorist form from φέρω.

[7] In English, when we want to negate a word, we can often add "ir-" or "un-" to the beginning of the word (e.g., "irreli
  gious," "unnecessary"). Greek does the same thing with "ἀ-" as in this word. It is called an "alpha privative." ἄλαλον i
  from α- and λάλος, the cognate noun to the verb λαλέω. What does ἄλαλον mean?

[8] οὖς, ὠτός, τό, *ear.*

[9] διοδεύω, *I travel through.*

[10] This is a special function of κατά. It is called the "distributive" function and it emphasizes that Jesus went to *each* city.

[11] παρρησιάζομαι, *I speak boldly.*

Aorist (Undefined) Adverbial Participles

arsing

Inflected	Person / Case	Number	Tense / Gender	Voice	Mood	Lexical form	Inflected form
μαρτυρήσασαν	A	S	F	A	part	μαρτυρέω	after bearing witness
μαρτυρήσαντες	N	P	M	A	part	μαρτυρέω	after testifying
ἐρχομένων	N	S	M	M	part	ἔρχομαι	after going
γραφείσης	G	S	F	A	part	γράφω	after writing
λαμβάνουσι (2x)	3 / D	P / P	P / M	A / A	I part	λαμβάνω	while / after taking, they take
ποιησάσῃ	D	S	F	A	part	ποιέω	after doing
ἀκουσάμεναι	N	P	F	P	part	ἀκούω	after hearing, they heard for themselves
εἰσελθόντος	G	S	M N	M	part	εἰσέρχομαι	after going in, he/it went
πιστευθέντες	N	P	M	~~A~~ P	part	πιστεύω	after believing, they were believed
ἐπίστευσας	~~A~~ 2	~~P~~ S	~~F~~ aorist	A	~~part~~ I	πιστεύω	~~after believing~~ you believed

arm-up

εἶπεν τῷ ἀγγελῷ κράξαντι. He ~~said~~ spoke to the angel after ~~it calling~~ called out.

ἐλθόντες εἰς τὴν οἰκίαν εἶδον τὸ παιδίον μετὰ Μαρίας. After going into the house, they saw the boy with Mary.

προσελθὼν εἷς γραμματεὺς εἶπεν αὐτῷ· διδάσκαλε. One scribe, after coming, said to him After going to the scribe he said to him, "Teacher."

ἀρξάμενος ἀπὸ τῆς Γαλιλαίας after ~~starting away from~~ he began in Galilee

εἶπον τῷ ἀνδρὶ ἀποστείλαντι ὑμᾶς πρός με. I spoke to the man ~~sending~~ after he sent you to me.

ἐλθούσῃ εἰς τὴν οἰκίαν λέγει αὐτῇ. After ~~going~~ she went into the house he ~~spoke~~ speaks to her.

ἄγγελον τοῦ θεοῦ εἰσελθόντα πρὸς αὐτὸν καὶ εἰπόντα αὐτῷ

angels of God after going to him and after saying to him
After an angel of God came to him and spoke to him

Translation

There are 1,586 aorist active participles in the New Testament. 1,359 are nominative (86%). If it appears the exercises are heavy on the nominative, this is why.

1. καὶ εὐθὺς τοῖς σάββασιν[1] εἰσελθὼν εἰς τὴν συναγωγὴν ἐδίδασκεν.

   And immediately on the Sabbath he taught (~~was teaching~~) after going into the synagogue

2. εὐθὺς κράξας ὁ πατὴρ τοῦ παιδίου ἔλεγεν· πιστεύω.

   Immediately ~~after~~ crying out, the child's father said, "I believe."

3. ἐλθόντι δὲ εἰς τὴν οἰκίαν προσῆλθον αὐτῷ.

   And after he went ~~going~~ into the house they went to him.

4. ἀσπασάμενοι τοὺς ἀδελφοὺς ἐμείναμεν ἡμέραν μίαν παρ' αὐτοῖς.

   After greeting the brothers we remained one day in their presence.

5. προσελθόντες δὲ οἱ δοῦλοι τοῦ οἰκοδεσπότου (owner) εἶπον αὐτῷ· κύριε, οὐχὶ καλὸν

   σπέρμα (seed) ἔσπειρας;

   But after the owner's servants had come they said to him

   "Master, did you not sow good seed?"

6. ἀκούσας δὲ ὁ Ἡρῴδης ἔλεγεν, Ὃν ἐγὼ ἀπεκεφάλισα (I beheaded) Ἰωάννην, οὗτος ἠγέρθη.

   And after he had listened, Herod said

   I beheaded John, this one was raised up

   The one I beheaded - John -

---

[1] This is an example of the "dative of time when." See discussion in exercise 12, sentence 8.

ὁ δὲ Σίμων καὶ αὐτὸς ἐπίστευσεν, καὶ βαπτισθεὶς ἦν προσκαρτερῶν[2] τῷ Φιλίππῳ, θεωρῶν τε

σημεῖα καὶ δυνάμεις μεγάλας. And Simon ~~and they~~ *himself* believed, and *after being baptized*

he followed after Phillip, looking at signs and great miracles.

καὶ ἀποκριθεῖσα ἡ μήτηρ αὐτοῦ εἶπεν· οὐχί, ἀλλὰ κληθήσεται Ἰωάννης.

And after she had answered, the mother said, " Not so, but he shall

be called John. "

    And his mother answered and said

καὶ ἰδὼν τὸν Ἰησοῦν ἀπὸ μακρόθεν (afar) ἔδραμεν (he/she/it ran) καὶ προσεκύνησεν αὐτῷ καὶ

κράξας φωνῇ μεγάλῃ λέγει, Τί ἐμοὶ καὶ σοί,[3] Ἰησοῦ υἱὲ τοῦ θεοῦ τοῦ ὑψίστου (the Highest);

And seeing Jesus from afar he ran and worshipped him and

calling out in a loud voice he says, " Who are you to me, Jesus

Son of the Highest God? "

Καὶ ἀποκριθεὶς ὁ Ἰησοῦς ἔλεγεν διδάσκων ἐν τῷ ἱερῷ· πῶς λέγουσιν οἱ γραμματεῖς ὅτι ὁ

Χριστὸς υἱὸς Δαυίδ ἐστιν; αὐτὸς Δαυίδ εἶπεν ἐν τῷ πνεύματι τῷ ἁγίῳ· εἶπεν κύριος τῷ κυρίῳ

μου· κάθου (Sit!) ἐκ[4] δεξιῶν μου ἕως ἂν θῶ (I place) τοὺς ἐχθρούς (enemies) σου ὑποκάτω[5] τῶν

ποδῶν σου. And after he had answered, Jesus ~~said~~ *spoke* while teaching in the

     " How do the scribes say that *the* Christ is the son of David?

     David *himself* spoke in the Holy Spirit ' The Lord ~~spoke~~ *said* to my lord

     Sit at my right ~~while~~ *until* I place your enemies under

     your feet.

dditional

ἀσπασάμενα τοὺς πατρὰς καὶ τὰς μητρὰς αὐτῶν τὰ παιδία ἐξῆλθεν σὺν τοῖς ἄλλοις τέκνοις.

he children went out with the other children after saluting their ~~fathers~~ & mothers.

ὁ δὲ Ἰησοῦς ἐκ τῆς οἰκίας καὶ εἰς τὸ ἱερὸν ἐλθὼν ἔκραξεν ἐν μεγάλῃ φωνῇ· πάντες οἱ εἰς ἐμὲ
πιστεύουσιν σωθήσονται ἀπὸ τῆς ἐξουσίας τοῦ πονηροῦ. After going out of the house and into
the temple, Jesus called in a loud voice," All who believe in me will be saved from
     the power-/authority of evil. "

ἦν προσκαρτερῶν means "he followed after" and is followed by a dative.

This idiomatic use of the dative is common in this type of question. See exercise 21, sentence 6.

This is an unusual use of the preposition ἐκ. Translate it as "at."

A preposition meaning "under" that takes an object in the genitive.

13. ἰδόντες δὲ οἱ υἱοὶ τοῦ θεοῦ τὰς θυγατέρας[6] τῶν ἀνθρώπων ὅτι καλαί εἰσιν, ἔλαβον ἑαυτοῖς γυναῖκας ἀπὸ πασῶν, ὧν ἐξελέξαντο.[7] *And after the sons of God had seen the daughters of men that they are good, they took wives to themselves from all, whom they ch*

14. καθὼς καὶ Μωϋσῆς προσηύξατο πρὸς κύριον καὶ κατέβη πῦρ ἐκ τοῦ οὐρανοῦ καὶ τὰ [8] τῆς θυσίας[9] ἐδαπάνησεν[10] οὕτως καὶ Σαλωμὼν προσηύξατο καὶ καταβὰν τὸ πῦρ τὰ τῆς θυσίας ἐδαπάνησεν. *And after Moses prayed to the Lord and fire from heaven came down, the offerings of the sacrifice were consumed and so Solomon prayed* Even as also

15. καὶ λαβοῦσα τοῦ καρποῦ αὐτοῦ[11] ἔφαγεν καὶ ἔδωκεν (he/she/it gave) καὶ τῷ ἀνδρὶ αὐτῆς μετ' αὐτῆς καὶ ἔφαγον. *And after taking its fruit she ate and gave it to her husb and he was eating with her and they ate.*

16. καὶ ἠγέρθη καὶ εὐθὺς ἄρας τὸν κράβαττον ἐξῆλθεν. *And he was raised up and immediately he went out carrying his bed.*

17. ἀκούσας δὲ ὁ βασιλεὺς Ἡρώδης ἐταράχθη καὶ πᾶσα Ἱεροσόλυμα μετ' αὐτοῦ. *And after listening King Herod was disturbed and all Jerusalem with him.*

18. καὶ πάλιν ἀπελθὼν προσηύξατο τὸν αὐτὸν λόγον εἰπών. καὶ πάλιν ἐλθὼν εὗρεν αὐτοὺς καθεύδοντας. *And again after departing he prayed saying the same word. And again after going he found them sleeping.*

19. εἶπεν· λάβετε (take!), τοῦτό ἐστιν τὸ σῶμά μου. καὶ λαβὼν ποτήριον εὐχαριστήσας ἔδωκεν (he/she/it gave) αὐτοῖς, καὶ ἔπιον ἐξ αὐτοῦ πάντες. *He said, "Take! This is my body. And af taking the cup he gave it to them after he had given thanks, and all drank out of it*

20. αὐτὸς δὲ ἐκβαλὼν πάντας παραλαμβάνει τὸν πατέρα τοῦ παιδίου καὶ τὴν μητέρα καὶ τοὺς μετ' αὐτοῦ καὶ εἰσπορεύεται ὅπου ἦν τὸ παιδίον. *And after throwing them all out he is taking the child's father & mother and those with him and he is going into where the child was.*

References

α. —; β. Mt 2:11; γ. Mt 8:19; δ. Lk 23:5; ε. —; ζ. —; η. Ac 10:3; **1.** Mk 1:21; **2.** Mk 9:24; **3.** Mt 9:28; **4.** Ac 21:7; **5.** M 13:27; **6.** Mk 6:16; **7.** Ac 8:13. **8.** Lk 1:60; **9.** Mk 5:6-7; **10.** Mk 12:35-36; **11.** —; **12.** —; **13.** Gen 6:2; **14.** (2 Mac 2:10 **15.** Gen 3:6; **16.** Mk 2:12; **17.** Mt 2:3; **18.** Mk 14:39-40; **19.** Mk 14:22-23; **20.** Mk 5:40.

---

[6]   θυγάτηρ, -τρος, ἡ, *daughter.*

[7]   ἐκλέγομαι, *I choose, select.*

[8]   What word is missing here?

[9]   θυσία, -ας, ἡ, *sacrifice, offering.*

[10]   δαπανάω, *I consume.*

[11]   The antecedent of αὐτοῦ is the tree of knowledge of good and evil.

Adjectival Participles

Parsing

Inflected	Person / Case	Number	Tense / Gender	Voice	Mood	Lexical form	Inflected meaning
φερούσης	G	S	F			φέρω	
ἐνεχθέντι	D						
σαρξίν	D					σάρξ	
ποίησαν							
βαλόμεναι	N	P	F			βάλλω	
προσελθόντων						προσέρχομαι	
ἐποίησαν	3	S	A	A	I	ποιέω	
γράψασιν	3					γράφω	
κηρύσσουσι (2x)	3 / D	P	P / MN	A	I / part		
10. βαπτιζομένου	G	S	MN	1		βαπτίζω	

Warm-up

ὁ ζῶν πατήρ   the living Father

τῷ πατρὶ τῷ πέμψαντι ἡμᾶς   to the Father who sends us

δέχεται τὸν ἀποστείλαντά με.   He receives the one who sends me.

τῷ ἐκ νεκρῶν ἐγερθέντι   to the one raised from the dead.

περὶ τοῦ ῥήματος τοῦ λαληθέντος   according to the word of the one who spok

τῇ ἐρχομένῃ ἡμέρᾳ   to the coming day

θεὸν τὸν γεννήσαντά σε   God who begot you

Translation

Try to differentiate between the adjectival and the adverbial participles.

1. βλέπει τὸν Ἰησοῦν ἐρχόμενον[1] πρὸς αὐτόν καὶ λέγει· ἴδε ὁ ἀμνὸς (lamb) τοῦ θεοῦ ὁ αἴρων τὴν

   ἁμαρτίαν τοῦ κόσμου. He sees Jesus coming and says, " Behold the
   Lamb of God, the one which takes away the sins of the world."

2. ὁ λαὸς ὁ καθήμενος ἐν σκότει φῶς εἶδεν μέγα.

   The people sitting in darkness saw a great light.

3. καὶ ὁ θεωρῶν ἐμὲ θεωρεῖ τὸν πέμψαντά με.

   And the one looking at me looks at the one who sent me.

4. ὁ πιστεύσας καὶ βαπτισθεὶς σωθήσεται.

   The one who believes and is baptized will be saved.

5. Περιπατῶν δὲ παρὰ τὴν θάλασσαν τῆς Γαλιλαίας εἶδεν δύο ἀδελφούς, Σίμωνα τὸν λεγόμενο

                                                    casting   a   net   into the sea
   Πέτρον καὶ Ἀνδρέαν τὸν ἀδελφὸν αὐτοῦ, βάλλοντας ἀμφίβληστρον (net) εἰς τὴν θάλασσαν.

   Walking around the Sea of Galilee, he saw two brothers, Simon the one
   called Peter and Andrew his brother, casting a net into the sea.

6. καὶ ἔρχονται φέροντες πρὸς αὐτὸν παραλυτικὸν (paralytic) αἰρόμενον[2] ὑπὸ τεσσάρων (four).

   And they went carrying to him a paralytic raised up by four (men).

---

[1]   When you come across an article–noun–participle construction (i.e., the participle is in the predicate position) and
      participle does not make sense when you insert the "is," the participle is usually adverbial.

[2]   Your normal definition of this word does not quite fit here. You can look up the word in a lexicon for a further definiti
      or in this case it is safe to modify the meaning you do know in light of the context.

      What is different between this participle and ἐρχόμενον in sentence 1? Right. The preceding noun (παραλυτικόν) is an
      throus. So is αἰρόμενον functioning as an attributive or adverbial? In this case you must rely on the sense of the passa
      and in this case αἰρόμενον appears to be telling us something about the paralytic and not about the verb.

ὁ ἔχων τὰς ἐντολάς μου καὶ τηρῶν αὐτὰς ἐκεῖνός ἐστιν ὁ ἀγαπῶν με· ὁ δὲ ἀγαπῶν με

ἀγαπηθήσεται ὑπὸ τοῦ πατρός μου, κἀγὼ ἀγαπήσω αὐτόν.

The one having my commandments and fulfilling them — that one is the one
who loves me.

οἱ δὲ ἰδόντες αὐτὸν ἐπὶ τῆς θαλάσσης περιπατοῦντα ἔδοξαν ὅτι φάντασμά (ghost) ἐστιν.

But the ones seeing him walking around on the sea   that it was
                                                               a ghost

Ὁ δεχόμενος ὑμᾶς ἐμὲ δέχεται, καὶ ὁ ἐμὲ δεχόμενος δέχεται τὸν ἀποστείλαντά με. ὁ δεχόμενος

προφήτην εἰς ὄνομα προφήτου μισθὸν (reward) προφήτου λήμψεται, καὶ ὁ δεχόμενος δίκαιον[3] εἰς

ὄνομα δικαίου μισθὸν δικαίου λήμψεται. The one receiving you receives me and
the one receiving me receives the one who sent me. The one who receives
a prophet in the name of the prophet will receive the prophet's reward and
the one who receives the righteous in the name of the righteous will receive
the reward of the righteous.

ὅτε δὲ ἐπίστευσαν τῷ Φιλίππῳ εὐαγγελιζομένῳ περὶ τῆς βασιλείας τοῦ θεοῦ καὶ τοῦ ὀνόματος

Ἰησοῦ Χριστοῦ, ἐβαπτίζοντο ἄνδρες τε καὶ γυναῖκες. And when they believed Philip preaching
about the kingdom of God and the name of Jesus Christ, men and women were
baptized.

dditional

                                                    in a great fire coming
οἱ ἑπτὰ οἱ περὶ τὴν γῆν πορευθέντες πολλὰς ἡμέρας ἀπεκτάνθησαν ἐν μεγάλῳ πυρὶ ἐρχόμενοι
from heaven to their houses
ἀπὸ τῶν οὐρανῶν πρὸς τοὺς οἴκους αὐτῶν.

                                                        raised from the dead
οἱ φαγόντες τε καὶ πιόντες μετὰ τοῦ κυρίου αὐτῶν ζῶντος ἐχάρησαν ἰδόντες τὸν ἐγερθέντα ἐκ
τῶν νεκρῶν. The ones eating and drinking with the Lord

καὶ ἐκάλεσεν Ἀδὰμ τὸ ὄνομα τῆς γυναικὸς αὐτοῦ Ζωὴ ὅτι αὕτη μήτηρ πάντων τῶν ζώντων.
And Adam called the name of his wife "Life" for she was the mother of all the living.

εἶπεν αὐτῷ· σὺ εἶ ὁ ἀνὴρ ὁ λαλήσας πρὸς τὴν γυναῖκα; καὶ εἶπεν ὁ ἄγγελος· ἐγώ.
He said to him, "Are you the man who called to my wife?" And the angel said, "I am."

δίκαιος, -αία, -αιον, *right, just, righteous*.

15. καὶ εἶπεν ὁ θεὸς τῷ Νῶε καὶ τοῖς υἱοῖς αὐτοῦ μετ᾽ αὐτοῦ λέγων· ἐγὼ ἰδοὺ ἀνίστημι (I am establishing) τὴν διαθήκην[4] μου ὑμῖν καὶ τῷ σπέρματι[5] ὑμῶν μεθ᾽ ὑμᾶς καὶ πάσῃ ψυχῇ τῇ ζώσ μεθ᾽ ὑμῶν ἀπὸ ὀρνέων[6] καὶ ἀπὸ κτηνῶν[7] ... ὅσα μεθ᾽ ὑμῶν ἀπὸ πάντων τῶν ἐξελθόντων ἐκ τῆ κιβωτοῦ.[8] *And God said to Noah and his sons with him, saying,* "*Behold, I am establishing.*

16. εἰ οὖν ὑμεῖς πονηροὶ ὄντες οἴδατε δόματα[9] ἀγαθὰ διδόναι (to give) τοῖς τέκνοις ὑμῶν, πόσῳ μᾶλλον ὁ πατὴρ ὑμῶν ὁ ἐν τοῖς οὐρανοῖς δώσει (he/she/it will give) ἀγαθὰ τοῖς αἰτοῦσιν αὐτό
Then if you being evil know how to give good gifts to your children, how much m will your Father in heaven give good things to those who

17. Ὁ ἄνωθεν ἐρχόμενος ἐπάνω πάντων ἐστίν· ὁ ὢν ἐκ τῆς γῆς ἐκ τῆς γῆς ἐστιν καὶ ἐκ τῆς γῆς λαλεῖ.

18. καὶ οἱ γραμματεῖς οἱ ἀπὸ Ἱεροσολύμων καταβάντες ἔλεγον ὅτι Βεελζεβοὺλ ἔχει καὶ ὅτι ἐν τ ἄρχοντι τῶν δαιμονίων ἐκβάλλει τὰ δαιμόνια.

★ 19. εἶπεν αὐτῇ ὁ Ἰησοῦς· ἐγώ εἰμι ἡ ἀνάστασις καὶ ἡ ζωή· ὁ πιστεύων εἰς ἐμὲ κἂν[10] ἀποθάνῃ (he she/it might die) ζήσεται, καὶ πᾶς ὁ ζῶν καὶ πιστεύων εἰς ἐμὲ οὐ μὴ ἀποθάνῃ εἰς τὸν αἰῶνα· πιστεύεις τοῦτο; λέγει αὐτῷ· ναί, κύριε, ἐγὼ πεπίστευκα ὅτι σὺ εἶ ὁ Χριστὸς ὁ υἱὸς τοῦ θεοῦ εἰς τὸν κόσμον ἐρχόμενος.

20. ὁ μὴ τιμῶν τὸν υἱὸν οὐ τιμᾷ τὸν πατέρα τὸν πέμψαντα αὐτόν. Ἀμὴν ἀμὴν λέγω ὑμῖν ὅτι ὁ τὸ λόγον μου ἀκούων καὶ πιστεύων τῷ πέμψαντί με ἔχει ζωὴν αἰώνιον καὶ εἰς κρίσιν οὐκ ἔρχετα ἀλλὰ μεταβέβηκεν[11] ἐκ τοῦ θανάτου εἰς τὴν ζωήν. ἀμὴν ἀμὴν λέγω ὑμῖν ὅτι ἔρχεται ὥρα κα νῦν ἐστιν ὅτε οἱ νεκροὶ ἀκούσουσιν τῆς φωνῆς τοῦ υἱοῦ τοῦ θεοῦ καὶ οἱ ἀκούσαντες ζήσουσι

References

α. Jn 6:57; β. —; γ. Lk 9:48; δ. Rom 7:4; ε. Lk 2:17; ζ. Ac 21:26; η. Ode 2:18; **1.** Jn 1:29; **2.** Mt 4:16; **3.** Jn 12:45; **4.** M 16:16; **5.** Mt 4:18; **6.** Mk 2:3; **7.** Jn 14:21; **8.** Mk 6:49; **9.** Mt 10:40-41; **10.** Ac 8:12; **11.** —; **12.** —; **13.** Gen 3:20; **14.** Ju 13:11; **15.** Gen 9:8-10; **16.** Mt 7:11; **17.** Jn 3:31; **18.** Mk 3:22; **19.** Jn 11:25-27; **20.** Jn 5:23-25.

18. *And the scribes who were going down from Jerusalem were saying that he had Beelzebub and that he was casting out demons in the ___ of the demons.*

19. *Jesus said to her, "I am the resurrection and the life. The one who believes in me, even though he might die, will be saved. And all the ones living and believing in me will by no means die forever. Do you believe this?" She said to him, "Yes, Lord, I have believed that you are the Christ, the Son of God who is coming into the world*

20. *The one who does not fear the Son does not fear the Father who sent him. Amen, a I tell you that the one who hears my word and believes in the one who sent me has eternal life and does not come into ___ but ___ from death into life. Amen, amen, I tell y*

---

[4] διαθήκη, -ης, ἡ, *covenant.*

[5] σπέρμα, -ατος, τό, *descendant.*

[6] ὄρνεον, -ου, τό, *bird.*

[7] κτῆνος, -ους, τό, *domesticated animal.*

[8] κιβωτός, -οῦ , ἡ, *ark.*

[9] δόμα, δόματος, τό, *gift.*

[10] In this context κἂν can be translated as *even though.*

[11] Hint: This is the perfect of a compound verb that added ιν to its root to form the present tense stem.

that the hour is coming and now is when the dead will hear the voice of the Son of God

Perfect Participles and Genitive Absolutes

Parsing

Inflected	Person / Case	Number	Tense / Gender	Voice	Mood	Lexical form	Inflected meaning
ἠγαπημένων	N	S	M	P	part	ἀγαπάω	
γεγεννηκότος	N	P	M		part	γεννάω	
πεπληρωμένη	D	S	F	M	part	πληρέω	
πεπίστευκεν	3	S	Perf	A	~~part~~ I	πιστεύω	
λελυκυία	D	S	F	A	part	λύω	
βεβαπτισμένοις	D	P	M	M	part	βαπτίζω	
πεποιήκοσι	D	P	M	A	part	ποιέω	
βεβλημένην	A	S	F	M	part	βάλλω	
βεβαπτισμένου	G	S	M/N	M	part	βαπτίζω	
0. ἀπεσταλμέναις	D	P	F	M	part	ἀποστέλλω	

Warm-up

ὁ Ἰησοῦς εἶπεν τοῖς πρεσβυτέροις λελυκόσι τὸ ἱερόν. Jesus spoke to the elders after they had destroyed the temple

οἱ καταβεβηκότες ἀπὸ Ἱεροσολύμων the ones who have gone up to Jerusalem

πρὸς τοὺς πεπιστευκότας αὐτῷ to the ones who have believed in him

ἐστὶν γεγραμμένον· ἔφαγεν ἄρτον ἐκ τοῦ οὐρανοῦ. It is written: he ate bread from heaven

Ἔλεγεν ... τῷ κεκληκότι αὐτόν He spoke ... to the one who called (on) him

After the Sabbath had begun
γενομένου σαββάτου αὐτὸς ἔρχεται εἰς τὸν συναγωγήν.
~~Since it was~~ the Sabbath he went into the synagogue.

μὴ εἰδότες τὰς γραφὰς μηδὲ τὴν δύναμιν τοῦ θεοῦ
not seeing the Scriptures and not (seeing) the power of God.

Translation

1. πεπιστεύκοτες δὲ ἠκολούθησαν αὐτῷ οἱ ὄχλοι.

   Having believed, the crowds followed /were following him

2. ὁ ἑωρακὼς ἐμὲ ἑώρακεν τὸν πατέρα.

   me   *the Father*

   The one who looks at me looks at the Father.

3. *no connecting vowel = perfect*

   Ἐγένετο[1] ἄνθρωπος, ἀπεσταλμένος παρὰ θεοῦ, ὄνομα αὐτῷ[2] Ἰωάννης.

   A man came into being, v sent by God, named John.

   having been

   There was a man who had been sent by God & his name was John

4. τὸ γεγεννημένον ἐκ τῆς σαρκὸς σάρξ ἐστιν, καὶ τὸ γεγεννημένον ἐκ τοῦ πνεύματος πνεῦμά

   That which has been born

   ἐστιν. *The one having been born of the flesh is flesh and the*

   That which is born   *from*

   one having been born from the spirit is spirit.

5. καὶ ἐξεπλήσσοντο (they were amazed) ἐπὶ τῇ διδαχῇ (teaching) αὐτοῦ· ἦν γὰρ διδάσκων αὐτοὺς

   ὡς ἐξουσίαν ἔχων καὶ οὐχ ὡς οἱ γραμματεῖς. *And they were amazed at his teaching;*

   for he was teaching them like one having authority and not as the scribes.

6. Καὶ εὐθὺς ἔτι αὐτοῦ λαλοῦντος παραγίνεται (comes) Ἰούδας εἷς τῶν δώδεκα καὶ μετ' αὐτοῦ

   ὄχλος. *And immediately, while he is still speaking, Judas comes to the*

   twelve and the crowd with them.

---

[1] Remember, there are two basic meanings for γίνομαι, "to be" and "to come into being."

[2] This use of the dative is idiomatic and a common way of specifying someone's name. See exercise 21, sentence 6, and exercise 28, sentence 9.

οὔπω (not yet) γὰρ ἦν βεβλημένος εἰς τὴν φυλακὴν (prison) ὁ Ἰωάννης.

For John was not yet thrown into prison.
For John had not yet been

καὶ ἐγένετο ἐκ τοῦ οὐρανοῦ ἦχος (sound) ... καὶ ἐπλήρωσεν ὅλον τὸν οἶκον οὗ ἦσαν καθήμενοι.

And there was a sound from heaven.... and it filled the whole house
where they were sitting.

Ταῦτα αὐτοῦ λαλοῦντος πολλοὶ ἐπίστευσαν εἰς αὐτόν. ἔλεγεν οὖν ὁ Ἰησοῦς πρὸς τοὺς
πεπιστευκότας αὐτῷ Ἰουδαίους· ἐὰν ὑμεῖς μείνητε (you remain) ἐν τῷ λόγῳ τῷ ἐμῷ, ἀληθῶς
(truly) μαθηταί μού ἐστε.

While he was speaking these things, many believed
in him. Then Jesus said to the Jews who had believed in him
"If you remain in my word, truly you are my disciples."

. καὶ οἱ προάγοντες (ones going before) καὶ οἱ ἀκολουθοῦντες ἔκραζον·

ὡσαννά·

εὐλογημένος[3] ὁ ἐρχόμενος ἐν ὀνόματι κυρίου·

εὐλογημένη ἡ ἐρχομένη βασιλεία τοῦ πατρὸς ἡμῶν Δαυίδ·

ὡσαννὰ ἐν τοῖς ὑψίστοις (highest).

And the ones going before and the ones following were calling out:
Hosanna!
Blessed is the one coming in the name of the Lord
Blessed is the coming kingdom of our father David
Hosanna in the highest

This participle is used as an exclamation of blessing. The verb is assumed.

The ones who have believed in Christ are called Christians

for they know him as Christ and as Lord.

Additional

11. οἱ δὲ πρεσβύτεροι τῶν Ἰουδαίων εἰδότες τὸν Ἰησοῦν μετὰ τῶν μαθητῶν ἐδέξαντο ἕνα ἐκείνω
ὃς τὴν ἐπαγγελίαν ἐποίησεν αὐτὸν παραδοῦναι (to betray).

12. οἱ πεπιστευκότες εἰς τὸν Ἰησοῦν Χριστιανοὶ[4] καλοῦνται ὅτι αὐτὸν ὡς τὸν Χριστόν τε καὶ τὸ
κύριον γινώσκουσιν.

13. Ἡ χάρις τοῦ κυρίου ἡμῶν Ἰησοῦ Χριστοῦ μεθ᾽ ὑμῶν καὶ μετὰ πάντων πανταχῆ[5] τῶν
κεκλημένων ὑπὸ τοῦ θεοῦ καὶ δι᾽ αὐτοῦ. The grace of our Lord Jesus Christ with
everyone everywhere who has been called by God and through him.

14. καὶ μετὰ ταῦτα οὕτως ἀνέγνω (he/she/it read) Ἰησοῦς πάντα τὰ ῥήματα τοῦ νόμου τούτου ...
κατὰ πάντα τὰ γεγραμμένα ἐν τῷ νόμῳ. And after these things Jesus read all the words
of this name
according to all the things that have been written in the name

15. Προσευξαμένου μου ἐν τῷ οἴκῳ εἰσῆλθεν ἀνήρ καὶ ἠσπάσατό με, κἀγὼ ἠσπασάμην αὐτόν.
While praying to me   a man went into the house and   greeted me, and I greeted him.

16. οἱ πατέρες ἡμῶν τὸ μάννα ἔφαγον ἐν τῇ ἐρήμῳ, καθώς ἐστιν γεγραμμένον· ἄρτον ἐκ τοῦ οὐρανοῦ
ἔδωκεν (he/she/it gave) αὐτοῖς φαγεῖν (to eat). Our fathers were eating manna in the desert
even as it is written: he gave them bread from heaven to eat.

17. ταῦτα οὐκ ἔγνωσαν αὐτοῦ οἱ μαθηταὶ τὸ πρῶτον,[6] ἀλλ᾽ ὅτε ἐδοξάσθη Ἰησοῦς τότε ἐμνήσθησα
(they remembered) ὅτι ταῦτα ἦν ἐπ᾽ αὐτῷ γεγραμμένα καὶ ταῦτα ἐποίησαν αὐτῷ.
The disciples did not know these things at first, but when

18. ἐλθόντος τοῦ λόγου γνώσονται τὸν προφήτην ὃν ἀπέστειλεν αὐτοῖς κύριος ἐν πίστει.

19. Καὶ ἔρχονται πάλιν εἰς Ἱεροσόλυμα. καὶ ἐν τῷ ἱερῷ περιπατοῦντος αὐτοῦ ἔρχονται πρὸς αὐτὸ
οἱ ἀρχιερεῖς καὶ οἱ γραμματεῖς καὶ οἱ πρεσβύτεροι καὶ ἔλεγον αὐτῷ· ἐν ποίᾳ ἐξουσίᾳ ταῦτα
ποιεῖς; And again he went to Jerusalem. And while he was walking around the temple, the
chief priests and the scribes and the elders came to him and were saying to him, " By what authority do
you do these things?"

20. [7] καλέσω τὸν οὐ λαόν μου λαόν μου καὶ τὴν οὐκ ἠγαπημένην ἠγαπημένην.
I will not call this people my people and this beloved (my) beloved

References

α. —; β. —; γ. Jn 8:31; δ. —; ε. Lk 14:12; ζ. —; η. Mk 12:24; **1.** —; **2.** Jn 14:9; **3.** Jn 1:6; **4.** Jn 3:6; **5.** Mk 1:22; **6.** Mk 14:
7. Jn 3:24; **8.** Ac 2:2; **9.** Jn 8:30-31; **10.** Mk 11:9-10; **11.** —; **12.** —; **13.**1 Clem 65:2; **14.** Josh 8:34; **15.** (Shep 25:1); **16.**
6:31; **17.** Jn 12:16; **18.** Jer 28:9 [LXX 35:9]; **19.** Mk 11:27-28; **20.** Rom 9:25.

18.

---

[4] You should be able to figure this one out.

[5] πανταχῆ, *everywhere*.

[6] Although the form is adjectival, τὸ πρῶτον is functioning adverbially. This is not uncommon.

[7] Hint: Diagram this sentence first to see what articles go with what nouns. τόν and τήν are acting as demonstratives.

Review #6

rammar

What determines the case, number, and gender of a participle?

a. Adjectival: the word it is modifying

b. Adverbial: agrees in GNC with a noun in the sentence but its action is directed towards the verb

What are the clues that a participle is being used in the following ways?

a. Adjectival usually articular

b. Adverbial anarthrous

c. Substantival articular, but there is nothing to modify

What are the seven questions you ask of any participle you meet?

1. gender   gender   case   number

2. case   adverbial   or   adjective

3. number   if adverbial → "while" or "after"?

4. aspect   if adjectival → attributive or substantival

5. antecedent   voice

6. aspect =   continuous or undefined?

7. what does the verb mean?

What is a genitive absolute?

an independent clause in which the subject appears in the genitive case it has no grammatical connection to the rest of the sentence.

How do you form the following periphrastic verbal forms?

a. Present: present tense of εἰμί + present participle

b. Future: future tense of εἰμί + present participle

c. Perfect: present tense of εἰμί + perfect participle

6. Write out the nominative and genitive singular forms of the participle morpheme (with tense formative an case endings) of all three genders for the following tenses.

		masculine	feminine	neuter
a.	Present active	ων	ουσα	ον
		οντος	ουσης	οντος
b.	First aorist active	σασ	σασα	σαν
		σαντος	σασης	σαντος
c.	First aorist passive	θεις	θεισα	θεν
		θεντος	θεισης	θεντος
d.	Second aorist middle	ομενος	ομενη	ομενον
		ομενου	ομενης	ομενου
e.	First perfect active	κως	κυια	κος
		κοτος	κυιας	κοτος
f.	Perfect middle/passive	μενος	μενη	μενον
		μενου	μενης	μενου

Parsing

1. θέλοντος   MN G S   present active participle   while wanting / willing

2. γραφεῖσι   MN D P   aorist passive participle   after ~~they were written~~ being written

3. λελαληκότες   M N P   perfect active participle   after having ~~when they have~~ spoken

4. πιστευομένας   F A P   present middle participle   while being believed before believing

5. ὄν   N NA S   present active participle   while being

6. βαλόντα   N NA P   aorist active participle   after ~~they~~ threw throwing

7. δεχθέντα   N NA P   aorist passive participle   after ~~they were taken~~ being received

8. βεβληκότα   N NA P   perfect active participle   after having thrown ~~when they have thrown~~

9. λυθείσῃ   F D S   aorist passive participle   after ~~the/it was~~ being loosed destroye

10. βλέψασα   F N S   aorist active participle   after ~~she saw~~ looking

Translation: Mark 1:1-22

1:1 Ἀρχὴ τοῦ εὐαγγελίου Ἰησοῦ Χριστοῦ [υἱοῦ θεοῦ]. 1:2 Καθὼς γέγραπται ἐν τῷ Ἡσαΐα τῷ
The beginning of the gospel of Jesus Christ (the Son of God)

προφήτῃ· ἰδοὺ ἀποστέλλω τὸν ἄγγελόν μου πρὸ προσώπου σου, ὃς κατασκευάσει τὴν ὁδόν σου·
Behold I send my messenger before your face, which

φωνὴ βοῶντος ἐν τῇ ἐρήμῳ· ἑτοιμάσατε (prepare!) τὴν ὁδὸν κυρίου, εὐθείας[1] ποιεῖτε (make!) τὰς
voice calling in the desert: Prepare the way of the Lord, make his paths straight.

τρίβους[2] αὐτοῦ, 1:4 ἐγένετο Ἰωάννης [ὁ] βαπτίζων ἐν τῇ ἐρήμῳ καὶ κηρύσσων βάπτισμα μετανοίας
John the Baptist was in the desert and   preaching baptism of repentance

ς ἄφεσιν ἁμαρτιῶν. 1:5 καὶ ἐξεπορεύετο πρὸς αὐτὸν πᾶσα ἡ Ἰουδαία χώρα καὶ οἱ Ἰεροσολυμῖται
the forgiveness of sins. And all the land of Judea and all the Jerusalemites came out to him

άντες, καὶ ἐβαπτίζοντο ὑπ' αὐτοῦ ἐν τῷ Ἰορδάνῃ ποταμῷ ἐξομολογούμενοι τὰς ἁμαρτίας αὐτῶν.
d they were baptized by them in the Jordan River   their sins.

καὶ ἦν ὁ Ἰωάννης ἐνδεδυμένος τρίχας[3] καμήλου[4] καὶ ζώνην[5] δερματίνην[6] περὶ τὴν ὀσφὺν[7] αὐτοῦ,
ohn was wearing camel hair and a leather belt around his waist

ὶ ἐσθίων ἀκρίδας[8] καὶ μέλι[9] ἄγριον.[10] 1:7 Καὶ ἐκήρυσσεν λέγων· ἔρχεται ὁ ἰσχυρότερός (greater
d eating locusts and wild honey.   And he preached saying, "One greater than me is coming

an) μου ὀπίσω μου, οὗ οὐκ εἰμὶ ἱκανὸς κύψας[11] λῦσαι (to loosen) τὸν ἱμάντα[12] τῶν ὑποδημάτων
after me, where I am not able stooping to loosen the strap of his sandal.

ὐτοῦ· 1:8 ἐγὼ ἐβάπτισα ὑμᾶς ὕδατι, αὐτὸς δὲ βαπτίσει ὑμᾶς ἐν πνεύματι ἁγίῳ.
I baptized you by water, but he will baptized you in the Holy Spirit.

1:9 Καὶ ἐγένετο ἐν ἐκείναις ταῖς ἡμέραις ἦλθεν Ἰησοῦς ἀπὸ Ναζαρὲτ τῆς Γαλιλαίας καὶ
And it happened in those days (that) Jesus went to Nazareth in Galilee and

βαπτίσθη εἰς τὸν Ἰορδάνην ὑπὸ Ἰωάννου. 1:10 καὶ εὐθὺς ἀναβαίνων ἐκ τοῦ ὕδατος εἶδεν
was baptized in the Jordan by John.   And coming up immediately from the water he saw

ιζομένους τοὺς οὐρανοὺς καὶ τὸ πνεῦμα ὡς περιστερὰν καταβαῖνον εἰς αὐτόν· 1:11 καὶ φωνὴ
litting the heavens   and the spirit which   was coming down to him
like a dove

εὐθύς, εὐθεῖα, εὐθύ, genitive, -έως, straight.

τρίβος, -ου, ἡ, path.

θρίξ, τριχός, ἡ, hair.

κάμηλος, -ου, ὁ and ἡ, camel.

ζώνη, -ης, ἡ, belt.

δερμάτινος, η, ον, (made of) leather.

ὀσφῦς, -ύος, ἡ, waist.

ἀκρίς, -ίδος, ἡ, locust.

μέλι, -ιτος, τό, honey.

ἄγριος, -ία, -ον, wild.

κύπτω, I bow, stoop.

ἱμάς, -άντος, ὁ, strap or thong.

ἐγένετο ἐκ τῶν οὐρανῶν· σὺ εἶ ὁ υἱός μου ὁ ἀγαπητός, ἐν σοὶ εὐδόκησα.
And there was a voice from heaven: "You are my beloved Son; in you

1:12 Καὶ εὐθὺς τὸ πνεῦμα αὐτὸν ἐκβάλλει εἰς τὴν ἔρημον. 1:13 καὶ ἦν ἐν τῇ ἐρήμῳ
And immediately, the spirit cast him out into the desert. And he was in the desert

τεσσεράκοντα ἡμέρας πειραζόμενος ὑπὸ τοῦ σατανᾶ, καὶ ἦν μετὰ τῶν θηρίων, καὶ οἱ ἄγγελοι
forty   days   tempted   by   Satan,

διηκόνουν αὐτῷ.

1:14 Μετὰ δὲ τὸ παραδοθῆναι τὸν Ἰωάννην[13] ἦλθεν ὁ Ἰησοῦς εἰς τὴν Γαλιλαίαν κηρύσσω
After John had been betrayed, Jesus went into Galilee preaching the gospel

τὸ εὐαγγέλιον τοῦ θεοῦ 1:15 καὶ λέγων ὅτι πεπλήρωται ὁ καιρὸς καὶ ἤγγικεν ἡ βασιλεία τοῦ θεοῦ
of God.
and announced the kingdom of G

μετανοεῖτε (repent!) καὶ πιστεύετε (believe!) ἐν τῷ εὐαγγελίῳ.
" Repent and believe in the gospel."

1:16 Καὶ παράγων παρὰ τὴν θάλασσαν τῆς Γαλιλαίας εἶδεν Σίμωνα καὶ Ἀνδρέαν τὸν
Sea of Galilee he saw Simon and Andrew the

ἀδελφὸν Σίμωνος ἀμφιβάλλοντας[14] ἐν τῇ θαλάσσῃ· ἦσαν γὰρ ἁλιεῖς.[15] 1:17 καὶ εἶπεν αὐτοῖς ὁ
brother of Simon casting into the sea, for they were fishermen.   And Jesus said to the

Ἰησοῦς· δεῦτε (follow!) ὀπίσω μου, καὶ ποιήσω ὑμᾶς γενέσθαι (to be) ἁλιεῖς ἀνθρώπων. 1:18 καὶ εὐθὺ
" Follow after me, and I will make you to be fishermen of men/humans." And

ἀφέντες (after leaving) τὰ δίκτυα ἠκολούθησαν αὐτῷ. 1:19 Καὶ προβὰς[16] ὀλίγον εἶδεν Ἰάκωβον τὸν
immediately after leaving the fishnets   they followed him.   he saw Jacob, s

τοῦ Ζεβεδαίου καὶ Ἰωάννην τὸν ἀδελφὸν αὐτοῦ, καὶ αὐτοὺς ἐν τῷ πλοίῳ καταρτίζοντας τὰ
of Zebedee and John his brother,

δίκτυα, 1:20 καὶ εὐθὺς ἐκάλεσεν αὐτούς. καὶ ἀφέντες (after leaving) τὸν πατέρα αὐτῶν Ζεβεδαῖον ε
After leaving their father Zebedee in the boat with the

τῷ πλοίῳ μετὰ τῶν μισθωτῶν[17] ἀπῆλθον ὀπίσω αὐτοῦ.
hired men   they   were coming after him

1:21 Καὶ εἰσπορεύονται εἰς Καφαρναούμ. καὶ εὐθὺς τοῖς σάββασιν εἰσελθὼν εἰς τὴν
And they went into Capernaum.   And immediately on the Sabbath he taught

συναγωγὴν ἐδίδασκεν. 1:22 καὶ ἐξεπλήσσοντο ἐπὶ τῇ διδαχῇ αὐτοῦ, ἦν γὰρ διδάσκων αὐτοὺς ὡς
going into the synagogue. And they   at his teaching, for he was teaching them

ἐξουσίαν ἔχων καὶ οὐχ ὡς οἱ γραμματεῖς.
like one having authority and not like the scribes.

---

[13] μετὰ τὸ παραδοθῆναι τὸν Ἰωάννην means "After John had been betrayed."

[14] ἀμφιβάλλω, *I cast.*

[15] ἁλιεύς, -έως, ὁ, *fisherman.*

[16] προβαίνω, *I go on, advance.*

[17] μισθωτός, -οῦ, ὁ, *hired man.*

Subjunctive

Parsing

Inflected	Person / Case	Number	Tense / Gender	Voice	Mood	Lexical form	Inflected meaning
βαπτίζωμεν	1	P	P	A	S	βαπτίζω	that we might baptize
ἀκούῃ (3x)	3 / 2	s / s	P	A / M/P	S / I	ἀκούω	he might hear / you might be heard
ἔλθωμεν	1	P	A	M	S	ἔρχομαι	that ~~they~~ might have gone *let us go*
περιπατήσητε	2	P	A	A	S	περιπατέω	that you might have walked around
διδαχθῶσι	3	P	A	P	S	διδάσκω	that they might have been taught
κρινῶ	1	S	P	A	S	κρίνω	that I may judge
σώσῃς	2	S	P	A	S	σώζω	that you may save
προσελθώμεθα	1	P	A	M	S	προσέρχομαι	that we might have gone *let us go for ourselves*
ἐγείρωσι	3	P	P	A	S	ἐγείρω	that ~~they~~ might raise up
ποιηθῇ	3	S	A	P	S	ποιέω	that it might be ~~have been~~ done

Warm-up

ἵνα ἀγαπῶμεν ἀλλήλους   that we might love each other

ὅταν ἔλθῃ ἐν τῇ δόξῃ τοῦ πατρὸς αὐτοῦ   whenever he goes   in the glory of his father

ταῦτα λέγω ἵνα ὑμεῖς σωθῆτε.   I say these things that you might be saved

θέλομεν ἵνα ὃ ἐὰν αἰτήσωμέν σε ποιήσῃς ἡμῖν.   We desire that *you would do for us* whatever we may ask of you

ἵνα ἀποστέλλῃ αὐτούς   that he might send them

ἦραν οὖν λίθους ἵνα βάλωσιν ἐπ᾽ αὐτόν.   Then they picked up stones that they might throw them at him

τί αἰτήσωμαι;   What should we ask for? shall I ask for myself?

Translation

1. Καὶ ἐν τούτῳ γινώσκομεν ὅτι ἐγνώκαμεν αὐτόν, ἐὰν τὰς ἐντολὰς αὐτοῦ τηρῶμεν.
    And in this we know that we might know, if we keep his commandments.
    him

2. ἀμὴν λέγω ὑμῖν, ὃς ἂν μὴ δέξηται τὴν βασιλείαν τοῦ θεοῦ ὡς παιδίον, οὐ μὴ εἰσέλθη[1] εἰς αὐτή
    Amen I say to you, whoever does not receive the kingdom of God like a child, shall
    DEFINITELY NOT go into it.

3. ἠρώτα αὐτὸν ἵνα τὸ δαιμόνιον ἐκβάλη ἐκ τῆς θυγατρὸς (daughter) αὐτῆς.
    He raised him up that he might cast the demon out of her daughter.
    She was asking him

4. αὕτη δέ ἐστιν ἡ αἰώγιος ζωὴ ἵνα[2] γινώσκωσιν σὲ τὸν μόνον ἀληθινὸν (true) θεὸν καὶ ὃν
    ἀπέστειλας Ἰησοῦν Χριστόν. And this is eternal life, that they know you,
    only true God and which sent Jesus Christ, whom you sent.

5. καὶ πάντα ὅσα ἂν αἰτήσητε ἐν τῇ προσευχῇ πιστεύοντες[3] λήμψεσθε.
    And all things as much as you ask in prayer, believing, you shall receive.
    while

6. μετὰ τοῦτο λέγει τοῖς μαθηταῖς· ἄγωμεν[4] εἰς τὴν Ἰουδαίαν πάλιν.
    After this he said to the disciples, "Go into Judea again."
    Let us
    In this manner

7. (Οὕτως) γὰρ ἠγάπησεν ὁ θεὸς τὸν κόσμον, ὥστε τὸν υἱὸν τὸν (μονογενῆ) (only) ἔδωκεν (he/she/it
    gave), ἵνα πᾶς ὁ πιστεύων εἰς αὐτὸν μὴ ἀπόληται (he/she/it might perish) ἀλλ᾽ ἔχη ζωὴν αἰώνιο
    οὐ γὰρ ἀπέστειλεν ὁ θεὸς τὸν υἱὸν εἰς τὸν κόσμον ἵνα κρίνη τὸν κόσμον, ἀλλ᾽ ἵνα σωθῇ ὁ κόσμο
    δι᾽ αὐτοῦ. For God so loved the world, that he gave his only son, that all those
    every one
    believing in him might not perish but have eternal life. For God did not sen
    his son into the world that he might judge the world, but that he
    might save the world through him.
    might be saved

---

[1] How does the strength of this emphatic negative help you understand what Jesus is saying?

[2] Here is another good example of ἵνα meaning "that," not "in order that." Some call this the "epexegetical" use of ἵνα which the ἵνα clause is describing, exegeting, the previous statement (cf. Wallace, 476).

[3] Another use of the participle is to indicate a condition; hence it is called a "conditional participle." The particip describes a condition applied to the verb the participle is modifying. You can use the key "if" in your translation.

[4] Our usual definition of ἄγω obviously does not work here. "Go" is acceptable.

καὶ ἐζήτουν οἱ ἀρχιερεῖς καὶ οἱ γραμματεῖς πῶς αὐτὸν ... ἀποκτείνωσιν.
And the high priests and the scribes were seeking how they might ... kill him.

οἱ πατέρες ὑμῶν ἔφαγον ἐν τῇ ἐρήμῳ (desert) τὸ μάννα καὶ ἀπέθανον· οὗτός ἐστιν ὁ ἄρτος ὁ ἐκ

τοῦ οὐρανοῦ καταβαίνων, ἵνα τις ἐξ αὐτοῦ φάγῃ καὶ μὴ ἀποθάνῃ. ἐγώ εἰμι ὁ ἄρτος ὁ ζῶν ὁ ἐκ

τοῦ οὐρανοῦ καταβάς· ἐάν τις φάγῃ ἐκ τούτου τοῦ ἄρτου ζήσει εἰς τὸν αἰῶνα, καὶ ὁ ἄρτος δὲ

ὃν ἐγὼ δώσω (I will give) ἡ σάρξ μού ἐστιν ὑπὲρ τῆς τοῦ κόσμου ζωῆς. Ἐμάχοντο (they were

quarreling) οὖν πρὸς ἀλλήλους οἱ Ἰουδαῖοι λέγοντες· πῶς δύναται οὗτος ἡμῖν δοῦναι (to give)

τὴν σάρκα [αὐτοῦ] φαγεῖν (to eat); εἶπεν οὖν αὐτοῖς ὁ Ἰησοῦς· ἀμὴν ἀμὴν λέγω ὑμῖν, ἐὰν μὴ

φάγητε τὴν σάρκα τοῦ υἱοῦ τοῦ ἀνθρώπου καὶ πίητε αὐτοῦ τὸ αἷμα, οὐκ ἔχετε ζωὴν ἐν ἑαυτοῖς.
Your fathers ate manna in the desert and died. This is the bread which is coming down from heaven, that whoever eats of it might not die. I am the bread of life which came down from heaven. Whoever eats this bread is saved forever, and the bread which I will give, is my flesh (on behalf of the life of the world)
Then they were quarreling among themselves saying, "How can this man give us his flesh to eat?" Then Jesus said to them, "Amen, amen, I say to you, if you do not eat the flesh of the Son of Man and drink his blood, you do not have life in yourselves." (the Jews)

0. εἰ νεκροὶ οὐκ ἐγείρονται, φάγωμεν καὶ πίωμεν, αὔριον (tomorrow) γὰρ ἀποθνήσκομεν.[5]
If the dead are not raised, let us eat and drink, for tomorrow we die.

Additional

1. ποιῶμεν πολὺ ἔργον ἐν τῇ γλώσσῃ ταύτῃ ἵνα γενώμεθα οἱ κηρύσσοντες τὸν λόγον τοῦ θεοῦ ἐν πάσῃ ἀληθείᾳ. *We do much work in this tongue that we might become preachers* (that you might become the preachers of the word of God in all truth)

2. ὅταν βλέψω τὰ παιδία μου ἀγαπῶντα ἀλλήλους, ἡ ἐμὴ καρδία χαίρει καὶ ἡ ἐμὴ ψυχὴ προσεύχεται τῷ θεῷ. *Whenever I will see my children loving each other, my heart rejoices and my soul worships (prays to) God.*

3. ἐὰν δὲ μὴ πιστεύσωσίν σοι μηδὲ ἀκούσωσιν τῆς φωνῆς τοῦ σημείου τοῦ πρώτου πιστεύσουσίν σοι τῆς φωνῆς τοῦ σημείου τοῦ ἐσχάτου.

Notice how Paul uses the present tense to describe an event that will occur in the future. There are several possible explanations for this. The present can be used for a future action to emphasize the vividness or certainty of the action. The present is also used to make a gnomic statement, an axiom, "a general principle (denoting an occurrence which may take place at any time), but with the context focusing on a particular outworking of this principle at a point in the future" (Fanning, 224).

14. καὶ λατρεύσετε⁶ ἐκεῖ θεοῖς ἑτέροις, ἔργοις χειρῶν ἀνθρώπων ξύλοις⁷ καὶ λίθοις, οἳ οὐκ
ὄψονται⁸ οὐδὲ μὴ ἀκούσωσιν οὔτε μὴ φάγωσιν. *And you worship other gods, works of human
hands of stone and wood, which neither see nor hear and do not eat.*

15. τὸν κύριον Ἰησοῦν Χριστόν, οὗ τὸ αἷμα ὑπὲρ ἡμῶν ἐδόθη (it was given), φοβώμεθα.
The Lord Jesus Christ, whose blood was given for us, let us fear.

16. Ὃς ἂν ἓν τῶν τοιούτων παιδίων δέξηται ἐπὶ τῷ ὀνόματί μου, ἐμὲ δέχεται· καὶ ὃς ἂν ἐμὲ
δέχηται, οὐκ ἐμὲ δέχεται ἀλλὰ τὸν ἀποστείλαντά με. *Whoever receives one of these child*
In my name receives me; and whoever receives me receives not me but the one who sent me.

17. ἀμὴν δὲ λέγω ὑμῖν, ὅπου ἐὰν κηρυχθῇ τὸ εὐαγγέλιον εἰς ὅλον τὸν κόσμον, καὶ ὃ ἐποίησεν αὐτ
λαληθήσεται εἰς μνημόσυνον⁹ αὐτῆς. *But verily I tell you, wherever the gospel is preache*
the whole world and that which she did will be spoken of in her memory.
what this woman did

18. ἐὰν δὲ ἐν τῷ φωτὶ περιπατῶμεν ὡς αὐτός ἐστιν ἐν τῷ φωτί, κοινωνίαν ἔχομεν μετ᾿ ἀλλήλων κα
τὸ αἷμα Ἰησοῦ τοῦ υἱοῦ αὐτοῦ καθαρίζει ἡμᾶς ἀπὸ πάσης ἁμαρτίας. ἐὰν εἴπωμεν ὅτι ἁμαρτία
οὐκ ἔχομεν, ἑαυτοὺς πλανῶμεν καὶ ἡ ἀλήθεια οὐκ ἔστιν ἐν ἡμῖν.

19. ¹⁰ ἀμὴν λέγω ὑμῖν ὅτι οὐκέτι οὐ μὴ πίω ἐκ τοῦ γενήματος¹¹ τῆς ἀμπέλου¹² ἕως τῆς ἡμέρας
ἐκείνης ὅταν αὐτὸ πίνω καινὸν ἐν τῇ βασιλείᾳ τοῦ θεοῦ. *Verily, I tell you that whoever*
does not drink of the fruit of the vine in these days I will not drink... until that day when
in the kingdom of God. *drink it new*

20. ἀπεκρίθη Ἰησοῦς· ἐὰν ἐγὼ δοξάσω ἐμαυτόν, ἡ δόξα μου οὐδέν ἐστιν· ἔστιν ὁ πατήρ μου ὁ
δοξάζων με, ὃν ὑμεῖς λέγετε ὅτι θεὸς ἡμῶν ἐστιν, καὶ οὐκ ἐγνώκατε αὐτόν, ἐγὼ δὲ οἶδα αὐτόν
κἂν εἴπω¹³ ὅτι οὐκ οἶδα αὐτόν, ἔσομαι ὅμοιος ὑμῖν ψεύστης· ἀλλὰ οἶδα αὐτὸν καὶ τὸν λόγον
αὐτοῦ τηρῶ. *Jesus answered, "If I glorify myself, the glory is not mine. It is my*
Father who glorifies me, which you say that God is ours and you do not know him, I do
not know him. And if I say that I do not know him I would be a liar like you

Summary *But I know him and keep his word.*

1. Participles can apply a condition to a verb ("conditional participle"). You can use the key word "if" in th
   translation.

2. The present tense can be used to describe a future event, either to emphasize the vividness or the certaint
   of the action, or to state a principle that is always true but whose fulfillment lies in the future ("axiomatic"

References

α. 1 Jn 3:11; β. Mk 8:38; γ. Jn 5:34; δ. Mk 10:35; ε. Mk 3:14; ζ. Jn 8:59; η. Mk 6:24; **1.** 1 Jn 2:3; **2.** Mk 10:15; **3.** Mk 7:2
4. Jn 17:3; **5.** Mt 21:22; **6.** Jn 11:7; **7.** Mk 14:1; **8.** Jn 3:16-17; **9.** Jn 6:49-53; **10.** 1 Cor 15:32; **11.** —; **12.** —; **13.** (Ex 4:8
14. Dt 4:28; **15.** (1 Clem 21:6); **16.** Mk 9:37; **17.** Mk 14:9; **18.** 1 Jn 1:7-8; **19.** Mk 14:25; **20.** Jn 8:54-55.

18. And if we walk around in the light as he is in the light, we have fellowship with each
other and the blood of Jesus his son will purify us from all sins. If we say that we
have no sins we lie to ourselves and the truth is not in us.

---

⁶ λατρεύω, *I serve, worship.*

⁷ ξύλον, -ου, τό, *wood.*

⁸ The switch from the indicative ὄψονται to the following two subjunctives make the negations more emphatic.

⁹ μνημόσυνον, ου, τό, *memory.*

¹⁰ How does the double negative and the present tense of πίνω help you understand the full force of what Jesus is sayin

¹¹ γένημα, -ματος, τό, *fruit, product.*

¹² ἄμπελος, ου, ἡ, *vine, grapevine.*

¹³ Did you notice that εἴπω has not lost its augment? We already saw this in the participial forms, and it is true in the oth
nonindicative forms.

Infinitive

Inflected	Person / Case	Number	Tense / Gender	Voice	Mood	Lexical form	Inflected meaning
φαγεῖν			A		Inf	ἐσθίω	
λαλήσασθαι			A			λάλω	
πεπληρωκέναι			Perf			πληρόω	
λέγειν			P			λέγω	
σῶσαι			A			σώζω	
δοξάζεσθαι						δοξάζω	
τεθεωρῆσθαι			Perf			θεωρέω	
ἀγαπᾶν			P			ἀγαπάω	
γραφῆναι						γράφω	
0. πληρῶσαι			A			πληρόω	

ἀπέστειλεν αὐτοὺς κηρύσσειν τὴν βασιλείαν τοῦ θεοῦ. He sent them to preach the kingdom of God.

εἰς τὴν βασιλείαν τοῦ θεοῦ εἰσελθεῖν to go into the kingdom of God

τίς δύναται σωθῆναι; who can be saved?

δεῖ κηρυχθῆναι τὸ εὐαγγέλιον. it is necessary to preach the gospel

εἰς τὸ ἀποκτεῖναι αὐτόν in order to kill him

καὶ ἐν τῷ σπείρειν αὐτὸν and while he was sowing

ἀλλὰ μετὰ τὸ ἐγερθῆναί με but after I was raised

Translation

1. Καὶ πάλιν ἤρξατο διδάσκειν παρὰ τὴν θάλασσαν.
   And again he began to teach alongside of the sea.

2. ὃς γὰρ ἐὰν θέλῃ τὴν ψυχὴν αὐτοῦ σῶσαι ἀπολέσει (he/she/it will lose) αὐτήν.
   For whoever wishes to save his life will lose it.

3. καὶ λέγει αὐτοῖς· ἔξεστιν (it is lawful) τοῖς σάββασιν ἀγαθὸν ποιῆσαι ἢ κακοποιῆσαι,[1] ψυχὴν
   σῶσαι ἢ ἀποκτεῖναι; And he said to them, "Is it lawful on the Sabbath to do good
   or do evil, to save a life or to kill?"

4. ἦλθεν γὰρ ὁ υἱὸς τοῦ ἀνθρώπου ζητῆσαι καὶ σῶσαι τὸ ἀπολωλός (lost).
   For the Son of Man went to seek and to save the lost.

5. καὶ ἐποίησεν[2] δώδεκα ... ἵνα ὦσιν μετ᾽ αὐτοῦ καὶ ἵνα ἀποστέλλῃ αὐτοὺς κηρύσσειν καὶ ἔχειν
   ἐξουσίαν ἐκβάλλειν τὰ δαιμόνια. And he appointed twelve... that they might be
   with him and that he might send them to preach & to have authority to cast
   out demons.

6. ἀμὴν γὰρ λέγω ὑμῖν ὅτι πολλοὶ προφῆται καὶ δίκαιοι ἐπεθύμησαν (they desired) ἰδεῖν ἃ βλέπετε
   καὶ οὐκ εἶδαν, καὶ ἀκοῦσαι ἃ ἀκούετε καὶ οὐκ ἤκουσαν. For truly I tell you that
   many prophets and righteous people desired to see that which you see and
   do not know, and to hear that which you hear and they did not hear.

---

[1] This compound verb happens to carry the meaning you would expect from its two parts. What do you think it means?

[2] In this context ποιέω must mean "appoint." ποιέω is flexible in its meaning.

³ αὐτὸς δὲ Ἰησοῦς οὐκ ἐπίστευεν⁴ αὐτὸν αὐτοῖς διὰ τὸ αὐτὸν γινώσκειν πάντας.

But the same Jesus did not entrust ~him to~ them because he knew all things

(ἵνα ...) εὑρεθῶ ἐν αὐτῷ, μὴ ἔχων ἐμὴν δικαιοσύνην τὴν ἐκ νόμου ἀλλὰ τὴν διὰ πίστεως

Χριστοῦ, τὴν ἐκ θεοῦ δικαιοσύνην ἐπὶ τῇ πίστει, τοῦ γνῶναι⁵ αὐτὸν καὶ τὴν δύναμιν τῆς

ἀναστάσεως (resurrection) αὐτοῦ.

ἀλλὰ μετὰ τὸ ἐγερθῆναί με προάξω (I will go before) ὑμᾶς εἰς τὴν Γαλιλαίαν.

But after I am raised   I will go before you into Galilee.

0. Ἀβραάμ ... ἐπίστευσεν εἰς τὸ γενέσθαι αὐτὸν πατέρα πολλῶν ἐθνῶν.

Abraham believed in order that he might become father of many nations.

Additional

1. αὕτη ἡ γυνὴ λίθον καλὸν ἔχειν θέλει ἐπὶ τῇ χειρὶ αὐτῆς δεξαμένη αὐτὸν ἀπὸ τοῦ ἠγαπηκότος
αὐτήν. This woman wishes to have a beautiful ston on her hand *that* she received from the one who loves her.

2. πορευθῶμεν γὰρ πρὸς τὴν θαλάσσην εἰς τὸ εὑρίσκειν ὧδε τινὰς ἡμέρας ἀγαθὰς ἐν τῷ
ἡλίῳ.⁶ For we came to the sea in order to find here good days in the sun.

3. καὶ κατέβη κύριος ἰδεῖν τὴν πόλιν καὶ τὸν πύργον⁷ ὃν ᾠκοδόμησαν⁸ οἱ υἱοὶ τῶν ἀνθρώπων.
And the master went down to the city to see the tower which the sons of men were building.

Hint: Watch for the different meanings of αὐτός.

In this context, πιστεύω carries the meaning of "entrust."

Hint: Look for the verbal root.

ἥλιος, -ου, ὁ, *sun.*

πύργος, -ου, ὁ, *tower.*

οἰκοδομέω, *I build.*

14. εἶπεν δὲ Ἀβραὰμ περὶ Σάρρας τῆς γυναικὸς αὐτοῦ ὅτι ἀδελφή μού ἐστιν, ἐφοβήθη γὰρ εἰπεῖν ὅτι γυνή μού ἐστιν μήποτε[9] ἀποκτείνωσιν αὐτὸν οἱ ἄνδρες τῆς πόλεως δι᾽ αὐτήν.

15. καὶ εἶπεν κύριος ὁ θεός· οὐ μὴ καταμείνῃ[10] τὸ πνεῦμά μου ἐν τοῖς ἀνθρώποις τούτοις εἰς τὸν αἰῶνα διὰ τὸ εἶναι αὐτοὺς σάρκας, ἔσονται δὲ αἱ ἡμέραι αὐτῶν ἑκατὸν εἴκοσι ἔτη.[11]

16. [12] ἀπεκρίθη αὐτοῖς· εἶπον ὑμῖν ἤδη καὶ οὐκ ἠκούσατε· τί πάλιν θέλετε ἀκούειν; μὴ καὶ ὑμεῖς θέλετε αὐτοῦ μαθηταὶ γενέσθαι;

17. οἱ δὲ ἀρχιερεῖς καὶ ὅλον τὸ συνέδριον ἐζήτουν κατὰ τοῦ Ἰησοῦ μαρτυρίαν εἰς τὸ θανατῶσαι[13] αὐτόν, καὶ οὐχ ηὕρισκον. The high priests and the whole Sanhedrin were seeking a witness against Jesus, in order that they might put him to death, but they were not finding

18. καὶ εἶπεν αὐτοῖς ὁ Ἰησοῦς· δεῦτε (follow!) ὀπίσω μου, καὶ ποιήσω ὑμᾶς γενέσθαι ἁλιεῖς[14] ἀνθρώπων. And Jesus said to them," Follow after me, and I will make you to become fishermen of people."

19. ἔλεος θέλω καὶ οὐ θυσίαν· οὐ γὰρ ἦλθον καλέσαι δικαίους ἀλλὰ ἁμαρτωλούς. I desire mercy & not sacrifice, For I did not come to call the righteous, but sinners.

20. Ἀνέβη δὲ καὶ Ἰωσὴφ ἀπὸ τῆς Γαλιλαίας ἐκ πόλεως Ναζαρὲθ εἰς τὴν Ἰουδαίαν εἰς πόλιν Δαυὶδ ἥτις καλεῖται Βηθλέεμ, διὰ τὸ εἶναι αὐτὸν ἐξ οἴκου καὶ πατριᾶς[15] Δαυίδ. And Joseph came up to Galilee from the city of Nazareth in Judea into the city of David, which is called Bethlehem, for he was of the house and lineage

References of David.

α. Lk 9:2; β. Mk 10:24; γ. Mk 10:26; δ. Mk 13:10; ε. (Mk 14:55); ζ. Mt 13:4; η. Mk 14:28; **1**. Mk 4:1; **2**. Mk 8:35; **3**. Mk 3:4; **4**. Lk 19:10; **5**. Mk 3:14-15; **6**. Mt 13:17; **7**. Jn 2:24; **8**. Phil 3:9-10; **9**. Mk 14:28; **10**. Rom 4:16, 18; **11**. —; **12**. —; **13**. Gen 11:5; **14**. Gen 20:2; **15**. Gen 6:3; **16**. Jn 9:27; **17**. Mk 14:55; **18**. Mk 1:17; **19**. Mt 9:13; **20**. Lk 2:4.

14 And Abraham said concerning Sarah his wife, "She is my sister," for he feared to say," She is my wife," lest the men of the city kill him on account of her.

15 And the Lord God said, "My spirit will by no means stay in these people forever, because they are flesh," and their days were 120 years.

16 He answered them," I said to you again & you did not hear. Why do you wish to hear it ag[ ] You don't want to become his disciples, do you?"

17 And the chief priests and the whole Sanhedrin were seeking a witness against Jesus In order that they might put him to death, but they were not finding.

---

9 μήποτε, *lest.*

10 καταμένω, *I stay, live.*

11 ἑκατὸν εἴκοσι ἔτη, *120 years.*

12 Did the blind man believe that they wanted to become Jesus' disciples?

13 θανατόω, *I put to death.*

14 ἁλιεύς, -έως, ὁ, *fisherman.*

15 πατριά, -ᾶς, ἡ, *family, lineage.*

Imperative

arsing

Inflected	Person / Case	Number	Tense / Gender	Voice	Mood	Lexical form	Inflected meaning
ἄκουε	2	S	~~PRE~~ P	A	Imp	ακουω	hear!
γράφεσθε (2x)	2	P	P	M	I / Imp	γράφω	you write / write!
θέλησον	2	S	P	A	Imp	θέλω	wish!
βλεπέτωσαν	3	P	P	A	Imp	βλέπω	Let them see!
πιστεύεις	2	S	P	A	I	πιστεύω	you believe
εἴπετε (2x)	2	P	A	A	I / Imp	λέγω	speak!
αἰτῆσαι (2x)	2	S	P	P / A	Imp / Inf	αἰτέω	to ~~raise ask~~ be ~~raised~~ asked!
λαλοῦ	2	S	P	A	Imp	λάλω	speak!
ἐκβλήθητι	2	S	A	P	Imp	εκβάλλω	be cast out!
0. γνωσθήτωσαν	3	P	A	P	Imp	γινώσκω	let them be known!

Warm-up

. φέρετε αὐτὸν πρός με. Bring him to me.

. ἀκολούθει μοι. Follow me.

. μὴ φοβεῖσθε. Do not be afraid.

. αἴτησόν με ὃ ἐὰν θέλῃς. Ask me for anything/whatever you want

. ὕπαγε, ἡ πίστις σου σέσωκέν σε. Depart; your faith has saved you.

. ἐγείρεσθε, ἄγωμεν. Arise, let us go/be on our way.

. ὑπάγετε εἴπατε τοῖς μαθηταῖς αὐτοῦ
Depart and speak to his disciples.

Translation

1. ἄκουε, Ἰσραήλ, κύριος ὁ θεὸς ἡμῶν κύριος εἷς ἐστιν.

   Hear, O Israel, the Lord our God is One.

2. καὶ ἔλεγεν αὐτοῖς· ὅπου ἐὰν εἰσέλθητε εἰς οἰκίαν, ἐκεῖ μένετε ἕως ἂν ἐξέλθητε.

   And he was saying to them, "Whenever you go into a house, stay there until you go out."

3. μὴ φοβοῦ, μόνον πίστευε.   Do not fear, only believe.

4. εἴτε οὖν ἐσθίετε εἴτε πίνετε εἴτε τι ποιεῖτε, πάντα εἰς δόξαν θεοῦ ποιεῖτε.

   Then whether you eat or drink or whatever you do, do all things in the glory of God.

5. ἔξελθε ἐξ αὐτοῦ καὶ μηκέτι (no longer) εἰσέλθῃς εἰς αὐτόν.

   Come out of him and no longer enter him!

6. Μὴ ἀγαπᾶτε τὸν κόσμον μηδὲ τὰ ἐν τῷ κόσμῳ. ἐάν τις ἀγαπᾷ τὸν κόσμον, οὐκ ἔστιν ἡ ἀγάπη

   τοῦ πατρὸς[1] ἐν αὐτῷ. Love neither the world nor that which is in the world. Whoever loves the world, love for the Father is not in him.

---

[1] Is this a subjective or objective genitive?

If a word is a "subjective" genitive, it is the subject of the action implied by the word it is modifying and therefore *produces* the action. "The love of the Father" would mean "the love the Father produces," or, his love for me.

If a word is an "objective" genitive, it is the object of the action implied by the word it is modifying and therefore *receives* the action. "The love of the Father" would mean "the love the Father receives," or, my love for him.

τί γὰρ ἐστιν εὐκοπώτερον (easier), εἰπεῖν· ἀφίενταί (they are forgiven) σου αἱ ἁμαρτίαι, ἢ εἰπεῖν·

ἔγειρε καὶ περιπάτει; ἵνα δὲ εἰδῆτε ὅτι ἐξουσίαν ἔχει ὁ υἱὸς τοῦ ἀνθρώπου ἐπὶ τῆς γῆς ἀφιέναι

(to forgive) ἁμαρτίας — τότε λέγει τῷ παραλυτικῷ (paralytic)· ἐγερθεὶς ἆρόν σου τὴν κλίνην (bed)

καὶ ὕπαγε εἰς τὸν οἶκόν σου. For why is it easier to say, "Your sins are forgiven,"
than to say "Rise and walk?" That you might know that the Son of
Man has authority on earth to forgive sins —

and depart into your house.

2 καὶ ἀποκριθεὶς ὁ Ἰησοῦς λέγει αὐτοῖς· ἔχετε πίστιν θεοῦ.3 ἀμὴν λέγω ὑμῖν ὅτι ὃς ἂν εἴπῃ τῷ

ὄρει (mountain) τούτῳ· ἄρθητι καὶ βλήθητι εἰς τὴν θάλασσαν, καὶ μὴ διακριθῇ (he/she/it wavers)

ἐν τῇ καρδίᾳ αὐτοῦ ἀλλὰ πιστεύῃ ὅτι ὃ λαλεῖ γίνεται,4 ἔσται αὐτῷ. διὰ τοῦτο λέγω ὑμῖν, πάντα

ὅσα προσεύχεσθε καὶ αἰτεῖσθε, πιστεύετε ὅτι ἐλάβετε, καὶ ἔσται ὑμῖν. And answering, Jesus said
to them, "You have faith in God. Truly I tell you that whoever says to this mountain
"Be raised up and cast into the sea" and does not waver in his heart but
believes that that which he says will happen,   For this reason I
say to you, all that you pray and ask for, believe that

λέγει αὐτῷ ὁ Ἰησοῦς· ἐὰν αὐτὸν θέλω μένειν ἕως ἔρχομαι, τί πρὸς σέ; σύ μοι ἀκολούθει.
Jesus said to him, "   wishes to remain until I come, what is it to you?
Follow me."

10. καὶ γὰρ ἐγὼ ἄνθρωπός εἰμι ὑπὸ ἐξουσίαν ... καὶ λέγω τούτῳ· πορεύθητι, καὶ πορεύεται, καὶ

ἄλλῳ· ἔρχου, καὶ ἔρχεται, καὶ τῷ δούλῳ μου· ποίησον τοῦτο, καὶ ποιεῖ. For I am a man under-
authority ... and I say to this one "Go!" and he goes, and to another "Come!"
and he comes, and to my slave, "Do this!" and he does it.

---

2   Note carefully the shifting of tenses.

3   What kind of genitive is this? What is the precise relationship between πίστιν and θεοῦ?

4   Why is Mark using the present tense to indicate a future action?

Additional

11. οἱ περιπατοῦντες ἐν τῇ ὁδῷ τῆς δικασιοσύνης ἀπὸ τῶν κακῶν ἀπελθέτωσαν καὶ γινέσθωσαν
δοῦλοι τοῦ θεοῦ ἐν φόβῳ καὶ ἐλπίδι. *Those walking in the path of righteousness*
away from the evil ones   servants of God in fear and hope.

12. ὁ δὲ Παῦλος τοὺς ἐν ταῖς ἐκκλησίαις ἐδίδασκεν· πιστεύσατε εἰς τὸν Ἰησοῦν Χρίστον καὶ ζᾶτε
κατὰ τὸ θέλημα τοῦ κυρίου ἡμῶν. *And Paul taught those in the churches, " Believe*
in Jesus Christ and live according to the will of our Lord."

13. καὶ εἶπεν ὁ θεός· γενηθήτω φῶς, καὶ ἐγένετο φῶς.
And God said," Let there be light, and there was light."

14. εἰπάτωσαν πάντες οἱ φοβούμενοι τὸν κύριον ὅτι ἀγαθός ὅτι εἰς τὸν αἰῶνα ἡ ἀγάπη αὐτοῦ.
Let them speak all who fear the Lord because he is good and because his love is forever.

15. σὺ οὖν πίστευε τῷ δικαίῳ, τὸ γὰρ δίκαιον ὀρθὴν[5] ὁδὸν ἔχει. καὶ σὺ τῇ ὀρθῇ ὁδῷ πορεύου.
Then believe in the righteous, for the righteous has the straight path. Go in the
straight path!

16. [6] Χαίρετε ἐν κυρίῳ πάντοτε· πάλιν ἐρῶ, χαίρετε.
Rejoice in the Lord always: again I say rejoice!

17. ὃς ἔχει ὦτα[7] ἀκούειν ἀκουέτω.
He who has ears to hear — let him hear.

18. πορεύου, καὶ ἀπὸ τοῦ νῦν μηκέτι ἁμάρτανε.
Go and sin no more.

19. Ὡς οὖν παρελάβετε τὸν Χριστὸν Ἰησοῦν τὸν κύριον, ἐν αὐτῷ[8] περιπατεῖτε.
Then that which you took of the Lord Jesus Christ, walk in it.

20. Μὴ ταρασσέσθω[9] ὑμῶν ἡ καρδία· πιστεύετε εἰς τὸν θεόν καὶ εἰς ἐμὲ πιστεύετε.
Let not your heart be troubled: believe in God and believe in me.

Summary

1.   A subjective genitive produces the action of the noun; the objective genitive receives the action of the noun

References

α. Mk 9:19; β. Mk 2:14; γ. Mk 6:50; δ. Mk 6:22; ε. Mk 10:52; ζ. Mk 14:42; η. Mk 16:7; **1**. Mk 12:29; **2**. Mk 6:10; **3**. Mk
5:36; **4**. 1 Cor 10:31; **5**. Mk 9:25; **6**. 1 Jn 2:15; **7**. Mt 9:5-6; **8**. Mk 11:22-24; **9**. Jn 21:22; **10**. Mt 8:9; **11**. —; **12**. —; **13**. Gen
1:3; **14**. Ps 118:4 [LXX 117:4]; **15**. (Shep 35:2); **16**. Phil 4:4; **17**. Mk 4:9; **18**. Jn 8:11; **19**. Col 2:6; **20**. Jn 14:1.

---

[5]   ὀρθός, -ή, -όν, *straight, upright.*

[6]   What a great verse for Greek class!

[7]   οὖς, ὠτός, τό, *ear.*

[8]   Is this masculine or neuter? What is the difference in meaning?

[9]   ταράσσω, I *trouble.*

Exercise 34

μι Verbs; Indicative of δίδωμι

Inflected	Person / Case	Number	Tense / Gender	Voice	Mood	Lexical form	Inflected meaning
δίδωσι	3	S	P	A	I	δίδωμι	he/she/it gives ~~gave~~
ἔδωκαν	3	P	A	A	I	δίδωμι	they gave
δέδωκεν	3	S	Perf	A	I	δίδωμι	he she it has given
δώσετε	2	P	F	A	I	δίδωμι	you will give
ἐδίδους	2	S	I	A	I	δίδωμι	you were giving
διδόασι	3	P	P	A	I	δίδωμι	they give
δέδωκαν	3	P	Perf	A	I	δίδωμι	they have given
δώσω	1	S	F	A	I	δίδωμι	I will give
ἐδώκαμεν	1	P	A	A	I	δίδωμι	we gave
δεδώκαμεν	1	P	Perf	A	I	δίδωμι	we have given

What are the five rules for μι verbs?

μι verbs reduplicate their initial stem letter to form the present, and separate the reduplicated consonant with ι   δο → διδ

μι verbs generally do not use a thematic connecting vowel

μι verbs use 3 different personal endings in the present active indicative

the stem vowel of μι verbs can shorten, lengthen, or drop out

most μι verbs use κα as the tense formative in the aorist tense

Warm-up

α. ὁ δὲ θεὸς δίδωσιν αὐτῷ σῶμα.
But God gives a body to him.

β. διὰ τοῦ πνεύματος δίδοται λόγος σοφίας.
The word gives wisdom through the Spirit.

γ. δώσομεν αὐτοῖς φαγεῖν;
Shall we give them (something) to eat?

δ. καὶ ἔδωκα αὐτῇ χρόνον.
And I gave here the time.

ε. δώσουσιν σημεῖα μεγάλα.
They will give a great sign.

ζ. τὴν δόξαν τὴν ἐμήν, ἣν δέδωκάς μοι
my glory, which you have given to me.

η. ἐδόθη μοι πᾶσα ἐξουσία.
All authority was given to me.

Translation

1. ὁ δὲ ἀποκριθεὶς εἶπεν αὐτοῖς, ὅτι ὑμῖν δέδοται γνῶναι[1] τὰ μυστήρια (mysteries) τῆς βασιλεία

   τῶν οὐρανῶν, ἐκείνοις δὲ οὐ δέδοται. *And answering he said to them*
   "To you it is given to know the mysteries of the kingdom of heaven,
   but to those it is not given."

2. τὴν δύναμιν καὶ ἐξουσίαν αὐτῶν τῷ θηρίῳ (beast) διδόασιν.

   They give their power and authority to a beast.

3. οἱ πατέρες ἡμῶν τὸ μάννα ἔφαγον ἐν τῇ ἐρήμῳ, καθώς ἐστιν γεγραμμένον· ἄρτον ἐκ τοῦ οὐρανο

   ἔδωκεν αὐτοῖς φαγεῖν. εἶπεν οὖν αὐτοῖς ὁ Ἰησοῦς· ἀμὴν ἀμὴν λέγω ὑμῖν, οὐ Μωϋσῆς δέδωκε

   ὑμῖν τὸν ἄρτον ἐκ τοῦ οὐρανοῦ, ἀλλ᾽ ὁ πατήρ μου δίδωσιν ὑμῖν τὸν ἄρτον ἐκ τοῦ οὐρανοῦ τὸν

   ἀληθινόν (true). *Our fathers ate manna in the desert, just as it is written.*
   He gave them bread from heaven to dead. Then Jesus said to them,

   " Truly I tell you, Moses did not give you bread from heaven, but
   my Father gives you the true bread from heaven."

---

[1] Hint: What is the root of this verbal form?

[2] καὶ εἶπεν αὐτῷ ὁ διάβολος· (devil)· σοὶ δώσω τὴν ἐξουσίαν ταύτην ἅπασαν[3] καὶ τὴν δόξαν

αὐτῶν, ὅτι ἐμοὶ παραδέδοται καὶ ᾧ ἐὰν θέλω δίδωμι αὐτήν.

And the devil said to him, "I will give you all this authority

ὁ νόμος διὰ Μωϋσέως ἐδόθη, ἡ χάρις καὶ ἡ ἀλήθεια διὰ Ἰησοῦ Χριστοῦ ἐγένετο.

The law was given through Moses; the grace and truth was through
Jesus Christ

οἱ λοιποὶ ἔμφοβοι (terrified) ἐγένοντο καὶ ἔδωκαν δόξαν τῷ θεῷ τοῦ οὐρανοῦ.

The rest were terrified and gave glory to the God of heaven.

τὰ ῥήματα ἃ ἔδωκάς μοι δέδωκα αὐτοῖς, καὶ αὐτοὶ ἔλαβον καὶ ἔγνωσαν ἀληθῶς (truly) ὅτι

παρὰ σοῦ ἐξῆλθον, καὶ ἐπίστευσαν ὅτι σύ με ἀπέστειλας. The words which you gave me
I have given to them, and they received and truly knew that

came out from you and believed that you sent me.

βλέπετε οὖν πῶς ἀκούετε· ὃς ἂν γὰρ ἔχῃ, δοθήσεται[4] αὐτῷ, καὶ ὃς ἂν μὴ ἔχῃ, καὶ ὃ δοκεῖ ἔχειν

Give attention to / Watch how you are hearing

ἀρθήσεται ἀπ᾽ αὐτοῦ. Then you see how you hear: whoever has, it will be

given to him and whoever does not have, that which he seems to have?
will be taken from him.

εἰ οὖν ὑμεῖς πονηροὶ ὑπάρχοντες οἴδατε δόματα (gifts) ἀγαθὰ διδόναι (to give) τοῖς τέκνοις

ὑμῶν, πόσῳ (how much) μᾶλλον ὁ πατὴρ [ὁ] ἐξ οὐρανοῦ δώσει πνεῦμα ἅγιον τοῖς αἰτοῦσιν

αὐτόν. If you being evil   know to give good gifts to your children, how

much more your Father in heaven will give the Holy Spirit to those who ask for it.

Notice the shift in normal word order all the way through this verse.

ἅπας has the same meaning as πᾶς.

We did not discuss this specific form in the text, but if you learned the rules it should not be a problem for you.

10. διὰ τοῦτο λέγω ὑμῖν ὅτι ἀρθήσεται ἀφ᾽ ὑμῶν ἡ βασιλεία τοῦ θεοῦ καὶ δοθήσεται ἔθνει ποιοῦν·
    τοὺς καρποὺς αὐτῆς. *For this reason I tell you that the kingdom of heaven will be taken from you and will be given to a nation doing its fruits.*

Additional

↓

11. οἱ μὴ πιστεύοντες εἰς τὸν Ἰησοῦν ἀπώλεσαν τοὺς δύο πύργους[5] ἐν τῇ μεγάλῃ πόλει ἵνα πρὸς
    τὴν γῆν πέσωσιν καὶ πολλοὶ ἀποθάνωσιν.

12. τῶν ἀποστόλων εἰς τὸν ὅλον κόσμον ἀπελθόντων πόλλοὶ ὄχλοι τὰς καρδίας αὐτῶν τῷ κυρίῳ
    crowds their hearts to the Lord
    ἔδωκαν διὰ τὸν λόγον τὸν κηρυχθέντα αὐτοῖς.

13. καὶ λαβοῦσα τοῦ καρποῦ αὐτοῦ[6] ἔφαγεν καὶ ἔδωκεν καὶ τῷ ἀνδρὶ αὐτῆς μετ᾽ αὐτῆς καὶ ἔφαγο·
    And she took its fruit and ate and she gave (it) to her husband with her and they ate.

14. καὶ εἶπεν ὁ Ἀδάμ· ἡ γυνή ἣν ἔδωκας μετ᾽ ἐμοῦ αὕτη μοι ἔδωκεν ἀπὸ τοῦ ξύλου[7] καὶ ἔφαγον.
    And Adam said," The woman which you gave me - she gave to me from the tree and I ate."

15. τόπον ἔδωκεν ὁ δεσπότης[8] τοῖς βουλομένοις[9] ἐπιστραφῆναι[10] ἐπ᾽ αὐτόν.
    The master gave the place to those wishing to return to him.

16. καὶ ἔδωκαν κλήρους αὐτοῖς καὶ ἔπεσεν ὁ κλῆρος ἐπὶ Μαθθίαν.
    And they gave them lots and the lot fell on Matthias.

17. εὐλογήσω δὲ αὐτὴν καὶ δώσω σοι ἐξ αὐτῆς τέκνον καὶ εὐλογήσω αὐτόν καὶ ἔσται εἰς ἔθνη κα·
    βασιλεῖς ἐθνῶν ἐξ αὐτοῦ ἔσονται.

18. ᾧ[11] μὲν γὰρ διὰ τοῦ πνεύματος δίδοται λόγος σοφίας, ἄλλῳ δὲ λόγος γνώσεως κατὰ τὸ αὐτὸ
    πνεῦμα. *For to one was given the word of wisdom through the Spirit, to another the word after the same Spirit.*

19. εἶπεν αὐτῷ ὁ θεός· ἀναβλέψας τοῖς ὀφθαλμοῖς σου, ἴδε ἀπὸ τοῦ τόπου οὗ νῦν σὺ εἶ, πρὸς ...
    ἀνατολὰς καὶ θάλασσαν· ὅτι πᾶσαν τὴν γῆν ἣν σὺ ὁρᾷς, σοὶ δώσω αὐτὴν καὶ τῷ σπέρματί σο·
    ἕως αἰῶνος. *God said to him," You will open your eyes, see the place where now you are : that all the land which you see. I will give this to you and your descenda·*

20. τὸν κύριον Ἰησοῦν Χριστόν, οὗ τὸ αἷμα ὑπὲρ ἡμῶν ἐδόθη, ἐντραπῶμεν.[12]
    Let us respect the Lord Jesus Christ, whose blood was given on our behalf.

References

α. 1 Cor 15:38; β. 1 Cor. 12:8; γ. Mk 6:37; δ. Rev 2:21; ε. Mt 24:24; ζ. Jn 17:24; η. Mt 28:18; **1**. Mt 13:11; **2**. Rev 17:1·
3. Jn 6:31-32; **4**. Lk 4:6; **5**. Jn 1:17; **6**. Rev 11:13; **7**. Jn 17:8; **8**. Lk 18:18; **9**. Lk 11:13; **10**. Mt 21:43; **11**. —; **12**. —; **13**. Ge·
3:6; **14**. Gen 3:12; **15**. 1 Clem 7:5; **16**. Ac 1:26; **17**. Gen 17:16; **18**. 1 Cor 12:8; **19**. 1 Clem 10:4; **20**. 1 Clem 21:6.

---

[5] πύργος, -ου, ὁ, *tower.*

[6] This is the third (and last) time you will see this verse. The antecedent of αὐτοῦ is the tree of knowledge of good and evi·

[7] ξύλον, -ου, τό, *wood, tree.*

[8] δεσπότης, -ου, ὁ, *master, lord.*

[9] βούλομαι, *I wish, determine.*

[10] ἐπιστρέφω, *I turn to, return.* It has a second aorist passive, ἐπεστράφην.

[11] ᾧ μέν is used in conjunction with ἄλλῳ δέ to mean "to one ... to another."

[12] ἐντρέπω, *I respect.*

Additional μι Verbs; Nonindicative Forms

Inflected	Person / Case	Number	Tense / Gender	Voice	Mood	Lexical form	Inflected meaning
διδῶ	3	S	P	A	S	δίδωμι	that he she it might give
ἵστησι	3	S	P	A	I	ἵστημι	he she it stands
τίθετε	2	P	P	A	I	τίθημι	you put/place
δεικνύεις	2	S	P	A	I	δείκνυμι	you show/ explain
δῶτε	2	P	A	A	S	δίδωμι	that you might have give—
ἀφῆκας	2	S	A	A	I	ἀφίημι	you let go left permitted
ἐτέθη	3	S	A	A	I	τίθημι	he/she/it put placed
ἀναστήσομεν	1	P	F	A	I	ἀνίστημι	we will rise
διδότω	3	S	P	A	Imp	δίδωμι	let him/her/it give!
ἑσταμένου	G	S	N/M	M/P	Part	ἵστημι	of being stood

cause this is the last chapter without further chapters to help review this chapter, we have included more ex-
cises. It is well worth your time to work through all of them.

μηδὲ δίδοτε τόπον.   Don't give (the) place!

ὃ ἐὰν δοθῇ ὑμῖν ἐν ἐκείνῃ τῇ ὥρᾳ   whatever he might give you in that hour

δότε αὐτοῖς ὑμεῖς φαγεῖν.   Give them (something) to eat.

δοῦναι τὴν ψυχήν   to give life

διὰ πνεύματος ἁγίου τοῦ δοθέντος ἡμῖν   through the Holy Spirit which is given to us.

πῶς οὖν σταθήσεται ἡ βασιλεία αὐτοῦ;   Then how will his kingdom be established?

ἴδε ὁ τόπος ὅπου ἔθηκαν αὐτόν.   See the place where they laid him.

Translation

1. δίδοτε, καὶ δοθήσεται ὑμῖν.

   Give, and it will be given to you.

2. θήσω τὸ πνεῦμά μου ἐπ᾽ αὐτόν.

   I will place my Spirit on him

3. ἀπεκρίθησαν οὖν οἱ Ἰουδαῖοι καὶ εἶπαν αὐτῷ· τί σημεῖον δεικνύεις ἡμῖν ὅτι ταῦτα ποιεῖς;

   Then the Jews answered and said to him, "(by) what sign do you explain to us that you do these things?"

4. [1] Ταῦτα ἐλάλησεν Ἰησοῦς, καὶ ἐπάρας[2] τοὺς ὀφθαλμοὺς αὐτοῦ εἰς τὸν οὐρανὸν εἶπεν· πάτερ

   ἐλήλυθεν ἡ ὥρα· δόξασόν σου τὸν υἱόν, ἵνα ὁ υἱὸς δοξάσῃ σέ, καθὼς ἔδωκας αὐτῷ ἐξουσίαν

   πάσης[3] σαρκός, ἵνα πᾶν ὃ δέδωκας αὐτῷ δώσῃ αὐτοῖς ζωὴν αἰώνιον.

   Jesus said these things, and lifting his eyes to heaven said,

   "Father, the hour has come: they will glorify your Son, that the Son glorifies you,

   even as you gave him authority over all flesh, that all that you have

   given him gives them eternal life."

5. χάρις ὑμῖν καὶ εἰρήνη ἀπὸ[4] θεοῦ πατρὸς ἡμῶν καὶ κυρίου Ἰησοῦ Χριστοῦ τοῦ δόντος ἑαυτὸν

   ὑπὲρ τῶν ἁμαρτιῶν ἡμῶν. Grace to you and peace from God our Father

   and Jesus Christ who gave himself on behalf of

   ~~over~~ our sins.

---

[1]   Diagramming this verse will help.

[2]   ἐπαίρω, "I lift up," a compound verb formed from ἐπί and αἴρω.

[3]   The genitive case here signifies the sense of "over all."

[4]   Notice that ἀπό is not repeated before κυρίου. This is exegetically significant and present in Paul's salutations. If Paul thought of "God" and the "Lord" as two different entities, he would have had to repeat the preposition. The fact that he doesn't shows that he views both as the same entity. It is probably pushing the grammar too far to say that Paul equates Jesus and God, but it does show that Paul views them working in absolute harmony with each other, both being the single agent of grace and peace to the Galatians.

Τότε παραλαμβάνει (he/she/it took) αὐτὸν ὁ διάβολος (devil) εἰς τὴν ἁγίαν πόλιν καὶ ἔστησεν αὐτὸν ἐπὶ τὸ πτερύγιον (highest point) τοῦ ἱεροῦ. Then the devil took him into the holy city and stood him on the highest point of the temple.

Ἐγώ εἰμι ὁ ποιμὴν (shepherd) ὁ καλός· ὁ ποιμὴν ὁ καλὸς τὴν ψυχὴν αὐτοῦ τίθησιν ὑπὲρ τῶν προβάτων (sheep). I am the good shepherd: the good shepherd puts his life in behalf of his sheep.

ἔγραψεν δὲ καὶ τίτλον (inscription) ὁ Πιλᾶτος καὶ ἔθηκεν ἐπὶ τοῦ σταυροῦ (cross)· ἦν δὲ γεγραμμένον, Ἰησοῦς ὁ Ναζωραῖος ὁ βασιλεὺς τῶν Ἰουδαίων. Pilate wrote an inscription and placed it on the cross: and it had been written Jesus the Nazarite the King of the Jews

εἰ οὖν ὑμεῖς πονηροὶ ὄντες οἴδατε δόματα (gifts) ἀγαθὰ διδόναι τοῖς τέκνοις ὑμῶν, πόσῳ (how much) μᾶλλον ὁ πατὴρ ὑμῶν ὁ ἐν τοῖς οὐρανοῖς δώσει ἀγαθὰ τοῖς αἰτοῦσιν αὐτόν.[5] If you being evil know to give good gifts to your children, how much more our Father who is in heaven will give good things to those who ask for them.

εἰπέ μοι ποῦ (where) ἔθηκας αὐτόν, κἀγὼ αὐτὸν ἀρῶ. Tell me where you put him, and I will raise him up.

τὸν ἄρτον ἡμῶν τὸν ἐπιούσιον[6] δίδου. Give us our daily bread.

καὶ ἔστησαν ἐπὶ τοὺς πόδας αὐτῶν, καὶ φόβος μέγας ἐπέπεσεν[7] ἐπὶ τοὺς θεωροῦντας αὐτούς. And they stood on their feet and a great fear fell upon the ones looking at them.

In case this seems familiar, we translated its Lukan parallel (11:13) in the previous chapter.

ἐπιούσιον never occurs anywhere in Greek literature, except in discussions of this passage. It is therefore very difficult to define precisely. Guesses include "daily," "sufficient for today," "sufficient for tomorrow," and "day by day."

ἐπιπίπτω, *I fall upon.*

13. ἰδοὺ ἕστηκα[8] ἐπὶ τὴν θύραν (door) καὶ κρούω (I knock)· ἐάν τις ἀκούσῃ τῆς φωνῆς μου καὶ

    ἀνοίξῃ τὴν θύραν, [καὶ] εἰσελεύσομαι πρὸς αὐτὸν καὶ δειπνήσω (I will eat) μετ᾽ αὐτοῦ καὶ αὐτὸ•

    μετ᾽ ἐμοῦ. Behold I stand at the door and Knock: whoever hears my

    voice and opens the door

    and I will eat with him and he with me.

14. οὕτως γὰρ ἐντέταλται (he/she/it has commanded) ἡμῖν ὁ κύριος· τέθεικά σε εἰς φῶς ἐθνῶν τοῦ

    εἶναί σε εἰς σωτηρίαν (salvation) ἕως ἐσχάτου τῆς γῆς.

    For thus the Lord has commanded us : I have taken you into the

    light of nations which is

15. ἐθεάσαντο (they saw) τὸ μνημεῖον (tomb) καὶ ὡς ἐτέθη τὸ σῶμα αὐτοῦ.

    They saw the tomb and   how   his body was placed.

16. ἐζήτουν αὐτὸν εἰσενεγκεῖν (to bring) καὶ θεῖναι[9] [αὐτὸν] ἐνώπιον αὐτοῦ.

    They were seeking to bring him   and place it before him.

17. τρέχει (he/she/it runs) οὖν καὶ ἔρχεται πρὸς Σίμωνα Πέτρον καὶ πρὸς τὸν ἄλλον μαθητὴν ὃν

    ἐφίλει[10] ὁ Ἰησοῦς καὶ λέγει αὐτοῖς· ἦραν τὸν κύριον ἐκ τοῦ μνημείου (tomb) καὶ οὐκ οἴδαμεν

    ποῦ ἔθηκαν αὐτόν. Then she runs and goes to Simon Peter and to the

    disciple whom Jesus loved and says to them," They took the Lord

    out of the tomb and we do not know where they put him."

---

[8]   In the perfect, ἵστημι can have a present meaning.

[9]   Hint: Identify the root, and remember that the stem vowel can change.

[10] φιλέω means "I love." In classical Greek it actually referred to the highest form of love, but it eventually became assoc•
      ated with a kiss. In John's gospel, φιλέω and ἀγαπάω are synonyms, but in later Christian writings, φιλέω has been almo•
      entirely replaced by ἀγαπάω.

. δι᾽ οὗ καὶ τὴν προσαγωγὴν (access) ἐσχήκαμεν [τῇ πίστει] εἰς τὴν χάριν ταύτην ἐν ᾗ ἑστήκαμεν

καὶ καυχώμεθα (we boast) ἐπ᾽ ἐλπίδι τῆς δόξης τοῦ θεοῦ.

to this grace in which we stood

and we boast on the basis of the glory of God.

. Ταῦτα δὲ αὐτῶν λαλούντων αὐτὸς ἔστη ἐν μέσῳ αὐτῶν καὶ λέγει αὐτοῖς· εἰρήνη ὑμῖν.

Saying these things to them, he stood on the middle of
them and said to them, "Peace to you."

. [11] οὐχ ὑμεῖς με ἐξελέξασθε (you choose), ἀλλ᾽ ἐγὼ ἐξελεξάμην (I chose) ὑμᾶς καὶ ἔθηκα ὑμᾶς ἵνα

ὑμεῖς ὑπάγητε καὶ καρπὸν φέρητε καὶ ὁ καρπὸς ὑμῶν μένῃ, ἵνα ὅ τι ἂν αἰτήσητε τὸν πατέρα ἐν

τῷ ὀνόματί μου δῷ ὑμῖν. *You did not choose me, but I chose you and put you*
that you might depart and bear fruit and your fruit might remain,
that whoever

. εἶπεν δὲ πρὸς αὐτούς· οὐχ ὑμῶν[12] ἐστιν γνῶναι χρόνους ἢ καιροὺς οὓς ὁ πατὴρ ἔθετο[13] ἐν τῇ

ἰδίᾳ ἐξουσίᾳ. *And he said to them, "It is not for you to know the time or*
the age

. ἀπεκρίθη αὐτοῖς ὁ Ἰωάννης λέγων· ἐγὼ βαπτίζω ἐν ὕδατι· μέσος ὑμῶν ἕστηκεν ὃν ὑμεῖς οὐκ

οἴδατε. *John answered them saying, "I baptize in water; the one whom you*
do not know stood in your midst."

. μείζονα ταύτης ἀγάπην οὐδεὶς ἔχει, ἵνα τις τὴν ψυχὴν αὐτοῦ θῇ[14] ὑπὲρ τῶν φίλων (friends)

αὐτοῦ. *Greater love has noone than this, that someone put his*
life on behalf of his friends.

Does the scope of Jesus' saying apply only to the disciples or to all believers? Don't let your theology answer this one; stick with the text.

You can insert a "for" before ὑμῶν in this context.

τίθημι has the same basic meaning in the middle as it does in the active.

Hint: There is no reduplication, there is no augment, and θῇ occurs in a ἵνα clause.

24. τῷ δὲ θεῷ χάρις τῷ διδόντι ἡμῖν τὸ νῖκος (victory) διὰ τοῦ κυρίου ἡμῶν Ἰησοῦ Χριστοῦ.

But grace to God who gives us the victory through our Lord Jesus Christ.

25. εἰ δὲ καὶ ὁ σατανᾶς ἐφ᾽ ἑαυτὸν διεμερίσθη (he/she/it is divided), πῶς σταθήσεται ἡ βασιλεία αὐτοῦ; ὅτι λέγετε ἐν Βεελζεβοὺλ ἐκβάλλειν με τὰ δαιμόνια.

But if Satan is divided from himself, how does his kingdom stand? Since you say Beelzebub casts out demons (in my name)

26. If we stand in the way of sinners, we will not receive the grace of God
Additional but will perish in eternal fire.

26. ἐὰν ἱστῶμεν ἐπὶ τῇ ὁδῷ τῶν ἁμαρτανόντων, οὐ δεξόμεθα τὴν χάριν τοῦ θεοῦ ἀλλ᾽ ἀπολεσόμεθα ἐν τῷ αἰωνίῳ πυρί.

27. ἐπεὶ γινώσκομεν νῦν τὴν Ἑλληνικὴν[15] γλῶσσαν, ἀνοίξαντες τὴν καινὴν διαθήκην[16] διδασκώμεθα νῦν κηρύσσειν τοὺς λόγους τῆς ἀληθείας. Since we now know the Greek langu upon opening the New Testament now we will be taught to preach the words of truth.

28. καὶ ἔθετο αὐτοὺς ὁ θεὸς ἐν τῷ στερεώματι[17] τοῦ οὐρανοῦ, ὥστε φαίνειν ἐπὶ τῆς γῆς καὶ ἄρχειν τῆς ἡμέρας καὶ τῆς νυκτὸς καὶ διαχωρίζειν (to divide) ἀνὰ μέσον[18] τοῦ φωτὸς καὶ ἀνὰ μέσον τοῦ σκότους, καὶ εἶδεν ὁ θεὸς ὅτι καλόν.

29. καὶ εἶπεν ὁ Ἀδάμ· ἡ γυνή ἣν ἔδωκας μετ᾽ ἐμοῦ αὕτη μοι ἔδωκεν ἀπὸ τοῦ ξύλου καὶ ἔφαγον.

And Adam said, "The woman which you gave me, she gave to me from the tree and I ate."

30. καὶ ἔχθραν (enmity) θήσω ἀνὰ μέσον σου καὶ ἀνὰ μέσον τῆς γυναικὸς καὶ ἀνὰ μέσον τοῦ σπέρματός σου καὶ ἀνὰ μέσον τοῦ σπέρματος αὐτῆς, αὐτός σου τηρήσει κεφαλήν καὶ σὺ τηρήσεις αὐτοῦ πτέρναν.[19] And I will put enmity between you and the woman and between your seed and hers, he will crush your head and you will strike his heel.

Summary

1. When you find a preposition — noun — καί — noun construction, the single preposition "governs" the two nouns and shows you that the author thinks of them as a unit.

References

α. (Eph 4:27); β. Mk 13:11; γ. Mt 14:16; δ. Mt 20:28; ε. Rom 5:5; ζ. Mt 12:26; η. Mk 16:6; 1. Lk 6:38; 2. Mt 12:18; 3. 2:18; 4. Jn 17:1-2; 5. Gal 1:3-4; 6. Mt 4:5; 7. Jn 10:11; 8. Jn 19:19; 9. Mt 7:11; 10. Jn 20:15; 11. Lk 11:3; 12. Rev 11:1 13. Rev 3:20; 14. Ac 13:47; 15. Lk 23:55; 16. Lk 5:18; 17. Jn 20:2; 18. Rom 5:2; 19. Lk 24:36; 20. Jn 15:16; 21. Ac 1: 22. Jn 1:26; 23. Jn 15:13; 24. 1 Cor 15:57; 25. Lk 11:18; 26. —; 27. —; 28. Gen 1:17-18; 29. Gen 3:12; 30. Gen 3:15.

28. And God was putting them in the firmament of heaven, so that to shine on the earth and begin the day and the night and to divide between the light and the darkness, and God saw that it was good.

[15] Ἑλληνικός, -ή, -όν, *Greek.*

[16] διαθήκη, -κης, ἡ, *covenant, testament.*

[17] στερέωμα, -ματος, τό, *firmament.*

[18] ἀνὰ μέσον is an idiom that means *between.*

[19] πτέρνη, -ης, ἡ, *heel.*

Review #7

rammar

What is the basic significance of the tenses in non-indicative moods?   con tingency

What are the two ways a subjunctive verb is used in independent clauses?

a. hortatory = Let us ———!

b. deliberative = a question whose answer is uncertain

What are the two ways a subjunctive verb is used in dependent clauses?

a. ἵνα + subj. = purpose / in order that

b. ἐάν + subj = conditional statement
   forms the protasis in a ⬏

What are the two kinds of third class conditional sentences? How can you tell them apart?

a. future more probable

b. present general → verb in apodosis must be in present tense

How do you translate the following prepositions when they are used with an articular infinitive?

a. διά   because

b. εἰς   in order that
                        } purpose
c. πρός   in order that

What are the three ways in which you can indicate purpose with an infinitive?

a. articular infinitive w/ εἰς or πρός

b. articular infinitive w/ article in the genitive

c. the infinitive w/o preposition or article

7. What are the five ways to state a prohibition and other types of negation, and what are the nuances of ea

a. οὐ + indicative   simple negation

b. μή + present imperative   prohibition of a continuous action

c. μή + aorist Imperative   prohibition prohibition of a

d. μή + aorist subjunctive   stronger negation than a)

e. οὐ μή + aorist subjunctive   "by no means" "NOT" strongest negation of a future action

8. What are the five μι verb rules?

a. μι verbs reduplicate their initial stem letter to form the present and separate the reduplicated consonant with ι

b. μι verbs generally do not use a thematic connecting vowel

c. μι verbs use 3 different personal endings in the present active indicative

d. the stem vowels of μι verbs can ablaut

e. most μι verbs use κα as the tense formative in the aorist tense

Parsing

1. ποίησθε 2nd person plural future middle indicative
   You will do on behalf of yourselves

2. πιστεύειν present active infinitive   to believe

3. ἔρχηται 3rd person singular present middle subjuntive
   that he/she/it might go

4. γράψαι 3rd person singular future active indicative
   He/she/it will write

5. κρινέτωσαν 3rd person plural ~~aorist passive subjunctive~~ present active imperative
   that they might be answered   let them judge

6. ἔλθωμεν 1st person plural aorist active subjunctive
   that we might go

7. δίδωσι 3rd person singular present active indicative   he/she/it gives

8. ἀπεστάλθαι 2nd person singular perfect middle/passive indicative 2nd perfect
   you have been sent OR aorist middle infinitive

9. δέδωκεν 3rd person singular perfect active indicative
   He/she/it has given

10. παρακάλεσαι 2nd person singular perfect middle/passive indicative

τίθεμεν   *1st person plural   present active indicative   We put/place*

ἱστᾶσαι   *2nd person singular   aorist imperative   stand!*

Translation: Matthew 13:1-23

13.1 Ἐν τῇ ἡμέρᾳ ἐκείνῃ ἐξελθὼν ὁ Ἰησοῦς τῆς οἰκίας ἐκάθητο παρὰ τὴν θάλασσαν· 13.2 καὶ
On that day Jesus, ~~was~~ going out of the house, was sitting alongside of the sea.
(after)

νήχθησαν πρὸς αὐτὸν ὄχλοι πολλοί, ὥστε αὐτὸν εἰς πλοῖον ἐμβάντα καθῆσθαι, καὶ πᾶς ὁ ὄχλος
d many crowds were gathered to him, so that he embarked into the boat   *and all the*
in order to sit

ι τὸν αἰγιαλὸν[1] εἱστήκει (he/she/it stood).
owd stood on the shore.

13.3 Καὶ ἐλάλησεν αὐτοῖς πολλὰ ἐν παραβολαῖς λέγων· ἰδοὺ ἐξῆλθεν ὁ σπείρων τοῦ σπείρειν.
~~was speaking~~
And he ~~spoke~~ many things to them in parables, saying, "Behold, the sower ~~came~~ out to sow
Spoke   *went*   *sow*

· καὶ ἐν τῷ σπείρειν αὐτὸν ἃ[2] μὲν ἔπεσεν παρὰ τὴν ὁδόν, καὶ ἐλθόντα τὰ πετεινὰ κατέφαγεν αὐτά.
and as he was sowing, some fell along the way, and the birds came & ate them up.

ἄλλα δὲ ἔπεσεν ἐπὶ τὰ πετρώδη[3] ὅπου οὐκ εἶχεν γῆν πολλήν, καὶ εὐθέως ἐξανέτειλεν[4] διὰ τὸ μὴ
Some fell on the rocky where they did not have much soil, and they immediately   *from the earth*
ecause it did not have depth of soil.   Genitive Absolute   *sprang up*

ειν βάθος[5] γῆς· 13.6 ἡλίου δὲ ἀνατείλαντος[6] ἐκαυματίσθη[7] καὶ διὰ τὸ μὴ ἔχειν ῥίζαν ἐξηράνθη.
aving no depth.   And the sun coming up burned up and becaused it had no root it dried up.
After the sun rose, it was scorched

ἄλλα δὲ ἔπεσεν ἐπὶ τὰς ἀκάνθας, καὶ ἀνέβησαν αἱ ἄκανθαι καὶ ἔπνιξαν[8] αὐτά. 13.8 ἄλλα δὲ
But some fell among the thorns and the thorns came up and choked them. But ___ fell

εσεν ἐπὶ τὴν γῆν τὴν καλὴν καὶ ἐδίδου καρπόν, ὃ μὲν ἑκατόν, ὃ δὲ ἑξήκοντα,[9] ὃ δὲ τριάκοντα.
on the good soil and was giving fruit, some 100, some 60, some 30.

ὁ ἔχων ὦτα ἀκουέτω. *The one having ears, let him hear.*

13.10 Καὶ προσελθόντες οἱ μαθηταὶ εἶπαν αὐτῷ· διὰ τί ἐν παραβολαῖς λαλεῖς αὐτοῖς; 13.11 ὁ δὲ
nd going forth   the disciples said to him, "Why do you speak in parables?"
                                                             to them

οκριθεὶς εἶπεν αὐτοῖς· ὅτι ὑμῖν δέδοται γνῶναι τὰ μυστήρια τῆς βασιλείας τῶν οὐρανῶν,
d answering, he said to them, "   to you it is given to know the mysteries
of the kingdom of heaven."

αἰγιαλός - οῦ, ὁ, shore, beach.

The combinations of ὃς μέν, ὁ δέ, and ἄλλα δέ can be translated as "some."

πετρώδης, -ες, rocky, stony.

ἐξανατέλλω, I spring up.

βάθος, -ους, τό, depth.

ἀνατέλλω, I rise, spring up, dawn.

καυματίζω, I scorch, burn up.

πνίγω, I choke.

ἑξήκοντα, sixty.

ἐκείνοις δὲ οὐ δέδοται. 13.12 ὅστις γὰρ ἔχει, δοθήσεται αὐτῷ καὶ περισσευθήσεται· ὅστις δὲ οὐκ ἔχε
*has not been given   For whoever has, it will be given to him and he will be abounded
to them.*

καὶ ὃ ἔχει ἀρθήσεται ἀπ᾽ αὐτοῦ. 13.13 διὰ τοῦτο ἐν παραβολαῖς αὐτοῖς λαλῶ, ὅτι βλέποντες οὐ
*but whoever has not, that which he has   For this reason I speak to them in parables, since
will be taken from him.*

βλέπουσιν καὶ ἀκούοντες οὐκ ἀκούουσιν οὐδὲ συνίουσιν,[10] 13.14 καὶ ἀναπληροῦται[11] αὐτοῖς ἡ
seeing, they do not see, and hearing, they do not hear and they do not understand. And

προφητεία Ἠσαΐου ἡ λέγουσα·
to them is fulfilled the prophecy of Isaiah, which says:

      ἀκοῇ ἀκούσετε καὶ οὐ μὴ συνῆτε,
      Hearing you will hear   and you will NOT understand.

            καὶ βλέποντες βλέψετε καὶ οὐ μὴ ἴδητε.
            and   seeing you will see   and you will NOT see.

            13.15 ἐπαχύνθη[12] γὰρ ἡ καρδία τοῦ λαοῦ τούτου,
      For the heart of this people became dull

                  καὶ τοῖς ὠσὶν βαρέως[13] ἤκουσαν
                  and their ears heard with difficulty

                  καὶ τοὺς ὀφθαλμοὺς αὐτῶν ἐκάμμυσαν,[14]
                  and they closed their eyes

      μήποτε ἴδωσιν τοῖς ὀφθαλμοῖς
      lest they see with their eyes

            καὶ τοῖς ὠσὶν ἀκούσωσιν
            and ~~their ears will~~ hear with their ears

            καὶ τῇ καρδίᾳ συνῶσιν καὶ ἐπιστρέψωσιν
                              and will return

            καὶ ἰάσομαι αὐτούς.
            And I will heal them.

13.16 ὑμῶν δὲ μακάριοι οἱ ὀφθαλμοὶ ὅτι βλέπουσιν καὶ τὰ ὦτα ὑμῶν ὅτι ἀκούουσιν. 13.17 ἀμὴν γὰρ
And blessed are your eyes which see and your ears which see. For truly

λέγω ὑμῖν ὅτι πολλοὶ προφῆται καὶ δίκαιοι ἐπεθύμησαν ἰδεῖν ἃ βλέπετε καὶ οὐκ εἶδαν, καὶ
I tell you that many prophets and righteous people

---

[10] Hint: This is from συνίημι, a word occurring elsewhere in this passage.

[11] ἀναπληρόω, *I fulfill.*

[12] παχύνω, *I make dull, calloused.* Passive: *I become dull.*

[13] βαρέως, *with difficulty.*

[14] καμμύω, *I close.*

:ούσαι ἃ ἀκούετε καὶ οὐκ ἤκουσαν.

hear what you hear and they did not hear

13.18 Ὑμεῖς οὖν ἀκούσατε τὴν παραβολὴν τοῦ σπείραντος. 13.19 παντὸς ἀκούοντος τὸν λόγον

Therefore you will hear the parable of the sower. All hearing the word of the

ς βασιλείας καὶ μὴ συνιέντος ἔρχεται ὁ πονηρὸς καὶ ἁρπάζει τὸ ἐσπαρμένον ἐν τῇ καρδίᾳ αὐτοῦ,

ingdom and not understanding the evil man goes and seized the____ in his heart

τός ἐστιν ὁ παρὰ τὴν ὁδὸν σπαρείς. 13.20 ὁ δὲ ἐπὶ τὰ πετρώδη σπαρείς, οὗτός ἐστιν ὁ τὸν λόγον

is is the one which falls alongside And the one falling on this is the one hearing the
the road. rocky soil

:ούων καὶ εὐθὺς μετὰ χαρᾶς λαμβάνων αὐτόν, 13.21 οὐκ ἔχει δὲ ῥίζαν ἐν ἑαυτῷ ἀλλὰ

rd and immediately with joy receiving it, does not have roots in itself but

όσκαιρός[15] ἐστιν, γενομένης δὲ θλίψεως ἢ διωγμοῦ διὰ τὸν λόγον εὐθὺς σκανδαλίζεται. 13.22 ὁ δὲ

temporary, on account of the word and is immediately caused to sin.

; τὰς ἀκάνθας σπαρείς, οὗτός ἐστιν ὁ τὸν λόγον ἀκούων, καὶ ἡ μέριμνα[16] τοῦ αἰῶνος καὶ ἡ

he one falling in the thorns, this is the one hearing the word and anxiety of the age

:άτη[17] τοῦ πλούτου συμπνίγει[18] τὸν λόγον καὶ ἄκαρπος[19] γίνεται. 13.23 ὁ δὲ ἐπὶ τὴν καλὴν γῆν

deceitfulness of wealth chokes the word and it becomes barren. And the one that

αρείς, οὗτός ἐστιν ὁ τὸν λόγον ἀκούων καὶ συνιείς, ὃς δὴ[20] καρποφορεῖ[21] καὶ ποιεῖ ὃ μὲν ἑκατόν,

lls on good earth, this is the one hearing the word and understanding, which indeed

δὲ ἑξήκοντα, ὃ δὲ τριάκοντα.

d bears fruit, one a hundred, one sixty, and one thirty.

πρόσκαιρος, -ον, *temporary, transitory.*

μέριμνα, -ης, ἡ, *anxiety, worry.*

ἀπάτη, -ης, ἡ, *deceitfulness.*

συμπνίγω, *I choke.*

This word is formed with an alpha privative. What do you think it means?

δή, *indeed.*

καρποφορέω, *I produce a crop, bear fruit.*

Here is a famous Greek scholar who spent too much time studying and not enough time playing.

Present Active Indicative

arsing

Inflected	Person / Case	Number	Tense / Gender	Voice	Mood	Lexical form	Inflected meaning
λέγουσιν							
ἔχει							
πιστεύομεν							
λύεις							
ἀκούω							
βλέπουσι							
ἔργοις							
λέγετε							
λύει							
0. πιστεύεις							

arm-up

πιστεύω.

τὴν φωνὴν αὐτοῦ ἀκούεις.

πιστεύετε εἰς τὸν θεὸν.

τὸ πρόσωπον τοῦ ἀγαπητοῦ μου βλέπουσιν.

τότε ἀκούομεν τὸν νόμον μετὰ χαρᾶς.

τὸν δὲ νόμον τοῦ κυρίου οὐ λύετε.

βλέπει τὸν Ἰησοῦν.

Translation

1. τὴν ἀγάπην τοῦ θεοῦ οὐκ ἔχετε.

2. ὁ Πέτρος λέγει αὐτῷ· σὺ εἶ ὁ χριστός.

3. σὺ πιστεύεις εἰς τὸν υἱὸν τοῦ ἀνθρώπου;

4. ἐξουσίαν ἔχει ὁ υἱὸς τοῦ ἀνθρώπου ἀφιέναι (to forgive) ἁμαρτίας.

5. βλέπω Τωβιαν τὸν υἱόν μου.

6. εἶπεν αὐτοῖς ὁ Ἰησοῦς ... νῦν δὲ λέγετε ὅτι βλέπομεν.

7. οὐκ ἀκούετε, ὅτι ἐκ τοῦ θεοῦ οὐκ ἐστέ.

λέγουσιν τῷ τυφλῷ πάλιν (again)· τί (what) σὺ λέγεις περὶ[1] αὐτοῦ;

καὶ εἶπεν Δαυὶδ πρὸς Σαούλ· τί (why) ἀκούεις τῶν λόγων τοῦ ὄχλου;

). ὀφθαλμοὶ (eyes) αὐτοῖς[2] καὶ οὐ βλέπουσιν, ὦτα (ears) αὐτοῖς καὶ οὐκ ἀκούουσιν.

dditional

. ὅτι ἐν τῷ οἴκῳ ἐστὶν ὁ Ἰησοῦς, οἱ ὄχλοι ἀκούουσιν τῶν λόγων τοῦ θεοῦ καὶ οἱ τυφλοὶ βλέπουσιν.

. τὴν χαρὰν τοῦ κυρίου ἐν ταῖς καρδίαις τῶν ἀγαπητῶν βλέπεις;

. καὶ εἶπεν κύριος πρὸς Μωϋσῆν· τί (why?) οὐ πιστεύουσίν μοι ἐν πᾶσιν (all) τοῖς σημείοις[3] οἷς (that) βλέπουσιν ἐν αὐτοῖς;

. σὺ γὰρ ζωῆς καὶ θανάτου ἐξουσίαν ἔχεις.

. καὶ ἀκούουσιν οἱ ἀδελφοὶ αὐτοῦ καὶ ὁ οἶκος τοῦ πατρὸς (father) αὐτοῦ καὶ καταβαίνουσιν[4] πρὸς αὐτόν.

. ἀπὸ δὲ καρποῦ τοῦ ξύλου ὅ (which) ἐστιν ἐν μέσῳ τοῦ παραδείσου[5] εἶπεν ὁ θεός· οὐ φάγεσθε (you will eat) ἀπ᾽ αὐτοῦ.

. ἐγὼ δὲ ὅτι τὴν ἀλήθειαν λέγω, οὐ πιστεύετέ μοι.

. ἀλλὰ διὰ τῆς χάριτος (grace) τοῦ κυρίου Ἰησοῦ πιστεύομεν σωθῆναι (that we are saved).

. τότε λέγει αὐτῷ ὁ Πιλᾶτος· οὐκ[6] ἀκούεις πόσα (how many things) σου καταμαρτυροῦσιν;[7]

περί is a preposition meaning "about" that takes its object in the genitive.

You may need to be a little idiomatic in your translation of this dative.

σημεῖον, -ου, τό, *sign, miracle*.

καταβαίνω, *I go down, come down*.

παράδεισος, -ου, ὁ, *paradise*.

The οὐκ shows that the speaker anticipates a positive answer. This is discussed in detail in §31.19.

καταμαρτυρέω, *I testify against*. Takes a direct object in the genitive.

20. Ἰησοῦς δὲ ἔκραξεν (he/she/it cried out) καὶ εἶπεν· ὁ πιστεύων (one who believes) εἰς ἐμὲ οὐ πιστεύει εἰς ἐμὲ ἀλλὰ εἰς τὸν πέμψαντά (one who sent) με.

English to Greek

1. they say

2. you (plural) have

3. we believe

4. he sees

5. you (singular) hear

References

α. Mk 9:24; β. Jn 3:8; γ. Jn 14:1; δ. —; ε. —; ζ. —; η. Jn 1:29; **1**. Jn 5:42; **2**. Mk 8:29; **3**. Jn 9:35; **4**. Mk 2:10; **5**. Tob 11:1
6. Jn 9:41; **7**. Jn 8:47; **8**. (Jn 9:17); **9**. (1 Sam 24:10); **10**. Jer 5:21; **11**. —; **12**. —; **13**. (Num 14:11); **14**. Wsd 16:1
15. 1 Sam 22:1; **16**. Gen 3:3; **17**. Jn 8:45; **18**. Ac 15:11; **19**. (Mt 27:13); **20**. Jn 12:44.

Contract Verbs

arsing

Inflected	Person / Case	Number	Tense / Gender	Voice	Mood	Lexical form	Inflected meaning
λαλοῦμεν							
ἀγαπῶσι							
τηρῶ							
πληροῦτε							
ζητοῦσιν							
ἀγαπᾷ							
καλεῖς							
πληροῖ							
δαιμόνια	–						
0. ποιεῖ							

Warm-up

οὐ λαλῶ.

ἁμαρτίαν οὐ ποιεῖς.

αὐτοὺς ἀγαπῶσιν.

τὰς ἐντολὰς αὐτοῦ τηροῦμεν.

Ἰησοῦν ζητεῖτε.

Δαυὶδ καλεῖ αὐτὸν.

λέγουσιν γὰρ καὶ οὐ ποιοῦσιν.

Translation

1. ὁ πατὴρ (father) ἀγαπᾷ τὸν υἱόν.

2. οὐκ ἀνθρώποις λαλεῖ ἀλλὰ θεῷ.

3. οἶδα αὐτὸν καὶ τὸν λόγον αὐτοῦ τηρῶ.

4. οὐ γὰρ οἴδασιν τί (what) ποιοῦσιν.

5. Τί (why?) δέ με (me) καλεῖτε· κύριε, κύριε, καὶ οὐ ποιεῖτε ἃ (what) λέγω;

6. ἐκ τοῦ κόσμου λαλοῦσιν καὶ ὁ κόσμος αὐτῶν ἀκούει.

7. οἴδαμεν ὅτι μεταβεβήκαμεν (we have passed) ἐκ τοῦ θανάτου εἰς τὴν ζωήν, ὅτι ἀγαπῶμεν τοὺς
   ἀδελφούς (brothers).

λέγει τῷ Σίμωνι Πέτρῳ ὁ Ἰησοῦς· Σίμων Ἰωάννου,[1] ἀγαπᾷς με;[2]

λέγει οὖν αὐτῷ ὁ Πιλᾶτος· ἐμοὶ[3] οὐ λαλεῖς; οὐκ οἶδας ὅτι ἐξουσίαν ἔχω;

). σὺ πιστεύεις ὅτι εἷς (one) ἐστιν ὁ θεός, καλῶς (well) ποιεῖς· καὶ τὰ δαιμόνια πιστεύουσιν καὶ φρίσσουσιν (they tremble).

dditional

1. τοὺς νόμους καὶ τὰς ἐντολὰς τηροῦμεν, ὅτι ἀγαπῶμεν τὸν κύριον καὶ πιστεύομεν εἰς τὸν υἱὸν τοῦ θεοῦ.

2. ἐν τῇ πρώτῃ ἡμέρᾳ τοῦ σαββάτου τὸν λόγον τοῦ θεοῦ λαλῶ τοῖς πιστοῖς.

3. ἀκούεις μου, Ἰακώβ, καὶ Ἰσραήλ, ὃν (whom) ἐγὼ καλῶ· ἐγώ εἰμι πρῶτος καὶ ἐγώ εἰμι εἰς τὸν αἰῶνα.[4]

4. οὐ λαλεῖ περὶ[5] ἐμοῦ καλά ἀλλὰ ... κακά.

5. λέγει δὲ κύριος· ἰδού (behold), ποιῶ τὰ ἔσχατα ὡς (like) τὰ πρῶτα.

6. εἰ οὖν Δαυὶδ καλεῖ αὐτὸν κύριον, πῶς υἱὸς αὐτοῦ ἐστιν;

7. ὁ μὴ ἀγαπῶν (one who loves) με τοὺς λόγους μου οὐ τηρεῖ· καὶ ὁ λόγος ὃν (that) ἀκούετε οὐκ ἔστιν ἐμὸς ἀλλὰ τοῦ ... πατρός.[6]

The word that Ἰωάννου would normally be modifying has been left out. It would specify the relationship between Σίμων and Ἰωάννου.

με is the accusative of ἐγώ.

ἐμοι is the dative of ἐγώ.

εἰς τὸν αἰῶνα is an idiom meaning "forever."

περί is a preposition meaning, in this case, "concerning," and takes its object in the genitive.

πατρός means "Father" and is genitive.

18. καὶ κατεδίωξεν[7] αὐτὸν Σίμων καὶ οἱ μετ᾽ αὐτοῦ, καὶ εὗρον (they found) αὐτὸν καὶ λέγουσιν αὐτῷ ὅτι πάντες (all) ζητοῦσίν σε.

19. οἱ μαθηταὶ λέγουσιν αὐτῷ· διὰ τί[8] ἐν παραβολαῖς λαλεῖς αὐτοῖς;

20. ὁ δοῦλος οὐκ οἶδεν τί (what) ποιεῖ αὐτοῦ ὁ κύριος.

Summary

1. διὰ τί means "Why?" (sentence 19).

References

α. Jn 14:10; β. (1 Jn 3:9); γ. Lk 6:32; δ. 1 Jn 3:22; ε. Mk 16:6; ζ. Mt 22:45; η. Mt 23:3; **1.** Jn 3:35; **2.** 1 Cor 14:2; **3.** Jn 8:5 **4.** Lk 23:34; **5.** Lk 6:46; **6.** 1 Jn 4:5; **7.** 1 Jn 3:14; **8.** Jn 21:15; **9.** Jn 19:10; **10.** Jas 2:19; **11.** —; **12.** —; **13.** (Isa 48:1 **14.** (1 Kgs 22:8); **15.** Barn 6:13; **16.** Mt 22:45; **17.** Jn 14:24; **18.** Mk 1:36-37; **19.** (Mt 13:10); **20.** Jn 15:15.

---

[7] κατεδίωξεν means "he/she/it sought intently." It describes a searching done in earnest. How does knowing this help yo better understand the passage?

κατά is often used to form a compound verb, and carries with it an intensifying force. It is called the "perfective" use the preposition. For example, ἐργάζομαι means "I work" while κατεργάζομαι means "I work out thoroughly, I accor plish." ἐσθίω means "I eat" while κατεσθίω means "I eat up thoroughly, I devour." Likewise, διώκω means "I search fo while καταδιώκω means "I search for thoroughly, I seek intently." (For other examples of the perfective use of prepo tions see *Metzger*, 81-85.) There is a danger here, though. You cannot always assume that a compound word carries t meaning of its parts. That is called the "Root Fallacy" (see Carson, *Exegetical Fallacies*). Sometimes a compound verb h the same meaning as the simple form of the verb. As always, let context be your guide.

[8] διὰ τί is an idiom meaning "Why?" but you could probably guess from the meaning of the two words.

Present Middle/Passive Indicative

arsing

Inflected	Person / Case	Number	Tense / Gender	Voice	Mood	Lexical form	Inflected meaning
ἀκούεται							
λύεσθε							
ἔρχομαι							
ἀποκρίνεται							
πορεύονται							
ἔρχεσθε							
ἀποκρίνῃ							
συνάγει							
ἀγαπώμεθα							
0. δύνανται							

arm-up

συνάγεται πρὸς αὐτὸν ὄχλος.

ἔρχεται εἰς οἶκον.

καλεῖται Βηθλέεμ.

λέγουσιν αὐτῷ· ἐρχόμεθα.

ὁ δὲ Ἰησοῦς ἀποκρίνεται αὐτοῖς.

ἔρχονται πρὸς τὸν Ἰησοῦν.

καὶ πορεύεσθε εἰς τὸν τόπον.

Translation

The non-deponent verbs we know occur rarely in the middle or passive in the New Testament (and even the LXX), and hence the paucity of examples below. δύναμαι and ἔρχομαι are common deponents.

1. Καὶ συνάγονται οἱ ἀπόστολοι πρὸς τὸν Ἰησοῦν.

2. λέγουσιν αὐτῷ· δυνάμεθα.

3. Τότε ἔρχεται μετ᾽ αὐτῶν ὁ Ἰησοῦς.

4. ὅπου εἰμὶ ἐγὼ ὑμεῖς (you) οὐ δύνασθε ἐλθεῖν (to go).

5. πορεύομαι ἑτοιμάσαι (to prepare) τόπον ὑμῖν (for you).

6. νῦν δὲ πρὸς σὲ (you) ἔρχομαι καὶ ταῦτα (these things) λαλῶ ἐν τῷ κόσμῳ.

7. μὴ γὰρ ἐκ τῆς Γαλιλαίας ὁ χριστὸς ἔρχεται;

λέγει αὐτοῖς ὁ Ἰησοῦς· πιστεύετε ὅτι δύναμαι τοῦτο ποιῆσαι (to do); λέγουσιν αὐτῷ· ναί (yes).

καὶ γὰρ ἐγὼ ἄνθρωπός εἰμι ὑπὸ ἐξουσίαν, καὶ λέγω τούτῳ (to this one)· πορεύθητι (go!), καὶ πορεύεται, καὶ ἄλλῳ· ἔρχου (come!), καὶ ἔρχεται, καὶ τῷ δούλῳ μου· ποίησον (do!) τοῦτο, καὶ ποιεῖ.

. καὶ εἶπεν αὐτῇ ὁ ἄγγελος κυρίου· Ἁγὰρ ... πόθεν (from where?) ἔρχῃ καὶ ποῦ (where?) πορεύῃ· καὶ εἶπεν· ἀπὸ προσώπου Σάρας τῆς κυρίας.[1]

dditional

. εἰς τὴν οἰκίαν ἐρχόμεθα, οἴδαμεν γὰρ ὅτι ὁ Ἰησοῦς τοῖς ὄχλοις ἐκεῖ (there) λαλεῖ.

. ὁ δὲ Ἰησοῦς ἀποκρίνεται τοῖς πονηροῖς ὅτι ὑπὸ τῶν πιστῶν ἀγαπᾶται.

. καὶ ἔρχονται οἱ ἄγγελοι εἰς τὸν τόπον ἐκεῖνον[2] καὶ λαλοῦσιν τοὺς λόγους εἰς τὰ ὦτα[3] τοῦ ὄχλου.

. οὐκ εἰσὶν λόγοι ὅτι οὐκ ἀκούονται αἱ φωναὶ αὐτῶν.

. γενεὰ[4] πορεύεται καὶ γενεὰ ἔρχεται καὶ ἡ γῆ[5] εἰς τὸν αἰῶνα ἕστηκεν (he/she/it remains).

You should be able to guess what this word means based on its gender.

ἐκεῖνος, -η, -ο, *that, those.*

οὖς, ὠτός, τό, *ear.*

γενεά, -ᾶς, ἡ, *generation.*

16. καρδίᾳ γὰρ πιστεύεται εἰς δικαιοσύνην, στόματι[6] δὲ ὁμολογεῖται εἰς σωτηρίαν.

17. καὶ εἶπεν ὁ ἀνὴρ ὁ πρεσβύτης· ποῦ πορεύῃ καὶ πόθεν ἔρχῃ;

18. τί οὗτος οὕτως λαλεῖ; βλασφημεῖ· τίς δύναται ἀφιέναι (to forgive) ἁμαρτίας εἰ μὴ εἷς ὁ θεός;

19. πιστεύονται τὰ ἔργα τοῦ σατανᾶ, κοσμῷ λύεται δὲ ἡ κακὴ ζῶν αὐτοῦ τῷ Ἰησοῦ.

20. καὶ εἶπεν αὐτῷ Ναθαναήλ· ἐκ Ναζαρὲτ δύναταί τι (what) ἀγαθὸν εἶναι (to come);

References

α. Mk 4:1; β. Mk 3:20; γ. Lk 2:4; δ. Jn 21:3; ε. Jn 12:23; ζ. Mk 5:15; η. 1 Sam 29:10; **1.** Mk 6:30; **2.** Mt 20:22; **3.** Mt 26:3○
4. Jn 7:34; **5.** Jn 14:2; **6.** Jn 17:13; **7.** Jn 7:41; **8.** Mt 9:28; **9.** Lk 7:8; **10.** Gen 16:8; **11.** —; **12.** —; **13.** (1 Sam 11:4); **14.** (F
19:3 [LXX 18:4]); **15.** Eccl 1:4; **16.** Rom 10:10; **17.** Judg 19:17; **18.** Mk 2:7; **19.** —; **20.** Jn 1:46.

---

[5]   γῆ, γῆς, ἡ, *earth, land.*

[6]   στόματι is the dative singular of the word meaning "mouth."

Imperfect Indicative

arsing

Inflected	Person / Case	Number	Tense / Gender	Voice	Mood	Lexical form	Inflected meaning
. ἐπίστευες							
. ἠκούετε							
. ἠκολουθοῦμεν							
. ἤρχετο							
. ἐπορεύοντο							
. ἐπληροῦ							
. ἐδιδάσκετε							
. ἐπορευόμην							
. περιεπάτει							
10. ἐπηρώτων							

Warm-up

. ἐζητοῦμεν αὐτόν.

. ἐποίεις τὸν κόσμον.

. ἠκολούθουν αὐτῷ.

. οἱ Φαρισαῖοι ἔβλεπον πρὸς αὐτόν.

. ἐγὼ δὲ ... ἠρχόμην ἐκ Μεσοποταμίας.

. ἐπορεύοντο καὶ ἐλάλουν.

. οἱ νόμοι τοῦ θεοῦ ὑπὸ τοῦ Ἰησοῦ ἐποιοῦντο.

Translation

1. αὐτὸς ἐδίδασκεν[1] ἐν ταῖς συναγωγαῖς αὐτῶν.

2. ἐποίει ὡς ἤθελε.

3. ὁ ἄνθρωπος υἱὸς[2] θεοῦ ἦν.

4. παραβολαῖς πολλαῖς (many) ἐλάλει αὐτοῖς τὸν λόγον καθὼς ἠδύναντο ἀκούειν (to listen).

5. καὶ αὐτὴ ἐλάλει ἐν τῇ καρδίᾳ αὐτῆς ... καὶ φωνὴ αὐτῆς οὐκ ἠκούετο.

6. ὁ ... Πέτρος ἐτηρεῖτο ἐν τῇ φυλακῇ (prison).

---

[1] It is permissable to add the word "began" before your translation of the imperfect if it fits the context. This is a special use of the tense called the "inceptive imperfect" that emphasizes the beginning of an action.

[2] The Roman centurion is speaking. Are you going to put "the" in front of this word?

ἠγάπα[3] δὲ ὁ Ἰησοῦς τὴν Μάρθαν καὶ τὴν ἀδελφὴν[4] αὐτῆς καὶ τὸν Λάζαρον.

[5] ἠρώτων αὐτὸν οἱ περὶ (around) αὐτὸν σὺν (with) τοῖς δώδεκα (twelve) τὰς παραβολάς.

λέγει αὐτοῖς ὁ Ἰησοῦς· εἰ τέκνα (children) τοῦ Ἀβραάμ ἐστε, τὰ ἔργα τοῦ Ἀβραὰμ ἐποιεῖτε.[6]

0. Καὶ μετὰ ταῦτα[7] περιεπάτει ὁ Ἰησοῦς ἐν τῇ Γαλιλαίᾳ· οὐ γὰρ ἤθελεν ἐν τῇ Ἰουδαίᾳ (Judea)

περιπατεῖν (to walk), ὅτι ἐζήτουν αὐτὸν οἱ Ἰουδαῖοι (Jews) ἀποκτεῖναι (to kill).

Additional

1. ἐν ταῖς ἡμέραις τοῦ Ἰησοῦ οἱ πονηροὶ δαιμονίοις ἠκολούθουν ἀλλὰ οἱ ἀγαθοὶ τῷ κυρίῳ.

2. οἱ δὲ ἄγγελοι ἤκουον τοῦ ἀποστόλου, ἐδίδασκεν γὰρ τοὺς Φαρισαίους ἐν τῇ συναγωγῇ.

3. καὶ ἔλεγον· ἀγαθὴ ἡ γῆ (land).

4. οἱ Λευῖται ἐδίδασκον τὸν νόμον κυρίου.

5. ὁ ὄχλος ἤρχετο πρὸς αὐτόν, καὶ ἐδίδασκεν αὐτούς.

6. καὶ ἐπορεύεσθε ὀπίσω θεῶν ἀλλοτρίων.

Why is this verb in this tense?

Note the gender. ἀδελφή occurs twenty-six times in the New Testament, but it is easy to remember.

Hint: Locate the subject; it is a phrase.

This is what is called a "conditional sentence," which is an "if … then …" construction. It is also a special type of conditional sentence called "contrary to fact," where the speaker knows that the "if" clause is not true. In Classical Greek, a contrary to fact condition that related to a present situation had an imperfect tense in the "if" clause and an imperfect in the "then" clause. (Sentence 9 here, however, has a present tense in the "if" clause.) In English, we form this type of conditional sentence in the "then" clause using "would." We will discuss conditional sentences in detail in §31.14.

ταῦτα is the accusative plural neuter of οὗτος.

17. ὅτε ἤμην νήπιος, ἐλάλουν ὡς νήπιος.

18. ἐπηρώτα αὐτὸν καὶ λέγει αὐτῷ· σὺ εἶ ὁ χριστὸς ὁ υἱὸς τοῦ εὐλογητοῦ;

19. Ἀγαπητοί, οὐκ ἐντολὴν καινὴν γράφω ὑμῖν (to you) ἀλλ᾽ ἐντολὴν παλαιὰν ἣν (that) εἴχετε ἀπ᾽ ἀρχῆς.

20. καὶ εὐθὺς τοῖς σάββασιν[8] εἰσελθὼν (after entering) εἰς τὴν συναγωγὴν ἐδίδασκεν.

Summary

1. The imperfect can be used to emphasize the beginning of an action ("inceptive imperfect"). You can add th word "began" to your translation.

2. In Classical Greek, a contrary to fact condition that related to a present situation had an imperfect tense i both the "if" and "then" clauses. In English, we form this type of conditional sentence in the "then" claus using "would" and the imperfect will not be translated as past continuous

References

α. (Lk 2:48); β. Wsd 9:9; γ. Mk 2:15; δ. —; ε. Gen 48:7; ζ. 2 Kgs 2:11; η. —; **1.** Lk 4:15; **2.** Dan 8:4; **3.** Mk 15:39; **4.** M 4:33; **5.** 1 Sam 1:13; **6.** Ac 12:5; **7.** Jn 11:5; **8.** Mk 4:10; **9.** Jn 8:39; **10.** Jn 7:1; **11.** —; **12.** —; **13.** Dt 1:25; **14.** 1 Esdr 9:48 **15.** Mk 2:13; **16.** Jer 7:9; **17.** 1 Cor 13:11; **18.** Mk 14:61; **19.** 1 Jn 2:7; **20.** Mk 1:21.

---

[8] Treat this word as if it were σάββατοις. It will make sense in chapter 10 (i.e., it uses a third declension ending in the dative plural).

Review #3 — Track 2

rammar

Define the following three aspects, clearly differentiating among them.

a. Continuous

b. Undefined

c. Punctiliar

Write out the twelve forms of λύω, present active and passive.

	active		*passive*
1st sg		*1st sg*	
2nd sg		*2nd sg*	
3rd sg		*3rd sg*	
1st pl		*1st pl*	
2nd pl		*2nd pl*	
3rd pl		*3rd pl*	

Write out the Master Verb Chart

Tense	*Aug/Redup*	*Tense stem*	*Tense formative*	*Conn. vowel*	*Personal endings*	*First singular*
Pres act						
Pres mid/pas						
Imperf act						
Imperf mid/pas						

4. What are "The Big Five" contraction rules?

    a.

    b.

    c.

    d.

    e.

5. What vowels form the following contractions?

    a. ει

    b. ει

    c. α

    d. ου

    e. ου

    f. ου

    g. ω

6. How do you form the following English tenses with the verb "eat"?

    a. present active continuous

    b. present passive punctiliar

7. Define what a "deponent" verb is and give one example.

8. When are primary and secondary endings used?

    a. Primary:

    b. Secondary:

9. What are the three basic rules of augmentation?

    a. Verbs beginning with a consonant:

    b. Verbs beginning with a vowel:

    c. Verbs beginning with a diphthong:

rsing

ἀκούετε

ἤθελεν

πορεύεται

ἀγαθαί

πιστεύει

εἶχεν

τηροῦμαι

ἐδίδασκεν

ἠρώτουν

). ἀγαπῶμεν

ι. ἐδύνατο

2. λαλῶ

3. περιπατοῦμεν

4. πληροῖ

5. ἤρχοντο

ranslation: 1 John 1:5-2:5

1:5 Καὶ ἔστιν αὕτη (this) ἡ ἀγγελία[1] ἣν (which) ἀκηκόαμεν (we have heard) ἀπ᾽ αὐτοῦ καὶ

ἀναγγέλλομεν[2] ὑμῖν (to you), ὅτι ὁ θεὸς φῶς[3] ἐστιν καὶ σκοτία ἐν αὐτῷ οὐκ ἔστιν οὐδεμία (none).

6 Ἐὰν εἴπωμεν (we say) ὅτι κοινωνίαν ἔχομεν μετ᾽ αὐτοῦ καὶ ἐν τῷ σκότει (darkness) περιπατῶμεν

(we are walking), ψευδόμεθα[4] καὶ οὐ ποιοῦμεν τὴν ἀλήθειαν· 1:7 ἐὰν δὲ ἐν τῷ φωτὶ περιπατῶμεν ὡς

ἀγγελία, -ας, ἡ, message.
ἀναγγέλλω, I proclaim.
φῶς means "light." Its dative form is coming up: φωτί.

αὐτός ἐστιν ἐν τῷ φωτί, κοινωνίαν ἔχομεν μετ᾽ ἀλλήλων καὶ τὸ αἷμα Ἰησοῦ τοῦ υἱοῦ αὐτοῦ

καθαρίζει⁵ ἡμᾶς (us) ἀπὸ πάσης ἁμαρτίας. ¹:⁸ ἐὰν εἴπωμεν (we say) ὅτι ἁμαρτίαν οὐκ ἔχομεν,

ἑαυτοὺς (ourselves) πλανῶμεν⁶ καὶ ἡ ἀλήθεια οὐκ ἔστιν ἐν ἡμῖν (us). ¹:⁹ ἐὰν ὁμολογῶμεν (we confes

τὰς ἁμαρτίας ἡμῶν (our), πιστός ἐστιν καὶ δίκαιος, ἵνα ἀφῇ (he/she/it will forgive) ἡμῖν τὰς

ἁμαρτίας καὶ καθαρίσῃ (he/she/it will cleanse) ἡμᾶς ἀπὸ πάσης ἀδικίας. ¹:¹⁰ ἐὰν εἴπωμεν (we say

ὅτι οὐχ ἡμαρτήκαμεν (we have sinned), ψεύστην ποιοῦμεν αὐτὸν καὶ ὁ λόγος αὐτοῦ οὐκ ἔστιν ἐν

ἡμῖν.

2:1 Τεκνία⁷ μου, ταῦτα (these things) γράφω⁸ ὑμῖν (to you) ἵνα μὴ ἁμάρτητε (you might sin). κ

ἐάν τις (someone) ἁμάρτῃ (he/she/it sins), παράκλητον⁹ ἔχομεν πρὸς τὸν πατέρα (father) Ἰησοῦν

Χριστὸν δίκαιον· ²:² καὶ αὐτὸς ἱλασμός¹⁰ ἐστιν περὶ τῶν ἁμαρτιῶν ἡμῶν, οὐ περὶ τῶν ἡμετέρων¹

δὲ μόνον ἀλλὰ καὶ περὶ ὅλου¹² τοῦ κόσμου.

2:3 Καὶ ἐν τούτῳ (this) γινώσκομεν ὅτι ἐγνώκαμεν (we have known) αὐτόν, ἐὰν τὰς ἐντολὰς

αὐτοῦ τηρῶμεν. ²:⁴ ὁ λέγων (one who says) ὅτι ἔγνωκα (I have known) αὐτὸν καὶ τὰς ἐντολὰς αὐτοῦ

μὴ τηρῶν (is keeping), ψεύστης ἐστὶν καὶ ἐν τούτῳ¹³ ἡ ἀλήθεια οὐκ ἔστιν· ²:⁵ ὃς (who) δ᾽ ἂν τηρῇ

(he/she/it is keeping) αὐτοῦ τὸν λόγον, ἀληθῶς ἐν τούτῳ ἡ ἀγάπη τοῦ θεοῦ τετελείωται (he/she/it

has been perfected), ἐν τούτῳ γινώσκομεν ὅτι ἐν αὐτῷ ἐσμεν.

---

⁴   ψεύδομαι, *I lie.*

⁵   καθαρίζω, *I cleanse.*

⁶   πλανάω, *I deceive.*

⁷   τεκνίον, -ου, τό, *little child.*

⁸   γράφω, *I write.*

⁹   παράκλητος, -ου, ὁ, *mediator, intercessor, helper.*

¹⁰ ἱλασμός, -οῦ, ὁ, *expiation, atoning sacrifice.*

¹¹ ἡμέτερος, -α, -ον, *our.*

¹² ὅλος, -η, -ον, *whole.* A peculiarity of this adjective is that it occurs in the predicate position when it is functioning as a attributive.

¹³ τούτῳ is the dative of οὗτος. In this case it is masculine. Its next occurrence is neuter.

Third Declension

ite out the master paradigm of all case endings.

	masc	fem	neut		masc/fem	neut
n sg						
n sg						
t sg						
c sg						

	masc	fem	neut		masc/fem	neut
m pl						
n pl						
t pl						
c pl						

rsing

Inflected	Person / Case	Number	Tense / Gender	Voice	Mood	Lexical form	Inflected meaning
σαρκί							
πάσας							
σῶμα							
σαρξί							
πνεύματα							
ἕνα							
πᾶσιν							
σάρκες							
τίνας							
. οὐδένα							

Warm-up

α. πάντες ἔρχονται πρὸς αὐτόν.

β. διὰ τὸ ὄνομα μου

γ. τὴν σάρκα τοῦ υἱοῦ τοῦ ἀνθρώπου

δ. εἰς ὄνομα προφήτου

ε. Οὐ περὶ πάντων ... λέγω.

ζ. τινὰς ἐξ αὐτῶν

η. οὐδὲν ἀποκρίνῃ τί οὗτοι λέγουσιν;

Translation

1. πάντα δὲ ποιῶ διὰ τὸ εὐαγγέλιον.

2. ἔλεγεν περὶ τοῦ ναοῦ (temple) τοῦ σώματος αὐτοῦ.

3. πνεῦμα σάρκα καὶ ὀστέα (bones) οὐκ ἔχει.

4. τὸ γεγεννημένον[1] ἐκ τῆς σαρκὸς σάρξ ἐστιν, καὶ τὸ γεγεννημένον ἐκ τοῦ πνεύματος πνεῦμά ἐστιν.

5. ἀποκατήλλαξεν (he/she/it has reconciled) ἐν τῷ σώματι τῆς σαρκὸς αὐτοῦ διὰ τοῦ θανάτου.

6. τί με λέγεις ἀγαθόν; οὐδεὶς ἀγαθὸς εἰ μὴ εἷς ὁ θεός.

---

[1] τὸ γεγεννημένον means "that which has been born."

οὐκ ἐστὲ ἐν σαρκὶ ἀλλὰ ἐν πνεύματι, εἴπερ (if) πνεῦμα θεοῦ οἰκεῖ (he/she/it dwells) ἐν ὑμῖν (you). εἰ δέ τις πνεῦμα Χριστοῦ οὐκ ἔχει, οὗτος οὐκ ἔστιν αὐτοῦ.

ἔλεγον οὖν ἐκ τῶν Φαρισαίων τινές· οὐκ ἔστιν οὗτος παρὰ θεοῦ ... ὅτι τὸ σάββατον οὐ τηρεῖ.

Ἀγαπητοί, μὴ παντὶ πνεύματι πιστεύετε[2] ἀλλὰ δοκιμάζετε (test!) τὰ πνεύματα εἰ ἐκ τοῦ θεοῦ ἐστιν.... ἐν τούτῳ (this) γινώσκετε (you know) τὸ πνεῦμα τοῦ θεοῦ· πᾶν πνεῦμα ὃ (that) ὁμολογεῖ (he/she/it confesses) Ἰησοῦν Χριστὸν ἐν σαρκὶ ἐληλυθότα (has come) ἐκ τοῦ θεοῦ ἐστιν, καὶ πᾶν πνεῦμα ὃ μὴ ὁμολογεῖ τὸν Ἰησοῦν[3] ἐκ τοῦ θεοῦ οὐκ ἔστιν·[4] καὶ τοῦτό ἐστιν τὸ[5] τοῦ ἀντιχρίστου (antichrist), ὃ (which) ἀκηκόατε (you heard) ὅτι ἔρχεται, καὶ νῦν ἐν τῷ κόσμῳ ἐστὶν ἤδη.[6]

οἶδά σε (you) τίς εἶ, ὁ ἅγιος τοῦ θεοῦ.

πιστεύετε is actually an imperative stating a command, even though it looks just like an indicative.

Remember we said earlier that when there are two parallel thoughts, the author feels free to omit some of the words in the second phrase. They are assumed from the first phrase.

This heresy John is refuting became known as "docetism," formed from the Greek word δοκέω that means to "think," "appear," "seem." Docetism taught that Christ only appeared to be human. People have always had trouble understanding the Incarnation, and fortunately the church condemned docetism.

Because of the parallel structure of these verse, John in typical fashion has omitted the word that you would normally expect after τό. Do you know what that word would be? Hint: It must be neuter singular because of the article, but you knew that.

Right! πνεῦμα.

Notice how Greek can pile up adverbs to intensify their significance (νῦν ... ἤδη).

Additional

11. πάντες οἱ πιστοὶ σὺν τῷ κυρίῳ περιπατοῦσιν δία τὸν θάνατον τοῦ υἱοῦ τοῦ θεοῦ.

12. ὁ δὲ θεὸς οἶδεν τὰ ὀνόματα τῶν ἁγίων καὶ καλεῖ τοὺς ἀγαπητοὺς αὐτοῦ εἰς τὴν βασιλείαν το Χρίστου.

13. ὁ γὰρ λαλῶν (one who speaks) γλώσσῃ⁷ οὐκ ἀνθρώποις λαλεῖ ἀλλὰ θεῷ· οὐδεὶς γὰρ ἀκούει, πνεύματι δὲ λαλεῖ μυστήρια.⁸

14. τοῦτο νῦν ... σὰρξ ἐκ τῆς σαρκὸς μου.

15. ἐγὼ καὶ ὁ πατὴρ ἕν ἐσμεν.

16. οἴδαμεν ὅτι οἶδας πάντα.

17. τοῖς πᾶσιν γέγονα (I have become) πάντα.⁹

18. λέγει αὐτῷ [ὁ] Ἰησοῦς· ἐγώ εἰμι ἡ ὁδὸς καὶ ἡ ἀλήθεια καὶ ἡ ζωή· οὐδεὶς ἔρχεται πρὸς τὸν πατέρα (father) εἰ μὴ δι᾽ ἐμοῦ.

19. οὐκέτι λέγω ὑμᾶς (you) δούλους, ὅτι ὁ δοῦλος οὐκ οἶδεν τί ποιεῖ αὐτοῦ ὁ κύριος.

20. λέγει αὐτῷ ὁ Πιλᾶτος· τί ἐστιν ἀλήθεια; ... καὶ λέγει αὐτοῖς· ἐγὼ οὐδεμίαν εὑρίσκω ἐν αὐτῷ αἰτίαν.

References

α. Jn 3:26; β. Mt 10:22; γ. Jn 6:53; δ. Mt 10:41; ε. Jn 13:18; ζ. Rom 11:14; η. (Mt 26:62); **1.** 1 Cor 9:23; **2.** Jn 2:21; **3.** I 24:39; **4.** Jn 3:6; **5.** Col 1:22; **6.** Mk 10:18; **7.** Rom 8:9; **8.** (Jn 9:16); **9.** 1 Jn 4:1-3; **10.** Lk 4:34; **11.** —; **12.** —; **13.** 1 C 14:2; **14.** 1 Clem 6:3; **15.** Jn 10:30; **16.** Jn 16:30; **17.** 1 Cor 9:22; **18.** Jn 14:6; **19.** Jn 15:15; **20.** Jn 18:38.

---

⁷ γλῶσσα, -ης, ἡ, *tongue, language.*

⁸ μυστήριον, -ου, τό, *mystery.*

⁹ Hint: The first πᾶς is masculine and the second is neuter.

First and Second Person Personal Pronouns

rsing

Inflected	Person / Case	Number	Tense / Gender	Voice	Mood	Lexical form	Inflected meaning
σοι							
ἡμῶν							
ὑμεῖς							
ἐλπίδα							
σε							
χάριτας							
ἡμᾶς							
πίστεως							
ὑμῖν							
πατρός							

arm-up

οὐκ οἶδα ὑμᾶς.

σὺ ἔρχῃ πρός με;

ἔχετε πίστιν;

ἐν τῷ ὀνόματι τοῦ πατρός μου

διὰ πίστεως γὰρ περιπατοῦμεν.

ὑμεῖς ἐστε τὸ φῶς τοῦ κόσμου.

οὐδὲν ἀποκρίνῃ;

Translation

1. ἀπεκρίθη Θωμᾶς καὶ εἶπεν αὐτῷ· ὁ κύριός μου καὶ ὁ θεός μου.

2. Παῦλος ἀπόστολος Χριστοῦ Ἰησοῦ κατ᾽ ἐπιταγὴν (command) θεοῦ σωτῆρος (savior) ἡμῶν κο
   Χριστοῦ Ἰησοῦ τῆς ἐλπίδος ἡμῶν.

3. Παῦλος καὶ Σιλουανὸς καὶ Τιμόθεος τῇ ἐκκλησίᾳ Θεσσαλονικέων ἐν θεῷ πατρὶ ἡμῶν καὶ
   κυρίῳ Ἰησοῦ Χριστῷ.

4. λέγω δὲ ὑμῖν ὅτι οὐδὲ Σολομὼν ἐν πάσῃ τῇ δόξῃ αὐτοῦ περιεβάλετο (he/she/it was clothed) ὡς
   τούτων (of these).

5. οὐ τὸ ἔργον μου ὑμεῖς ἐστε ἐν κυρίῳ;[1]

6. μισθὸν (reward) οὐκ ἔχετε παρὰ τῷ πατρὶ ὑμῶν τῷ ἐν τοῖς οὐρανοῖς.

7. Δικαιωθέντες (having been justified) οὖν ἐκ πίστεως εἰρήνην (peace) ἔχομεν πρὸς τὸν θεὸν διὰ τ
   κυρίου ἡμῶν Ἰησοῦ Χριστοῦ.

---

[1] The οὐ beginning this sentence is the Greek way of saying that the speaker expects the answer to be "Yes." We will
cuss this in detail in chapter 31.

ποιεῖτε τὰ ἔργα τοῦ πατρὸς ὑμῶν. εἶπαν (they said) [οὖν] αὐτῷ ... ἕνα πατέρα ἔχομεν τὸν θεόν.

καὶ εὑρεθῶ (I may be found) ἐν αὐτῷ, μὴ ἔχων (having) ἐμὴν δικαιοσύνην (righteousness) τὴν ἐκ νόμου ἀλλὰ τὴν διὰ πίστεως Χριστοῦ, τὴν ἐκ θεοῦ δικαιοσύνην ἐπὶ τῇ πίστει.

ἰδοὺ ἡ μήτηρ σου καὶ οἱ ἀδελφοί σου [καὶ αἱ ἀδελφαί[2] σου] ἔξω ζητοῦσίν σε. καὶ ἀποκριθεὶς (answering) αὐτοῖς λέγει· τίς ἐστιν ἡ μήτηρ μου καὶ οἱ ἀδελφοί [μου]; ... ἴδε ἡ μήτηρ μου καὶ οἱ ἀδελφοί μου. ὃς (who) [γὰρ] ἂν ποιήσῃ (he/she/it does) τὸ θέλημα τοῦ θεοῦ, οὗτος (this one) ἀδελφός μου καὶ ἀδελφὴ καὶ μήτηρ ἐστίν.

dditional

ὅτι ὁ πατὴρ καὶ ἡ μήτηρ ἡμῶν ἡμᾶς ἀγαπῶσιν, δυνάμεθα χαρὰν ἐν ταῖς καρδίαις ἡμῶν εὑρίσκειν (to find).

ἐπὶ τῇ ἡμέρᾳ οἱ ἄνδρες πορεύονται πρὸς τοὺς τόπους τοῦ ἔργου καὶ ἐπὶ τῇ νυκτὶ ἔρχονται εἰς τοὺς οἴκους αὐτῶν.

Τίμα (Honor!) τὸν πατέρα σου καὶ τὴν μητέρα σου.

Οὐ πᾶς ὁ λέγων[3] μοι· κύριε[4] κύριε, εἰσελεύσεται (he/she/it will enter) εἰς τὴν βασιλείαν τῶν οὐρανῶν, ἀλλ᾽ ὁ ποιῶν (one who is doing) τὸ θέλημα τοῦ πατρός μου τοῦ ἐν τοῖς οὐρανοῖς.

This actual word does not occur fifty or more times; but by knowing that it follows natural gender, you should be able to determine its meaning.

In this context, ὁ λέγων together mean "the one who says."

Do you recognize the case ending? You shouldn't. It is the vocative, the fifth and final case, which we will meet in chapter 13. It is used when addressing a person directly. Translate it as "Lord."

15. εἷς γάρ ἐστιν ὑμῶν ὁ διδάσκαλος,[5] πάντες δὲ ὑμεῖς ἀδελφοί ἐστε.

16. ἀπεκρίθη αὐτοῖς ὁ Ἰησοῦς· εἶπον (I told) ὑμῖν καὶ οὐ πιστεύετε. τὰ ἔργα ἃ (that) ἐγὼ ποιῶ ἐν 1 ὀνόματι τοῦ πατρός μου ταῦτα (these things) μαρτυρεῖ[6] περὶ ἐμοῦ. ἀλλὰ ὑμεῖς οὐ πιστεύετε, ὅ οὐκ ἐστὲ ἐκ τῶν προβάτων τῶν ἐμῶν.

17. Εὐχαριστῶ τῷ θεῷ μου ... ἀκούων (because I hear of) σου τὴν ἀγάπην καὶ τὴν πίστιν, ἣν (whic ἔχεις πρὸς τὸν κύριον Ἰησοῦν καὶ εἰς πάντας τοὺς ἁγίους.

18. Πάντα μοι παρεδόθη (they were given) ὑπὸ τοῦ πατρός μου, καὶ οὐδεὶς ἐπιγινώσκει[7] τὸν υἱὸν μὴ ὁ πατήρ, οὐδὲ τὸν πατέρα τις ἐπιγινώσκει εἰ μὴ ὁ υἱός.

19. καὶ ἐπηρώτα αὐτόν· τί ὄνομά σοι; καὶ λέγει αὐτῷ· Λεγιὼν ὄνομά μοι, ὅτι πολλοί ἐσμεν.

20. πέντε γὰρ ἄνδρας ἔσχες (you have had) καὶ νῦν ὃν (whom) ἔχεις οὐκ ἔστιν σου ἀνήρ.

English to Greek

Every once in a while I have found it helpful to go English to Greek. Personal pronouns are important and qu easy. It is especially good to confirm that you understand the different forms of the English pronouns.

1. to me   6. to you (plural)

2. our   7. I

3. us   8. your

4. you   9. we

5. my   10. you (plural)

References

α. Mt 25:12; β. Mt 3:14; γ. Mk 4:40; δ. Jn 5:43; ε. 2 Cor 5:7; ζ. Mt 5:14; η. Mt 26:62; **1**. Jn 20:28; **2**. 1 Tim 1:1; **3**. 2 1:1; **4**. Mt 6:29; **5**. 1 Cor 9:1; **6**. Mt 6:1; **7**. Rom 5:1; **8**. Jn 8:41; **9**. Phil 3:9; **10**. Mk 3:32-35; **11**. —; **12**. —; **13**. Mk 7: **14**. Mt. 7:21; **15**. Mt 23:8; **16**. Jn 10:25-26; **17**. Phlm 1:4-5; **18**. Mt 11:27; **19**. Mk 5:9; **20**. Jn 4:18.

---

[5] διδάσκαλος, -ου, ὁ, *teacher*.

[6] μαρτυρέω, *I witness*. Why is the verb singular but the subject plural? What does this tell you about the author's inte (See 1 Jn 4:1-4 in exercise 10 for the discussion of the grammatical construction.)

[7] ἐπιγινώσκω, *I know*. ἐπιγινώσκω can describe a more complete knowledge than does γινώσκω, or the process of comin know.

Exercise 12 — Track 2

αὐτός

Inflected	Person / Case	Number	Tense / Gender	Voice	Mood	Lexical form	Inflected meaning
αὐτό							
αὐτοῦ							
σοι							
αὐτήν							
ἐμοῦ							
αὐτῷ							
ἡμῖν							
θανάτου							
αὐτῆς							
ὑμῶν							

arm-up

αὐτός ἐστιν Ἠλίας.

ἐγὼ δὲ οἶδα αὐτήν.

καὶ αὐτὸς ἐπηρώτα αὐτούς.

ἡ αὐτὴ σάρξ

ἐν αὐτῇ τῇ ὥρᾳ

ὁ διδάσκαλος αὐτῶν ἐστιν μαθητὴς αὐτοῦ.

αὐτὸς Δαυὶδ εἶπεν ἐν τῷ πνεύματι τῷ ἁγίῳ.

Translation

1. καὶ εὐθὺς λέγουσιν αὐτῷ περὶ αὐτῆς.

2. καὶ λέγει αὐτοῖς· τίνα ζητεῖτε;

3. καὶ γὰρ ποιεῖτε αὐτὸ εἰς πάντας τοὺς ἀδελφούς.

4. Οὐκ ἔστιν μαθητὴς ὑπὲρ τὸν διδάσκαλον οὐδὲ δοῦλος ὑπὲρ τὸν κύριον αὐτοῦ.

5. [1] οὐ πᾶσα σὰρξ ἡ αὐτὴ σάρξ.

6. λέγουσιν οὖν τῷ τυφλῷ πάλιν· τί σὺ λέγεις περὶ αὐτοῦ, ὅτι ἠνέῳξέν (he/she/it opened) σου τοὺ ὀφθαλμούς; ὁ δὲ εἶπεν ὅτι προφήτης ἐστίν.

7. αὐτὸ τὸ πνεῦμα συμμαρτυρεῖ (he/she/it witnesses with) τῷ πνεύματι ἡμῶν ὅτι ἐσμὲν τέκνα θεοὶ

---

[1] This sentence is a little tricky. You will have to supply a verb. What is the subject?

[2] τὰ αὐτὰ γὰρ ἐποίουν τοῖς προφήταις οἱ πατέρες αὐτῶν.

αὐτὸς δὲ Ἰησοῦς οὐκ ἐπίστευεν[3] αὐτὸν αὐτοῖς.

καὶ πολλοὶ ἦλθον (they came) πρὸς αὐτὸν καὶ ἔλεγον ὅτι Ἰωάννης μὲν σημεῖον ἐποίησεν

(he/she/it did) οὐδέν, πάντα δὲ ὅσα εἶπεν Ἰωάννης περὶ τούτου (him) ἀληθῆ (true) ἦν.

dditional

καλὸς διδάσκαλος τοῖς αὐτοῖς μαθηταῖς ἀποκρίνεται ὅτι δεῖ αὐτοῖς τὸ ἔργον αὐτῶν
ποιεῖν (to do).

εἰ οὐ τὰ ἱμάτια[4] ἐπὶ τῷ σώματι τοῦ βασίλεως[5] βλέπω, εἰμὶ πονηρός;

ἀνέβη (he/she/it went up) δὲ Ἀβρὰμ ἐξ Αἰγύπτου, αὐτὸς καὶ ἡ γυνὴ[6] αὐτοῦ καὶ πάντα τὰ αὐτοῦ
καὶ Λὼτ μετ᾽ αὐτοῦ εἰς τὴν ἔρημον.[7]

διέμειναν (they have continued) πάσας τὰς ἡμέρας τῆς ζωῆς αὐτῶν ἐν τῇ αὐτῇ φρονήσει.[8]

οὐκ αὐτός μοι εἶπεν· ἀδελφή μού ἐστιν, καὶ αὐτή μοι εἶπεν· ἀδελφός μού ἐστιν;

[9] Ἰησοῦς Χριστὸς ἐχθὲς (yesterday) καὶ σήμερον ὁ αὐτός καὶ εἰς τοὺς αἰῶνας.

Παρακαλῶ δὲ ὑμᾶς, ἀδελφοί, διὰ τοῦ ὀνόματος τοῦ κυρίου ἡμῶν Ἰησοῦ Χριστοῦ, ἵνα τὸ αὐτὸ
λέγητε (you might say) πάντες.

Hint: What is the subject? How does the ordering of the words help you understand the point of the passage?

πιστεύω can also mean "I entrust."

ἱμάτιον, -ου, τό, garment.

βασιλεύς, -έως, ὁ, king.

γυνή, γυναικός, ἡ, woman, wife.

ἔρημος, -ον, adj: solitary, deserted; noun: desert, wilderness.

φρόνησις, -εως, ἡ, way of thinking, (frame of) mind.

By now you should be accustomed to supplying verbs in sentences. We will not point out the need any longer.

18. Διαιρέσεις[10] δὲ χαρισμάτων εἰσίν, τὸ δὲ αὐτὸ πνεῦμα· καὶ διαιρέσεις διακονιῶν εἰσιν, καὶ αὐτὸς κύριος· καὶ διαιρέσεις ἐνεργημάτων[11] εἰσίν, ὁ δὲ αὐτὸς θεός ὁ ἐνεργῶν (one who work τὰ πάντα ἐν πᾶσιν.[12]

19. τὸν νόμον τῶν ἐντολῶν ἐν δόγμασιν[13] καταργήσας,[14] ἵνα τοὺς δύο κτίσῃ (he might create) ἐν αὐ εἰς ἕνα καινὸν ἄνθρωπον ποιῶν (thus making) εἰρήνην.

20. Αὐτὸς δὲ ὁ κύριος ἡμῶν Ἰησοῦς Χριστὸς καὶ [ὁ] θεὸς ὁ πατὴρ ἡμῶν ὁ ἀγαπήσας (one who love ἡμᾶς καὶ δοὺς (one who gave) παράκλησιν αἰωνίαν καὶ ἐλπίδα ἀγαθὴν ἐν χάριτι, παρακαλέσαι (may he comfort) ὑμῶν τὰς καρδίας καὶ στηρίξαι (may he strengthen) ἐν παντὶ ἔρ καὶ λόγῳ ἀγαθῷ.

English to Greek

Write out the Greek equivalent of these English pronouns.

1. him   6. his

2. its   7. to it

3. to them   8. she

4. their   9. they

5. hers   10. he

References

α. Mt 11:14; β. —; γ. Mk 8:29; δ. 1 Cor 15:39; ε. Lk 12:12; ζ. —; η. Mk 12:36; θ. —; **1.** Mk 1:30; **2.** Jn 18:4; **3.** 1 Th 4 **4.** Mt 10:24; **5.** 1 Cor 15:39; **6.** Jn 9:17; **7.** Rom. 8:16; **8.** Lk 6:23; **9.** Jn 2:24; **10.** Jn 10:41; **11.** —; **12.** —; **13.** Gen 1 **14.** Shep 106:2; **15.** Gen 20:5; **16.** Heb 13:8; **17.** 1 Cor 1:10; **18.** 1 Cor 12:4-6; **19.** Eph 2:15; **20.** 2 Th 2:16-17.

---

[10] διαίρεσις, -εως, ἡ, *division, variety.*

[11] ἐνέργημα, -ματος, τό, *activity, working, experience.*

[12] Is πᾶσιν masculine or neuter?

[13] δόγμα, -ματος, τό, *ordinance, decision, command.*

[14] καταργήσας is actually a participle, but you can translate it here as "he has abolished."

Demonstratives

Inflected	Person / Case	Number	Tense / Gender	Voice	Mood	Lexical form	Inflected meaning
τούτων							
αὐτή							
με							
ἐκείνας							
ἑνί							
ταῦτα							
ἐκεῖνο							
αὕτη							
τούτου							
ἡμᾶς							

οὐκ οἶδα τὸν ἄνθρωπον τοῦτον.

οὐκ οἴδατε τὴν παραβολὴν ταύτην;

τὸ φῶς τοῦ κόσμου τούτου βλέπει.

αὕτη ἐστὶν ἡ ἐντολὴ ἡ ἐμή.

οὐκ ἦν ἐκεῖνος τὸ φῶς.

ἄνδρες, τί ταῦτα ποιεῖτε;

ἐν δὲ ταῖς ἡμέραις ἐκείναις

Translation

1. οὗτος ὁ ἄνθρωπος υἱὸς θεοῦ ἦν.

2. αὕτη ἐστὶν ἡ μεγάλη[1] καὶ πρώτη ἐντολή.

3. εἰ ταῦτα οἴδατε, μακάριοί ἐστε ἐὰν ποιῆτε (you do) αὐτά.

4. Τῶν δὲ δώδεκα ἀποστόλων τὰ ὀνόματά ἐστιν ταῦτα.

5. ὑμεῖς[2] ἐκ τούτου τοῦ κόσμου ἐστέ, ἐγὼ οὐκ εἰμὶ ἐκ τοῦ κόσμου τούτου.

6. διὰ τοῦτο[3] ὑμεῖς οὐκ ἀκούετε, ὅτι ἐκ τοῦ θεοῦ οὐκ ἐστέ.

7. εἶπεν δὲ ὁ Πέτρος· κύριε, πρὸς ἡμᾶς τὴν παραβολὴν ταύτην λέγεις ἢ καὶ πρὸς πάντας;

---

[1]   Did you notice that the positive degree of the adjective is used as a superlative?

[2]   Notice the emphatic position of the two personal pronouns. What does that tell you about what Jesus is saying?

[3]   διὰ τοῦτο means "for this reason." It is a common idiom, much like ἐν τούτῳ.

εἶπον (they said)· σὺ μαθητὴς εἶ ἐκείνου, ἡμεῖς δὲ τοῦ Μωϋσέως ἐσμὲν μαθηταί.

οὐκ ἔστιν οὗτος[4] παρὰ θεοῦ ὁ ἄνθρωπος, ὅτι τὸ σάββατον οὐ τηρεῖ.

Περὶ δὲ τῆς ἡμέρας ἐκείνης ἢ τῆς ὥρας οὐδεὶς οἶδεν, οὐδὲ[5] οἱ ἄγγελοι ἐν οὐρανῷ οὐδὲ ὁ υἱός, εἰ μὴ[6] ὁ πατήρ.

dditional

ἐὰν ἀγαπῶμεν τὸν κύριον, τηροῦμεν τὰς ἐντολὰς ταύτας οὐ μόνον ἐν τοῖς σαββάτοις ἀλλὰ καὶ ἐν πᾶσιν ταῖς ἡμέραις.

ἐκεῖνοι οἱ ἄνδρες ζητοῦσιν τὰς γυναῖκας αὐτῶν ἐν τῇ ἀγορᾷ[7] τῆς μεγάλης πόλεως.

καὶ εἶπεν Ἀδάμ· τοῦτο νῦν ὀστοῦν[8] ἐκ τῶν ὀστέων μου καὶ σὰρξ ἐκ τῆς σαρκός μου· αὕτη κληθήσεται (he/she/it will be called) γυνή ὅτι ἐκ τοῦ ἀνδρὸς αὐτῆς ἐλήμφθη (he/she/it was taken) αὕτη.

καὶ ἐκάλεσεν (he/she/it called) Ἀδὰμ τὸ ὄνομα τῆς γυναικὸς αὐτοῦ Ζωὴ ὅτι αὕτη μήτηρ πάντων τῶν ζώντων.[9]

πολλαὶ γυναῖκες ἐκοπίησαν (they labored) διὰ τῆς χάριτος τοῦ θεοῦ αὐτῶν.

ἡ βασιλεία ἡ ἐμὴ οὐκ ἔστιν ἐκ τοῦ κόσμου τούτου.

τί ποιοῦμεν ὅτι οὗτος ὁ ἄνθρωπος πολλὰ ποιεῖ σημεῖα;

νῦν δὲ πρὸς σὲ ἔρχομαι καὶ ταῦτα λαλῶ ἐν τῷ κόσμῳ.

What word does οὗτος modify?

The two occurrences of οὐδέ act as "correlative conjunctions" meaning "neither ... nor."

In this context, εἰ μὴ means "only."

ἀγορά, -ᾶς, ἡ, marketplace.

ὀστέον, ου, τό, with the genitive plural ὀστέων, bone. Also occurs in its contracted form, ὀστοῦν, οῦ, τό (i.e., the εο has contracted to ου).

τῶν ζώντων means those who are living.

19. λέγει πρὸς αὐτὸν ἡ γυνή· κύριε, δός (give!) μοι τοῦτο τὸ ὕδωρ.

20. πάτερ, σῶσόν (save!) με ἐκ τῆς ὥρας ταύτης; ἀλλὰ διὰ τοῦτο ἦλθον (I came) εἰς τὴν ὥραν ταύτη πάτερ, δόξασόν (glorify!) σου τὸ ὄνομα. ... ἀπεκρίθη Ἰησοῦς καὶ εἶπεν· οὐ δι᾽ ἐμὲ ἡ φωνὴ αὕτ γέγονεν (he/she/it came) ἀλλὰ δι᾽ ὑμᾶς.

Summary

1. διὰ τοῦτο means "for this reason."

2. Two occurrences of οὐδέ can act as "correlative conjunctions" meaning "neither ... nor."

References

α. Mk 14:71; β. Mk 4:13; γ. Jn 11:9; δ. Jn 15:12; ε. Jn 1:8; ζ. Ac 14:15; η. Mt 3:1; **1**. Mk 15:39; **2**. Mt 22:38; **3**. Jn 13: **4**. Mt 10:2; **5**. Jn 8:23; **6**. Jn 8:47; **7**. Lk 12:41; **8**. Jn 9:28; **9**. Jn 9:16; **10**. Mk 13:32; **11**. —; **12**. —; **13**. Gen 2:23; **14**. G 3:20; **15**. (1 Clem 55:3); **16**. Jn 18:36; **17**. Jn 11:47; **18**. Jn 17:13; **19**. Jn 4:15; **20**. Jn 12:27-28, 30.

Relative Pronouns

arsing

Inflected	Person / Case	Number	Tense / Gender	Voice	Mood	Lexical form	Inflected meaning
ἅ							
ᾧ							
οὗ							
ὅ							
ἅς							
ἥ							
ἧς							
ὧν							
ἐκείνους							
ἥν							

arm-up

τὰ ῥήματα ἃ ἐγὼ λαλῶ

πιστεύουσιν ... τῷ λόγῳ ὃν εἶπεν ὁ Ἰησοῦς.

ἓν τῶν πλοίων, ὃ ἦν Σίμωνος

ἐν τῇ ὁδῷ ταύτῃ ᾗ ἐγὼ πορεύομαι

τὸ πνεῦμα τῆς ἀληθείας, ὃ ὁ κόσμος οὐ δύναται λαβεῖν (to receive)

καὶ πᾶς ὃς πορεύεται ἐπὶ χειρῶν

ὁ θεὸς τῆς εἰρήνης ὅς ἐστιν μεθ᾽ ὑμῶν

Translation

Be able to identify every relative pronoun, explain its case, number, and gender, and explain what word the ª
ative clause modifies and what function it performs in the sentence.

1. τί δέ με καλεῖτε· κύριε κύριε, καὶ οὐ ποιεῖτε ἃ λέγω;

2. τί ποιοῦσιν τοῖς σάββασιν ὃ οὐκ ἔξεστιν (it is lawful);

3. καὶ ἔλεγον· οὐχ οὗτός ἐστιν Ἰησοῦς ὁ υἱὸς Ἰωσήφ, οὗ ἡμεῖς οἴδαμεν τὸν πατέρα καὶ τὴν μητέρª

    πῶς νῦν λέγει ὅτι ἐκ τοῦ οὐρανοῦ καταβέβηκα (I have come down);

4. ἀλλ᾽ εἰσὶν ἐξ ὑμῶν τινες οἳ οὐ πιστεύουσιν.

5. ὃς γὰρ οὐκ ἔστιν καθ᾽ ἡμῶν, ὑπὲρ ἡμῶν ἐστιν.

6. χάριτι δὲ θεοῦ εἰμι ὅ εἰμι.

7. εἶπεν δὲ Ἡρῴδης· ... τίς δέ ἐστιν οὗτος περὶ οὗ ἀκούω;

Καὶ ἰδοὺ ἄνθρωπος ἦν ἐν Ἰερουσαλὴμ ᾧ ὄνομα Συμεὼν καὶ ὁ ἄνθρωπος οὗτος δίκαιος (just) ... καὶ πνεῦμα ἦν ἅγιον ἐπ᾽ αὐτόν.

Ἰωάννης ταῖς ἑπτὰ ἐκκλησίαις ταῖς ἐν τῇ Ἀσίᾳ· χάρις ὑμῖν καὶ εἰρήνη ... ἀπὸ τῶν ἑπτὰ πνευμάτων ἃ ἐνώπιον τοῦ θρόνου αὐτοῦ.

. οὐ πιστεύεις ὅτι ἐγὼ ἐν τῷ πατρὶ καὶ ὁ πατὴρ ἐν ἐμοί ἐστιν; τὰ ῥήματα ἃ ἐγὼ λέγω ὑμῖν ἀπ᾽ ἐμαυτοῦ (of myself) οὐ λαλῶ, ὁ δὲ πατὴρ ἐν ἐμοὶ μένων (who abides) ποιεῖ τὰ ἔργα αὐτοῦ.

dditional

. οἱ μαθηταὶ πάντας τοὺς ἐν τῇ συναγωγῇ ἐδίδασκον ὅτι ὅστις ἂν τὸν κύριον ἀγαπᾷ ζωὴν αἰώνιον ἔχει.

. ἐπαγγελίαν γὰρ ἔχομεν τῆς εἰρήνης καὶ τῆς δικαιουσύνης ἣν ὁ θεὸς πληροῖ ἐκείνοις οἳ εἰς αὐτὸν πιστεύουσιν.

. σώζεσθε,[1] ἀγάπης τέκνα καὶ εἰρήνης. ὁ κύριος τῆς δόξης καὶ πάσης χάριτος μετὰ τοῦ πνεύματος ὑμῶν.

. ἐγὼ δὲ ἀπεκρίθην (I answered)· τίς εἶ, κύριε; εἶπέν τε πρός με· ἐγώ εἰμι Ἰησοῦς ὁ Ναζωραῖος,[2] ὃν σὺ διώκεις.[3]

. οὐχ οὗτός ἐστιν ὃν ζητοῦσιν ἀποκτεῖναι (to kill);

. καὶ αὐτός ἐστιν ἡ κεφαλὴ τοῦ σώματος τῆς ἐκκλησίας· ὅς ἐστιν ἀρχή, πρωτότοκος[4] ἐκ τῶν νεκρῶν.

While this sentence does not have a relative pronoun, it is just too cool a verse not to include, and it does use a vocabulary word for this chapter. σώζεσθε is a plural imperative meaning *Be saved!* It is a way of saying *Farewell.* Be sure to use it when saying goodbye to your teacher and fellow students after class.

Ναζωραῖος, ου, ὁ, *an inhabitant of Nazareth.*

διώκω, *I pursue, persecute.*

πρωτότοκος, ον, *firstborn.*

17. καὶ αὕτη ἐστὶν ἡ ἐπαγγελία ἣν αὐτὸς ἐπηγγείλατο (he/she/it promised) ἡμῖν, τὴν ζωὴν τὴν αἰώνιον.

18. νῦν δὲ ζητεῖτέ με ἀποκτεῖναι (to kill) ἄνθρωπον ὃς τὴν ἀλήθειαν ὑμῖν λελάληκα (I have spoke» ἣν ἤκουσα (I heard) παρὰ τοῦ θεοῦ.

19. καταβὰς (after coming down) δὲ Πέτρος πρὸς τοὺς ἄνδρας εἶπεν· ἰδοὺ ἐγώ εἰμι ὃν ζητεῖτε.

20. ὥσπερ γὰρ ὁ πατὴρ ἐγείρει[5] τοὺς νεκροὺς καὶ ζῳοποιεῖ,[6] οὕτως καὶ ὁ υἱὸς οὓς θέλει ζῳοποιε

Summary

1. σῴζεσθα, οἱ μαθηταί.

References

α. (Jn 6:63); β. (Jn 2:22); γ. Lk 5:3; δ. Gen 28:20; ε. Jn 14:17; ζ. Lev 11:27; η. (Phil 4:9); 1. Lk 6:46; 2. Mk 2:24; 3. 6:42; 4. Jn 6:64; 5. Mk 9:40; 6. 1 Cor 15:10; 7. Lk 9:9; 8. Lk 2:25; 9. Rev 1:4; 10. Jn 14:10; 11. —; 12. —; 13. Barn 21 14. Ac 22:8; 15. Jn 7:25; 16. Col 1:18; 17. 1 Jn 2:25; 18. Jn 8:40; 19. Ac 10:21; 20. Jn 5:21.

---

[5] ἐγείρω, *I raise.*

[6] ζῳοποιέω, *I make alive.*

Future Active/Middle Indicative

Parsing

Inflected	Person / Case	Number	Tense / Gender	Voice	Mood	Lexical form	Inflected meaning
λύσει							
ἀκούσεις							
γεννήσομεν							
ζήσουσι							
πορεύσεται							
βλέψεις							
ἕξετε							
καλέσομεν							
ὅλους							
συνάξουσιν							

Warm-up

πάντες πιστεύσουσιν εἰς αὐτόν.

αὐτὸς περὶ ἑαυτοῦ λαλήσει.

συνάξω τοὺς καρπούς μου.

ἕξει τὸ φῶς τῆς ζωῆς.

σὺν ἐμοὶ πορεύσονται.

βλέψετε καὶ οὐ λαλήσει.

ἐπὶ Καίσαρα πορεύσῃ.

Translation

1. κύριον τὸν θεόν σου προσκυνήσεις.[1]

2. [2] βασιλεὺς Ἰσραήλ ἐστιν, καταβάτω (let him come down!) νῦν ἀπὸ τοῦ σταυροῦ (cross) καὶ πιστεύσομεν ἐπ᾽ αὐτόν.

3. ἡ γυνή σου Ἐλισάβετ γεννήσει υἱόν σοι καὶ καλέσεις τὸ ὄνομα αὐτοῦ Ἰωάννην.

4. ὁ δὲ θεός μου πληρώσει πᾶσαν χρείαν (need) ὑμῶν κατὰ τὸ πλοῦτος (riches) αὐτοῦ ἐν δόξῃ ἐν Χριστῷ Ἰησοῦ.

5. ἀμὴν ἀμὴν λέγω ὑμῖν ὅτι ἔρχεται ὥρα καὶ νῦν ἐστιν ὅτε οἱ νεκροὶ ἀκούσουσιν τῆς φωνῆς τοῦ υἱοῦ τοῦ θεοῦ καὶ οἱ ἀκούσαντες (ones who hear it) ζήσουσιν.

6. καὶ ἔσεσθε μισούμενοι (hated) ὑπὸ πάντων διὰ τὸ ὄνομά μου.

---

[1] Notice that although this is a future verb, it is being used as an imperative to state a command. This is a common use the future in both Greek and English. See the *Exegetical Insight* to this chapter.

[2] Hint: The people are probably taunting Jesus and being sarcastic. Interestingly, some manuscripts (A, 𝔐, Latin, Syria et al.) insert εἰ before βασιλεύς.

[3] ἀμὴν ἀμὴν λέγω ὑμῖν, ὁ πιστεύων (one who believes) εἰς ἐμὲ τὰ ἔργα ἃ ἐγὼ ποιῶ κἀκεῖνος (that one) ποιήσει καὶ μείζονα τούτων[4] ποιήσει, ὅτι ἐγὼ πρὸς τὸν πατέρα πορεύομαι.

ὑμεῖς προσκυνεῖτε ὃ οὐκ οἴδατε· ἡμεῖς προσκυνοῦμεν ὃ οἴδαμεν, ὅτι ἡ σωτηρία (salvation) ἐκ τῶν Ἰουδαίων ἐστίν. ἀλλὰ ἔρχεται ὥρα καὶ νῦν ἐστιν, ὅτε οἱ ἀληθινοὶ (true) προσκυνηταὶ (worshipers) προσκυνήσουσιν τῷ πατρὶ ἐν πνεύματι καὶ ἀληθείᾳ.

ζητήσετέ με, καὶ καθὼς εἶπον (I said) τοῖς Ἰουδαίοις ὅτι ὅπου ἐγὼ ὑπάγω (I go) ὑμεῖς οὐ δύνασθε ἐλθεῖν (to go), καὶ ὑμῖν λέγω.

. ἄκουε (Listen!), Ἰσραήλ, κύριος ὁ θεὸς ἡμῶν κύριος εἷς ἐστιν, καὶ ἀγαπήσεις κύριον τὸν θεόν σου ἐξ ὅλης τῆς καρδίας σου καὶ ἐξ ὅλης τῆς ψυχῆς σου καὶ ἐξ ὅλης τῆς διανοίας (mind) σου καὶ ἐξ ὅλης τῆς ἰσχύος (strength) σου.

This verse is a good example of John's repetitive style. He often describes the subject of the sentence with a clause, and then repeats the subject with a pronoun or some other word.

τούτων is an example of the "genitive of comparison." A comparative adjective such as μείζων is almost always followed by a word in the genitive to indicate comparison, and you can use the key word "than."

Additional

11. οἱ Ἰουδαῖοι συνάξουσιν ἐπὶ τῇ θαλάσσῃ τῆς Γαλιλαίας ὅτι ὁ Ἰησοῦς παραβολὰς λαλήσει.

12. πορευσόμεθα πρὸς τὴν βασιλείαν τοῦ Ἰσραήλ, ἀλλὰ ἀκούσομεν τοῦ εὐαγγελίου τῆς ἀγάπης τοῦ θεοῦ;

13. υἱοὺς καὶ θυγατέρας[5] γεννήσεις καὶ οὐκ ἔσονταί σοι.

14. οὐ προσκυνήσεις τοῖς θεοῖς αὐτῶν οὐδὲ ποιήσεις κατὰ τὰ ἔργα αὐτῶν.

15. καὶ εἶπεν κύριος τῷ Ἀβράμ· ἔξελθε (go out!) ἐκ τῆς γῆς[6] σου ... καὶ ἐκ τοῦ οἴκου τοῦ πατρός σου εἰς τὴν γῆν ἣν ἄν σοι δείξω (I will show) καὶ ποιήσω σε εἰς ἔθνος[7] μέγα καὶ εὐλογήσω[8] σε ... κα ἔσῃ εὐλογητός.[9]

16. ἔσεσθε οὖν ὑμεῖς τέλειοι ὡς ὁ πατὴρ ὑμῶν ὁ οὐράνιος[10] τέλειός ἐστιν.

17. δικαιοσύνη γὰρ θεοῦ ἐν αὐτῷ ἀποκαλύπτεται ἐκ πίστεως εἰς πίστιν, καθὼς γέγραπται (it is written)· ὁ δὲ δίκαιος ἐκ πίστεως ζήσεται.

18. ἐὰν ἀγαπᾶτέ με, τὰς ἐντολὰς τὰς ἐμὰς τηρήσετε.

19. εἴ τις θέλει πρῶτος εἶναι,[11] ἔσται πάντων ἔσχατος.

20. εὗρον (I have found) Δαυὶδ τὸν[12] τοῦ Ἰεσσαί, ἄνδρα κατὰ τὴν καρδίαν μου, ὃς ποιήσει πάντα τ θελήματά μου.

Summary

1. The future can be used to make a command.

2. A comparative adjective such as μείζων is almost always followed by a word in the genitive to indicate comparison. You can use the key word "than" in your translation.

References

α. Jn 11:48; β. Jn 9:21; γ. Lk 12:17; δ. Jn 8:12; ε. 1 Cor 16:4; ζ. —; η. Ac 25:12; **1.** Mt 4:10; **2.** Mt 27:42; **3.** Lk 1:13; **4.** Ph 4:19; **5.** Jn 5:25; **6.** Mk 13:13; **7.** Jn 14:12; **8.** Jn 4:22-23; **9.** Jn 13:33; **10.** Mk 12:29-31; **11.** —; **12.** —; **13.** Dt 28:41; **14.** (E 23:24); **15.** Gen 12:1-2; **16.** Mt 5:48; **17.** Rom 1:17; **18.** Jn 14:15; **19.** Mk 9:35; **20.** Ac 13:22.

---

[5] θυγάτηρ, -τρος, ἡ, *daughter.*

[6] γῆ, γῆ, ἡ, *earth, land, region.*

[7] ἔθνος, -ους, τό, *nation.*

[8] εὐλογέω, *I bless.*

[9] εὐλογητός, -ή, -όν, *blessed, praised.*

[10] οὐράνιος, -ον, *heavenly.*

[11] "To be." Takes a predicate nominative.

[12] The word τόν is modifying is often dropped out of this type of construction. What is the word?

Verbal Roots, and Other Forms of the Future

the verb is future, try to see what it would be in the present, and vice versa.

ırsing

Inflected	Person / Case	Number	Tense / Gender	Voice	Mood	Lexical form	Inflected meaning
ἀρεῖς							
ὄψεται							
ἐκβαλοῦμεν							
ἐγεροῦσιν							
ἀποκτενεῖτε							
σώσει							
ἀποστελεῖ							
βαπτίσεις							
ποιοῦσι							
0. κρινεῖτε							

Varm-up

.   ἐκεῖνος κρινεῖ αὐτὸν ἐν τῇ ἐσχάτῃ ἡμέρᾳ.

.   πολλοὶ γὰρ ἐλεύσονται ἐπὶ τῷ ὀνόματί μου.

.   ἐν τῷ ὀνόματί μου δαιμόνια ἐκβαλοῦσιν.

.   γνώσεσθε τὴν ἀλήθειαν.

.   ἐρῶ τῇ ψυχῇ μου.

.   αὐτὸς μένει ἐπὶ τὸν κόσμον ἀλλὰ σὺ μενεῖς εἰς τοὺς αἰῶνας.

.   πῶς πάσας τὰς παραβολὰς γνώσεσθε;

Translation

1. ἐγὼ ἐβάπτισα (I baptized) ὑμᾶς ὕδατι, αὐτὸς δὲ βαπτίσει ὑμᾶς ἐν πνεύματι ἁγίῳ.

2. ἀποστελεῖ ὁ υἱὸς τοῦ ἀνθρώπου τοὺς ἀγγέλους αὐτοῦ.

3. ἐκεῖ αὐτὸν ὄψεσθε, καθὼς εἶπεν ὑμῖν.

4. ἀπεκρίθη Ἰησοῦς καὶ εἶπεν αὐτῷ· ἐάν τις ἀγαπᾷ[1] με τὸν λόγον μου τηρήσει καὶ ὁ πατήρ μου ἀγαπήσει αὐτὸν καὶ πρὸς αὐτὸν ἐλευσόμεθα.

5. τέξεται (he/she/it will bear) δὲ υἱόν, καὶ καλέσεις τὸ ὄνομα αὐτοῦ Ἰησοῦν. αὐτὸς γὰρ σώσει τὸν λαὸν αὐτοῦ ἀπὸ τῶν ἁμαρτιῶν αὐτῶν.

6. ἢ οὐκ οἴδατε ὅτι οἱ ἅγιοι τὸν κόσμον κρινοῦσιν; ... οὐκ οἴδατε ὅτι ἀγγέλους κρινοῦμεν;

7. πάντες πιστεύσουσιν εἰς αὐτόν, καὶ ἐλεύσονται οἱ Ῥωμαῖοι καὶ ἀροῦσιν τὸν τόπον ἡμῶν.

---

[1]   This form is actually in the subjunctive mood (chapter 31), but in this case it is identical in form to the indicative and i translated the same way.

Ἀλλὰ ἐρεῖ τις· πῶς ἐγείρονται οἱ νεκροί; ποίῳ (in what sort of) δὲ σώματι ἔρχονται;

λέγει αὐτῷ· ἐκ τοῦ στόματός σου κρινῶ σε, πονηρὲ δοῦλε.

δ. διὰ τοῦτο καὶ ἡ σοφία τοῦ θεοῦ εἶπεν· ἀποστελῶ εἰς αὐτοὺς προφήτας καὶ ἀποστόλους, καὶ ἐξ αὐτῶν[2] ἀποκτενοῦσιν.

dditional

1. τί οἱ κακοὶ ἀποκτείνουσιν τοὺς ἀγαθούς, οἳ τηροῦσιν τὸν νόμον τοῦ θεοῦ καὶ ἀγαπῶσι πάντας;

2. ἐν τῷ στόματί μου μεγαλὴν σοφίαν λαλήσω καὶ κατὰ τὴν ὅλην ζωὴν ἐρῶ περὶ τῆς δικαιοσύνης τε καὶ τῆς ὁδοῦ τῆς ἀληθείας.

3. καὶ καλέσεις τὰ σάββατα ἅγια τῷ θεῷ σου καὶ οὐκ ἀρεῖς τὸν πόδα σου ἐπ᾽ ἔργῳ οὐδὲ λαλήσεις λόγον ἐν ὀργῇ[3] ἐκ τοῦ στόματός σου.

4. ὁ θεός ἐστιν κύριος, καὶ αὐτὸς οἶδεν, καὶ Ἰσραὴλ αὐτὸς γνώσεται.

5. τὸ ὕδωρ αὐτοῦ πιστόν· βασιλέα μετὰ δόξης ὄψεσθε, καὶ ἡ ψυχὴ ὑμῶν μελετήσει[4] φόβον[5] κυρίου.

6. καὶ τὰ τέκνα αὐτῆς ἀποκτενῶ ἐν θανάτῳ. καὶ γνώσονται πᾶσαι αἱ ἐκκλησίαι ὅτι ἐγώ εἰμι ὁ ἐραυνῶν (one who searches) νεφροὺς[6] καὶ καρδίας, καὶ δώσω (I will give) ὑμῖν ἑκάστῳ κατὰ τὰ ἔργα ὑμῶν.

7. Μὴ μόνον οὖν αὐτὸν καλῶμεν (let us call) κύριον, οὐ γὰρ τοῦτο σώσει ἡμᾶς.

αὐτῶν is called the "partitive genitive," where the word in the genitive indicates a larger group (αὐτῶν) and the word it is modifying represents a part of the smaller group. The problem here is that the noun it is modifying is unexpressed. Supply "some" in your translation for the smaller group.

ὀργή, -ῆς, ἡ, *wrath, anger.*

μελετάω, *I practice, cultivate.*

φόβος, -ου, ὁ, *fear, reverence.*

νεφρός, -οῦ, ὁ, *mind.*

18. [7]μακάριοι οἱ καθαροὶ τῇ καρδίᾳ, ὅτι αὐτοὶ τὸν θεὸν ὄψονται.

19. Ἀλλ᾽ ἐρεῖ τις· σὺ πίστιν ἔχεις, κἀγὼ ἔργα ἔχω. δεῖξόν (Show!) μοι τὴν πίστιν σου χωρὶς τῶν ἔργων, κἀγώ σοι δείξω (I will show) ἐκ τῶν ἔργων μου τὴν πίστιν. σὺ πιστεύεις ὅτι εἷς ἐστιν ὁ θεός, καλῶς ποιεῖς. καὶ τὰ δαιμόνια πιστεύουσιν καὶ φρίσσουσιν.[8]

20. ἐὰν τὰς ἐντολάς μου τηρήσητε (you keep), μενεῖτε ἐν τῇ ἀγάπῃ μου, καθὼς ἐγὼ τὰς ἐντολὰς το πατρός μου τετήρηκα (I have kept) καὶ μένω αὐτοῦ[9] ἐν τῇ ἀγάπῃ.

Summary

1. The partitive genitive indicates the larger group, and the word it modifies indicates the smaller group.

References

α. Jn 12:48; β. Mt 24:5; γ. Mk 16:17; δ. Jn 8:32; ε. Lk 12:19; ζ. —; η. Mk 4:13; **1.** Mk 1:8; **2.** Mt 13:41; **3.** Mk 16:7; **4.** 14:23; **5.** Mt 1:21; **6.** 1 Cor 6:2-3; **7.** (Jn 11:48); **8.** 1 Cor 15:35; **9.** Lk 19:22; **10.** Lk 11:49; **11.** —; **12.** —; **13.** (Is 58:13 **14.** (Josh 22:22); **15.** Barn 11:5; **16.** Rev 2:23; **17.** 2 Clem 4:1; **18.** Mt 5:8; **19.** Jas 2:18-19; **20.** Jn 15:10.

---

[7] You have to assume the verb in the first half of the sentence.

[8] φρίσσω, *I tremble.*

[9] Normally αὐτοῦ follows the word it modifies, but not always. How do you know what word it modifies?

Review #4 — Track 2

Grammar

Explain how the stem was modified in the following inflected forms. Start by writing out the word's stem, add the case ending, show the final form, and explain the changes.

a. σάρξ

b. ὄνομα

c. χάρισιν

d. πίστεως

e. πᾶς

Write out the seventh and eighth noun rules.

7.

8.

Describe what happens when you add a sigma to the following stops.

a. τ + σ ▸

d. π + σ ▸

b. β + σ ▸

e. γ + σ ▸

c. δ + σ ▸

f. κ + σ ▸

List the case endings

	first/second declension			third declension	
	masc	*fem*	*neut*	*masc/fem*	*neut*
nom sg					
gen sg					
dat sg					
acc sg					

	masc	fem	neut	masc/fem	neut
nom pl					
gen pl					
dat pl					
acc pl					

5.   What determines the case, number, and gender of a personal pronoun?

    a.   Case

    b.   Number/gender

6.   Write out the paradigm of the English personal pronouns

	first person	second person		first person	second person
subjective sg			subjective pl		
possessive sg			possessive pl		
objective sg			objective pl		

7.   What are the three uses of αὐτός?

    a.

    b.

    c.

8.   How do you distinguish the form of the feminine personal pronoun from the feminine demonstrative?

9.   In what adjectival position will you find the demonstratives when they are modifying nouns?

10. What are the four basic rules of the vocative?

    a.

    b.

    c.

    d.

. What determines the case, number, and gender of a relative pronoun?

a.   Case

b.   Number/gender

. How do you distinguish the form of the relative pronoun from the article?

. Write out the "Square of Stops," and what happens to each class of stop when followed by a sigma.

a.   labials:

b.   velars:

c.   dentals:

. What is the difference between a verbal "root" and "stem"?

a.   Root

b.   Stem

. What are the three basic ways in which the verbal root is used to form the present tense stem?

a.

b.

c.

. Write out the Master Verb Chart.

Tense	Aug/Redup	Tense stem	Tense formative	Conn. vowel	Personal endings	First singular
Pres act						
Imperf mid/pas						
Fut act						
Liquid fut act						
Fut mid						

Parsing

1. πόλεσιν

2. ὀνόματι

3. ἀροῦσιν

4. αὕτη

5. ζήσῃ

6. ἀκούσεις

7. οἷς

8. σώσω

9. γνώσεται

10. πολλοῖς

11. βλέψεται

12. ὄψονται

13. ποδί

14. γνώσονται

15. ὄψῃ

anslation: John 12:27-36

[12:27] Νῦν ἡ ψυχή μου τετάρακται (he/she/it has been troubled), καὶ τί εἴπω (I can say); Πάτερ,

ῳσόν (save!) με ἐκ τῆς ὥρας ταύτης; ἀλλὰ διὰ τοῦτο ἦλθον (I came) εἰς τὴν ὥραν ταύτην. [12:28] πάτερ,

ξασόν (glorify!) σου τὸ ὄνομα. ἦλθεν (he/she/it came) οὖν φωνὴ ἐκ τοῦ οὐρανοῦ· καὶ ἐδόξασα (I

orified) καὶ πάλιν δοξάσω. [12:29] ὁ οὖν ὄχλος ὁ ἑστὼς (one that was standing) καὶ ἀκούσας (hearing)

.εγεν βροντὴν γεγονέναι,[1] ἄλλοι ἔλεγον· ἄγγελος αὐτῷ λελάληκεν (he/she/it has spoken).

[30] ἀπεκρίθη Ἰησοῦς καὶ εἶπεν· οὐ δι᾽ ἐμὲ ἡ φωνὴ αὕτη γέγονεν (he/she/it came) ἀλλὰ δι᾽ ὑμᾶς.

[31] νῦν κρίσις ἐστὶν τοῦ κόσμου τούτου, νῦν ὁ ἄρχων τοῦ κόσμου τούτου ἐκβληθήσεται (he/she/it

ill be cast) ἔξω· [12:32] κἀγὼ ἐὰν ὑψωθῶ (I am lifted up) ἐκ τῆς γῆς, πάντας ἑλκύσω (I will draw) πρὸς

ιαυτόν. [12:33] τοῦτο δὲ ἔλεγεν σημαίνων (signifying) ποίῳ θανάτῳ ἤμελλεν ἀποθνήσκειν (to die).

[34] Ἀπεκρίθη οὖν αὐτῷ ὁ ὄχλος· ἡμεῖς ἠκούσαμεν (we heard) ἐκ τοῦ νόμου ὅτι ὁ Χριστὸς μένει εἰς

ν αἰῶνα, καὶ πῶς λέγεις σὺ ὅτι δεῖ ὑψωθῆναι (to be lifted up) τὸν υἱὸν τοῦ ἀνθρώπου;[2] τίς ἐστιν

ὗτος ὁ υἱὸς τοῦ ἀνθρώπου; [12:35] εἶπεν οὖν αὐτοῖς ὁ Ἰησοῦς· ἔτι μικρὸν χρόνον τὸ φῶς ἐν ὑμῖν ἐστιν.

ριπατεῖτε (walk!) ὡς τὸ φῶς ἔχετε, ἵνα μὴ σκοτία ὑμᾶς καταλάβῃ (he/she/it might overtake)· καὶ ὁ

ριπατῶν (one walking) ἐν τῇ σκοτίᾳ οὐκ οἶδεν ποῦ ὑπάγει. [12:36] ὡς τὸ φῶς ἔχετε, πιστεύετε (believe!)

ς τὸ φῶς, ἵνα υἱοὶ φωτὸς γένησθε (you might be).

βροντὴν γεγονέναι means "that it was thunder."

τὸν υἱὸν τοῦ ἀνθρώπου is acting as the subject of ὑψωθῆναι.

Discover the Basics of Greek with the Aid of a CD-ROM!

The Basics of Biblical Greek
Grammar–Second Edition

William D. Mounce

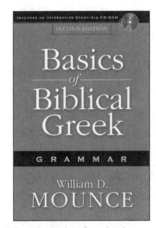

New, updated edition of the best-selling and most widely accepted textbook for learning biblical Greek.

William D. Mounce's *Basics of Biblical Greek Grammar*, the companion tool to this workbook, is by far the best-selling and most widely accepted textbook for learning New Testament Greek.

This excellent tool for studying New Testament Greek is now even better. As a result of feedback from professors, the author has made adjustments to his material. The CD-ROM is now easier to use and has even more information on it than the earlier edition. Some of the longer chapters have been shortened and some material has been moved elsewhere for easier learning.

Features include:

- Best-selling Greek language textbook
- Changes from the first edition made in response to ten years of use
- The CD-ROM is easier to navigate and now includes much more material
- A summary audio lecture for each lesson (7–9 minutes), which can help students with class preparation

Hardcover: 0-310-25087-0

Pick up a copy today at your favorite bookstore!

GRAND RAPIDS, MICHIGAN 49530 USA

WWW.ZONDERVAN.COM

GREEK FOR
THE REST OF US

William D. Mounce

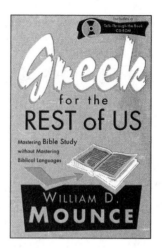

**You don't have to be a Greek student
to understand biblical Greek.**

If you'd love to learn Greek so you can
study your Bible better, but you can't spare two
years for college or seminary courses, then
Greek for the Rest of Us is for you. Developed
by renowned Greek teacher William Mounce,
this revolutionary crash-course on "baby Greek" will acquaint you with
the essentials of the language and deepen your understanding of God's
Word. You'll gain a sound knowledge of basic Greek, and you'll learn
how to use tools that will add muscle to your Bible studies.

In six sections, *Greek for the Rest of Us* will help you:

- Recite the Greek alphabet
- Read and pronounce Greek words
- Learn the Greek noun and verbal system
- Conduct Greek word studies
- Decipher why translations are different
- Read better commentaries

Greek for the Rest of Us broadens your knowledge still further with
an appendix on biblical Hebrew. It also includes a CD-ROM for your
computer, featuring the author's class lectures in audio, combined with
text and overheads.

You can start learning Greek right now. It won't take you forever to
grasp the basics, but the knowledge will serve you for a lifetime.

Hardcover: 0-310-23485-9

Pick up a copy today at your favorite bookstore!

ZONDERVAN™
GRAND RAPIDS, MICHIGAN 49530 USA
WWW.ZONDERVAN.COM

Discover the Basics of Greek with the Aid of a CD-ROM!

The Basics of Biblical Greek Grammar–Second Edition

William D. Mounce

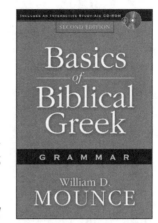

New, updated edition of the best-selling and most widely accepted textbook for learning biblical Greek.

William D. Mounce's *Basics of Biblical Greek Grammar*, the companion tool to this workbook, is by far the best-selling and most widely accepted textbook for learning New Testament Greek.

This excellent tool for studying New Testament Greek is now even better. As a result of feedback from professors, the author has made adjustments to his material. The CD-ROM is now easier to use and has even more information on it than the earlier edition. Some of the longer chapters have been shortened and some material has been moved elsewhere for easier learning.

Features include:

- Best-selling Greek language textbook
- Changes from the first edition made in response to ten years of use
- The CD-ROM is easier to navigate and now includes much more material
- A summary audio lecture for each lesson (7–9 minutes), which can help students with class preparation

Hardcover: 0-310-25087-0

Pick up a copy today at your favorite bookstore!

ZONDERVAN®

GRAND RAPIDS, MICHIGAN 49530 USA

WWW.ZONDERVAN.COM

GREEK FOR THE REST OF US

William D. Mounce

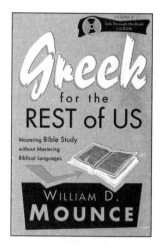

You don't have to be a Greek student to understand biblical Greek.

If you'd love to learn Greek so you can study your Bible better, but you can't spare two years for college or seminary courses, then *Greek for the Rest of Us* is for you. Developed by renowned Greek teacher William Mounce, this revolutionary crash-course on "baby Greek" will acquaint you with the essentials of the language and deepen your understanding of God's Word. You'll gain a sound knowledge of basic Greek, and you'll learn how to use tools that will add muscle to your Bible studies.

In six sections, *Greek for the Rest of Us* will help you:

- Recite the Greek alphabet
- Read and pronounce Greek words
- Learn the Greek noun and verbal system
- Conduct Greek word studies
- Decipher why translations are different
- Read better commentaries

Greek for the Rest of Us broadens your knowledge still further with an appendix on biblical Hebrew. It also includes a CD-ROM for your computer, featuring the author's class lectures in audio, combined with text and overheads.

You can start learning Greek right now. It won't take you forever to grasp the basics, but the knowledge will serve you for a lifetime.

Hardcover: 0-310-23485-9

Pick up a copy today at your favorite bookstore!

ZONDERVAN®

GRAND RAPIDS, MICHIGAN 49530 USA
WWW.ZONDERVAN.COM

A GRADED READER OF BIBLICAL GREEK

William D. Mounce

This multipurpose volume serves as a companion to *Basics of Biblical Greek, Greek Grammar Beyond the Basics,* and *Biblical Greek Exegesis.* It contains annotated readings from the New Testament designed for second-year Greek students. Sections from the Greek New Testament are presented in order of increasing difficulty, and unfamiliar forms and constructions are annotated.

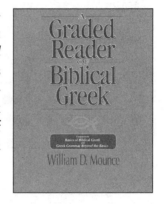

Softcover: 0-310-20582-4

Pick up a copy today at your favorite bookstore!

ZONDERVAN®

GRAND RAPIDS, MICHIGAN 49530 USA

WWW.ZONDERVAN.COM

*Build your New Testament Greek library
with these outstanding titles.*

THE ANALYTICAL LEXICON TO THE GREEK NEW TESTAMENT

William D. Mounce

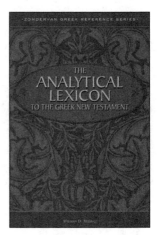

The Analytical Lexicon to the Greek New Testament was created to aid in the study of the Greek New Testament, using sophisticated computer resources to ensure an accurate, helpful, and in-depth analysis of the word forms that make up the New Testament. Its combination of features sets it apart from all previously published analytical lexicons:

- Based on one of the latest Greek texts (UBS 3d edition, revised)
- Includes both accepted and variant readings
- Up-to-date definitions
- Consistent with today's standard Greek lexicons
- Gives the frequency of each inflected form, verse references for forms that occur only once
- Includes Goodrick/Kohlenberger numbers for all words
- Includes principal parts for all verbs
- Contains grammatical section, with a discussion of paradigms and explanations as to why paradigms are formed as they are

Most significantly, *The Analytical Lexicon to the Greek New Testament* is keyed to *The Morphology of Biblical Greek,* which explains in detail why some Greek words follow certain patterns and other Greek words follow seemingly different patterns. In short, *The Analytical Lexicon to the Greek New Testament* is more than a tool for a quick reference—it is an index to another body of literature.

Hardcover: 0-310-54210-3

ZONDERVAN®

GRAND RAPIDS, MICHIGAN 49530 USA

WWW.ZONDERVAN.COM

THE NIV ENGLISH-GREEK
NEW TESTAMENT

William D. Mounce

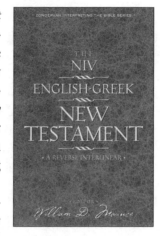

The NIV English-Greek New Testament allows you to immediately reference the original Greek words behind the English text of the New Testament. You don't need to know Greek in order to use this unique volume. Featuring today's best-loved translation, the *New International Version*, the reverse interlinear format allows you to read the English text in its normal order and consult corresponding Greek words as desired.

A Goodrick-Kohlenberger number provided with each Greek word lets you quickly key to the appropriate entry in *The NIV Theological Dictionary of New Testament Words*, the *Zondervan NIV Exhaustive Concordance*, Mounce's *Analytical Lexicon to the Greek New Testament*, or other study tools. A morphological tag analyzes each Greek form and gives parsing information. A cross-reference to Strong's numbers is also provided.

For Greek students and laypersons alike, *The NIV English-Greek New Testament* is a centerpiece for word studies that help you better understand the Bible. This is a New Testament no pastor should be without.

Hardcover: 0-310-20377-5

Pick up a copy today at your favorite bookstore!

ZONDERVAN®

GRAND RAPIDS, MICHIGAN 49530 USA

WWW.ZONDERVAN.COM

Learn on the Go

NEW TESTAMENT GREEK VOCABULARY

Jonathan T. Pennington

Students of biblical Greek will learn all Greek vocabulary words that occur ten times or more in the New Testament by interacting with this audio CD. Jonathan Pennington speaks all New Testament Greek words in descending order of frequency. Different tracks enable students to concentrate on different word groupings. After each citation is an opportunity for the user to give the gloss meaning of the word; then Pennington gives the gloss, confirming whether or not the user is correct. An accompanying printed guide supplements the learning process.

Unabridged Audio Pages® CD: 0-310-24382-3

BASICS OF BIBLICAL GREEK
FlashCards for Palm™ OS

Introducing a handy study tool that allows PDA users (Palm™, Handspring™, Sony, etc.) to quickly and easily learn biblical Greek words via the flash card method. The program is coordinated with and makes an excellent companion to the popular, widely used text *Basics of Biblical Greek Grammar* (Mounce), from which vocabulary words are derived.

This fun and easy-to-use electronic learning aid offers many exciting benefits:

- PDAs have a small, convenient size compared with large stacks of traditional flash cards.
- Automatic randomization of vocabulary words avoids manual shuffling of cards.
- Backlit screens of PDAs allow for study even in the dark.
- "Quiz mode" keeps track of right and wrong guesses and repeats words until learned, automatically removing memorized words.
- "Review mode" flips cards manually or automatically at specified time intervals.
- "Quick Lex" rapidly searches for words—Greek to English, or English to Greek.
- Verb charts allow choice of verb type, stem, tense/aspect.
- Select vocabulary words by textbook chapters, frequency of appearance, or patterns (e.g., all words starting with Nun letter).
- Filter verbs, nouns, adjectives, prepositions, and others.

ebook: ISBN 0-310-24836-1

Pick up a copy today at your favorite bookstore!

ZONDERVAN®
GRAND RAPIDS, MICHIGAN 49530 USA
WWW.ZONDERVAN.COM

We want to hear from you. Please send your comments about this book to us in care of zreview@zondervan.com. Thank you.

GRAND RAPIDS, MICHIGAN 49530 USA

ZONDERVAN.COM/
AUTHOR**TRACKER**